Childhood Pleasures

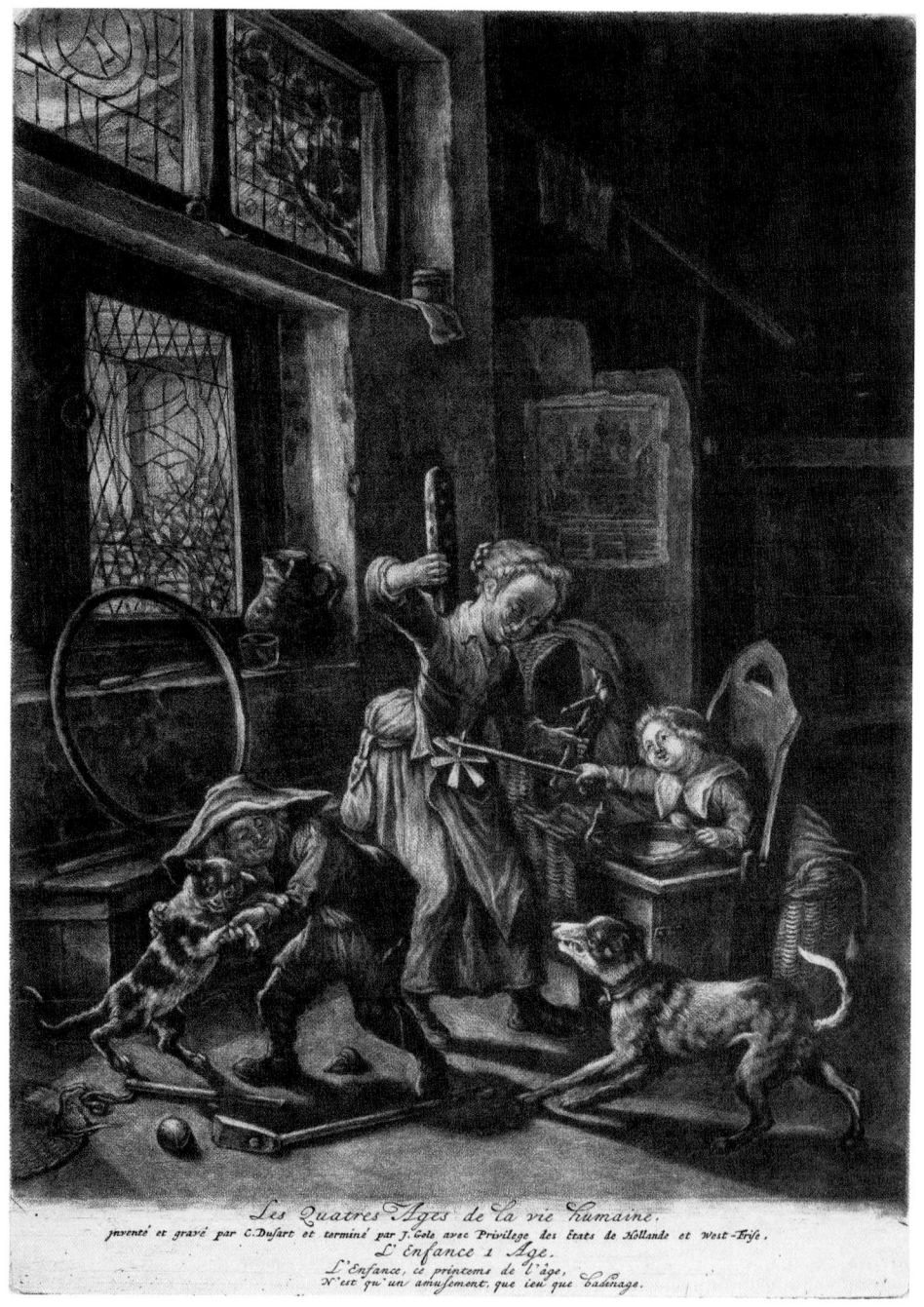

Les Quatres Ages de la vie humaine.
jnventé et gravé par C. Dusart et terminé par J. Gole avec Privilege des états de Hollande et West-Frise.
L'Enfance 1 Age.
L'Enfance, ce printems de l'âge,
N'est qu'un amusement, que ieu que badinage.

Cornelis Dusart, *L'Enfance* (Childhood), from *Les Quatres Ages de la vie humaine*
(The four ages of man). Print. Atlas van Stolk, Rotterdam.

Childhood Pleasures

DUTCH CHILDREN IN THE SEVENTEENTH CENTURY

Donna R. Barnes and Peter G. Rose

Foreword by Arthur K. Wheelock, Jr.

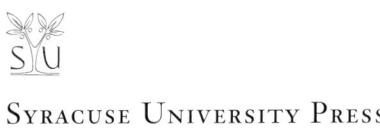

SYRACUSE UNIVERSITY PRESS

Syracuse University Press, Syracuse, NY 13244-5290

First Edition 2012

12   13   14   15   16   17   6   5   4   3   2   1

∞ The paper used in this publication meets the minimum requirements
of the American National Standard for Information Sciences—Permanence
of Paper for Printed Library Materials, ANSI Z39.48-1992.

For a listing of books published and distributed by Syracuse University Press,
visit our website at SyracuseUniversityPress.syr.edu.

ISBN: 978-0-8156-1002-1

Library of Congress Cataloging-in-Publication Data

Barnes, Donna R.
   Childhood pleasures : Dutch children in the seventeenth century / Donna R. Barnes
and Peter G. Rose ; foreword by Arthur K. Wheelock, Jr. — First Edition.
       p. cm.
   Includes bibliographical references and index.
   ISBN 978-0-8156-1002-1 (pbk. : alk. paper) 1. Children in art.   2. Art, Dutch—
17th century—Themes, motives.   3. Children—Netherlands—Social life and
customs—17th century.   I. Rose, Peter G.   II. Title.
   N7640.B37 2012
   704.94250949209032—dc23   2012023924

Contents

Illustrations

Foreword

ARTHUR K. WHEELOCK, JR.

The seventeenth-century Netherlands is a time and place that inspires our imagination. This maritime country, although small in scale and flat in terrain, conjures up images of windmills and dikes, picturesque farms, bustling cities, and harbors filled with ships having returned home from faraway lands, their holds bursting with spices and peppers. We also see in our mind's eye the Dutch people going about their daily lives, not only merchants selling their wares in the marketplace, proud farmers nurturing the land, rugged-looking travelers on rutted dirt roads, but also women caring for their homes, children at play, and tables laden with sumptuous cheeses, breads, and meat pies.

As is amply evident in the delightful images of paintings, drawings, and prints in this engaging book, Dutch artists have made it remarkably easy for us to transport ourselves back to that world. These artists drew their subjects from all aspects of the world about them, whether grazing cattle in a lush field, the active bustle of an outdoor vegetable market, the lively interior of a village school, or a festive family gathering. They studied the way people responded to different social situations and depicted their expressions and body language with great sensitivity. They also could render the textures of different materials, from the rough-hewn wood of beer vats in village taverns to the sheen of linens and satins in fine homes. They looked carefully at skies and clouds and could paint the wind rustling through the leaves of trees along sunlit inland waterways or whipping past skaters and *kolf* players on frozen lakes in the dead of winter. In short, they understood the magic of making paintings come alive, so much so that one can almost hear the voices of children laughing or men and women in quiet conversation, and even imagine the fragrance of warm waffles or freshly baked pies.

Artists help us envision how Dutch children enjoyed the games they played, but, in fact, many of these games, including rolling hoops, spinning tops, flying kites, and walking on stilts, still delight youngsters in the United

States and Europe. Similarly, today's children devour pancakes and apple tarts as enthusiastically as did their Dutch seventeenth-century counterparts. These similarities, however, mask differences in the way these games, and even certain types of food, were viewed in the Dutch Republic and in the modern world. Beyond the pleasures that they brought, games and foods often provided means for teaching deeply felt ethical and moral values that were broadly shared in Dutch society. For example, a number of authors stressed that a top will only spin as long as one tends it. Left alone, the top will wobble and fall to the ground. The lesson to be gained from this toy is that for children to become upright and responsible citizens, they must be properly, and consistently, reared and educated. On the other hand, a pinwheel, which relies on the direction of the wind to help it spin, symbolized fickleness and foolishness, while a hoop was a metaphor for a person whose life leads nowhere. One author wrote: "It is better to stand still than to make oneself tired with work that is useless."

Such moral associations, explicit and implicit, existed for virtually every Dutch toy. They are described in books, particularly emblem books, and are alluded to in prints and paintings. Even the images of children's games on Delft tiles, which seemingly celebrate the simple joys of childhood, also provided daily reminders of the lessons to be learned. Medical doctors similarly commented on the appropriateness of certain foods for a child's diet. For example, since apples and other soft-skinned fruit spoil easily, one author viewed them as being detrimental to good physical health and moral well-being.

In this environment, where so much educational guidance occurred in the home, the family, and particularly the mother, was especially important for guiding the moral upbringing of the next generation. The Dutch Republic, which was formed after the success of the Dutch revolt against Spanish control, was an entirely new political entity in the early seventeenth century. Freed from living under the yoke of the Spanish monarchy, the Dutch needed to shape their own institutions, laws, and traditions to create a viable social framework, and here the family played a significant role.

The country was fortunate to be led by the House of Orange (particularly Prince William the Silent, who led the initial phases of the Dutch Revolt, and his successors Prince Maurits and Prince Frederick Hendrick), and the States General (the governing body of representatives from the seven provinces that met in The Hague). These leaders soon established a political and legal system that provided a solid foundation for the Republic's political and economic success. Through their efforts, as well as those of writers, poets, teachers, and theologians, a cultural environment was established that nurtured individual growth and civic responsibility. Their efforts, however, would not have borne fruit without the support of parents, who through their own conduct and the teachings that they imparted to their children, reinforced the ideals that were fundamental to that country's social fabric. Parents often used tangible objects to impart moralizing lessons for their offspring, and among these were toys and food.

Many interrelated elements contributed to the peace and prosperity that allowed the Dutch to enjoy their "Golden Age." Important for this book, international trade brought to the Netherlands many of the fruits and vegetables that became the dietary staples for Dutch families. Dutch sailing vessels also brought back to port cities like Amsterdam and Rotterdam precious cargoes of spices and peppers and expensive collectors' items such as exotic flowers, shells, and porcelains. A vast network of inland river ways, moreover, allowed the Dutch to expand their trading network to Germany and other parts of Europe.

Foreign merchants and traders, as well as artists searching for markets in which to sell their paintings, immigrated to the Dutch Republic because of its economic success. A number of these new arrivals were Catholic, many of whom came from the Spanish-controlled Southern Netherlands. The Dutch, recognizing the importance of their contributions, and those of Jewish émigrés, developed a remarkably tolerant society that welcomed peoples of all religious backgrounds. Thus, while the Reformed Church was the official church of the Republic, Catholics and Jews were accepted as long as they worshipped privately. Some Catholic holiday traditions, such as Twelfth Night and Carnival, remained part of Dutch culture, and foods traditionally served at these occasions were eagerly anticipated by children and adults alike.

The enormous legacy of this remarkable period of the Dutch Republic, which artists, writers, and poets celebrated as its Golden Age, has enriched all of our lives. As we search for a fuller understanding of its unique character, we continually return to the central role of the family. Children are an essential part of that story, for how they were raised and taught, how they prayed and played, and what they ate and drank offer fundamental insights into Dutch life. In this book Donna Barnes and Peter Rose reveal the wonder of being a child in the seventeenth-century Netherlands and remind us of the basic human connections that exist between that distant world and ours. They also help us engage in that world by providing recipes for the foods that Dutch children enjoyed, whether breakfast, dinner, or dessert. These recipes are fun, easy to make, and tasty, and will provide as much delight and family enjoyment as any kite or pair of stilts could ever hope to achieve.

Preface

DONNA R. BARNES *and* PETER G. ROSE

Childhood Pleasures explores the pleasures of Dutch children living primarily in the province of Holland, the most prosperous and most important of the Seven United Provinces of the Netherlands. Our time focus is upon the seventeenth century and first decade of the eighteenth century. We draw much of our evidence from fascinating Dutch paintings, prints, and drawings that give visual clues to the lives of Dutch children and the behaviors and attitudes of Dutch people. Some evidence was also drawn from archeological digs, cookbooks, medical books, and diaries of the time period.

We combine our mutual interests in general historical patterns of Dutch social life, but also each author focuses attention on different dimensions. Donna Barnes explores connections between Dutch art, Dutch children's toys, games, and pleasurable amusements, and Dutch attitudes about children. Peter Rose probes connections between Dutch foodways and festive celebrations, answering the question: "what sweets and treats would bring pleasure to Dutch youngsters?"

We organize the images around eight major themes: infancy; Saint Nicholas, bringer of sweets and toys; celebrations and music; toys and games; animals as pets and companions; inventing fun, games, and mischief; shopping for food treats; and winter activities outdoors.

Brief biographies of the artists are provided as starting points for learning more about the particular artists whose imagery captured readers' attention. And we include a dozen recipes that can be used by adults working with children to create a taste of the past.

It is our hope that today's children and adults will discover that while some pleasures enjoyed by Dutch youngsters four hundred years ago have changed, some of those childhood pleasures remain sources of delight and amusement even in the twenty-first century.

Acknowledgments

Jointly the authors wish to express their thanks to The Netherland-America Foundation for a grant in support of this project and to Hofstra University for additional financial assistance. We thank Arthur K. Wheelock, Jr., curator of Northern Baroque paintings at the National Gallery of Art and professor of art history at the University of Maryland, for writing the illuminating foreword. Mary Selden Evans, executive editor of Syracuse University Press, and her assistant, Kelly Lynne Balenske, have been unfailingly kind and helpful to us and we thank them both.

Donna R. Barnes

Many images in this book have been drawn from Jan Luyken's emblem book, *Des Menschen Begin, Midden en Einde*, published after his death in 1712. Invited by the Amsterdam Historical Museum to organize an exhibition of Jan Luyken's prints and drawings for 1997, I relied heavily on these images. Special thanks to my colleagues there who not only worked with me on that exhibition, but also helped me bring many of those works to Hofstra University for an exhibition in 2004. In Amsterdam, I am especially grateful for the encouragement and cooperation provided by Pauline Kruseman, who had been director of the Amsterdam Historical Museum and who facilitated the loan of imagery for the present book. Other former or present staff members at the Amsterdam Historical Museum who have been invaluable in my efforts to understand Jan Luyken's oeuvre include: Joyce Edwards, Judith van Gent, Rob Jager, Michiel Jonker, Anneke van de Kieft, Renée Kistemaker, Nel Klaversma, Norbert Middelkoop, Frans Oehlen, Bert Vreeken, and Vanessa Vroon. The museum is now known as the Amsterdam Museum. Its current director, Paul Spies, also cooperated by granting permission to use imagery from the collection.

Hofstra University provided me time and support to research seventeenth-century Dutch art for many projects, including the present book. I am grateful to Provost Herman A. Berliner, former dean James Johnson, former acting dean Maureen Murphy, former Hofstra Museum director David Christman, and my chairpersons, Charol Shakehaft (now at Virginia Commonwealth University) and Karen Osterman. Graduate research assistance was also provided by Victoria Nesnick.

In Europe, other friends and colleagues have helped me understand more about Dutch art depicting children's lives, including their pleasures with toys and games as well as with foods. Cees Bakker, Lourens Bas, Pieter Biesboer, Jaap Bolten, Chris de Bruyn, Carl Nix, Michiel Plomp, Karin Wester, and Petra van den Born have all extended wise advice. Corry van de Wielen and Zeljko Latkovic made research time in Holland pleasurable.

I am grateful for the opportunity to work on this project with my good friend Peter Rose. We have worked together on many projects for more than twenty years. Always there is a sense of excitement that comes when we learn more and share our findings with each other. Her husband, Don Rose, has patiently listened to our enthusiasms.

My sister, Roberta Corbett, encouraged my interest in this project, while my friend Rusty Constine made some research travel possible. I wish to dedicate my portion of this book to the memory of my beloved friend Barbara Miller, who always encouraged my passion for Dutch art.

Peter G. Rose

I thank my coauthor, Donna R. Barnes, for a pleasant collaboration and a long friendship. My sincere thanks go also to Barbara Ketchum Wheaton for her valuable advice and input.

I am grateful to my friend Mary Beth (Chip) Kass for reading the manuscript and asking lots of questions. I value and admire her ability to bring cheerfulness and happiness to everyone's daily life. Debra Thimmesch not only read my section of the book but also helped with recipe testing. Stephen Schmidt is always a wonderfully knowledgeable and reliable source in answering baking questions. I thank all three of them for their help.

As always, my thanks and love go to our wonderful daughter, Peter Pamela, who considers a sandwich of *roggebrood* with butter and cheese, made by Mom, a true treat. Above all I want to express my deep love and thanks to my husband, Don, who makes everything possible. My section of this book is dedicated to them both and to the memory of my mother, who taught me to cook and to love food and history.

Childhood Pleasures

Children's Playful Pleasures

DONNA R. BARNES

Using art works (paintings, prints, and drawings) as visual sources of evidence, we can surmise that Dutch youngsters in the seventeenth century had many pleasures and enjoyed many playful activities throughout childhood.

For infants, pleasure was experienced when children were breast-fed and later learned to eat pap, and when they were hugged and cuddled. Babies enjoyed being rocked in cradles and listening to lullabies. Later, toddlers took delight in learning to walk with the assistance of their walkers (*loopwagens*) and were able to sit in special high chairs (*speelstoelen*) where they could eat meals, shake rattles, play with small toys, and nibble on sweet treats. Once children could walk and feed themselves, a whole world of new pleasurable possibilities opened for them.

Because some children lived in rural areas, many of their activities took place outdoors in the village square. Others played in the pasture lands or along the ditches that separated growing fields from pastures. Rural children might not have fully understood the technology involved in pumping the marshy Beemster, Purmer or Schermer lakes dry, but they recognized that new land was made available to their families for raising herds of dairy cows, flocks of sheep, or vegetable crops. With a system of dikes and ditches crisscrossing the polders, children had places to sail their toy boats, swing on wooden stiles separating fields, or use long poles to leap over the watery ditches.

Children played near the shorelines or in the water of Holland's lakes, rivers, and the North Sea. Youngsters played at the seaside dunes that stretched along the western coast from Den Helder in the North down toward Zeeland in the South.

Often country boys and girls amused themselves in the family barn or barnyard. Few wooded areas existed in Holland, so woodland activities were very limited. Where there were woods, or where families planted cherry, pear, or apple trees, we can be confident that boys climbed mature trees and swung on branches (as they have done around the world since time immemorial).

The majority of Dutch children, especially those in the more heavily populated province of Holland, lived in cities and towns. Their outdoor activities in Amsterdam, Leiden, Haarlem, Delft, Rotterdam, The Hague, Enkhuizen, Alkmaar, and Hoorn took place in the streets and city squares, on the family's household front door stoop, occasionally in the church or church yard, and, in wintertime, on the frozen canals and lakes.

Cities were expanding. More canals were dug; new structures (such as houses, churches, municipal buildings, warehouses, shipyards, factories, orphanages, and old-age facilities) were built; and children (especially boys) enjoyed visiting construction sites. Boys did so out of curiosity (also shared by adult males) and passed these sites sometimes when skipping rope or rolling hoops. Occasionally youngsters found discarded building materials, particularly pieces of wood or snips of roof flashing, which they took home to use in fashioning self-made toys.

No question about it, city-dwelling youngsters also enjoyed going out of the city on treks to the countryside for boat rides and picnics or to the beach. Some wealthy urban youngsters came from families who owned country houses to which they traveled in the hot summer months to escape the heat, humidity, stench, and flies of the city. Those rich children enjoyed "country pleasures" and might have "played" at being shepherds and shepherdesses with the lambs.

At their country homes, rich city children got a taste of rural pleasures, but while they might have a pet goat hitched to a fancy goat cart for a carefree jaunt along country lanes, farm children often had responsibilities for taking care of the goats and other farm animals. Feeding, grooming, milking, or mucking out the barn stable to form manure piles used as plant fertilizer was work, not play, for farmers' sons and daughters. Farmer children did not often think of farm animals as playful pets.

Farmers' children did not have gilded goat carts resembling fanciful mythological chariots. Nor did working farm children dress up in idealized antique shepherd or hunter costumes. But rich parents often had their children's portraits painted with the youngsters attired as make-believe shepherds and shepherdesses in pastoral settings.

Whether living in cities or the rural villages of Schoonhoven, Beverwyck, Edam, or Scheveningen, Dutch children relished local or regional fairs where they could watch traveling performers, bear-baiters, tight-rope walkers, itinerant musicians, puppeteers, and quacks selling their "medicinal" potions to gullible customers. Like their elders, children laughed at amateur comic farce performances by local men in the chambers of rhetoric. Boys and girls gawked at the merchandise available for sale at the fairs, whether that included paintings, live horses (as was the case at the Valkenburg Fair) and cattle, embroidered purses, feathered fans, brassware and glasses, or toys.

Just like their parents, children enjoyed going to horse fairs or markets devoted to the sale of cows or pigs. Adult men might bargain with each other for the sale of a horse to be used later to pull farm plows, hay wagons, and coaches or sleds transporting people. Families might purchase a cow or pig to be added to the farmer's herd or to be slaughtered for meat. Women might sell and buy live rabbits or ducks. But children enjoyed hearing the sounds and watching the movement made by the animals. Sometimes youngsters touched the animals, feeling how soft were the rabbits' ears or how silky were the horses' tails. Some grunted loudly at the pigs, imitating the sows' sounds.

Children also enjoyed going to local markets where food was sold. Seeing game and birds for sale or displayed fish and shellfish was visually interesting, especially if live crabs were scrambling over the display benches or roosters were squawking in cages. Laughing children sometimes crowed back at the roosters. But perhaps the most fun for children at the food markets was the opportunity to buy treats—pancakes and waffles, or mussels, or carrots and apples—and eat them on the spot. (These edible market pleasures are discussed further by Peter Rose.)

City-dwelling youngsters probably had more access to toys than their rural counterparts because toy sellers set up their stands at a *kermis* or fair. Peddlers bringing wooden toys into Holland from the producers in Nürnberg (Germany) might also sell toys at local open-air markets or wander door-to-door attempting to attract family buyers. Playing cards, printed in Amsterdam, were sold by book dealers and stationers. Those might have been purchased for, or by, children. Children played cards. Moralizing emblem book writers like Roemer Visscher cautioned parents against letting their children gamble with cards and dice, but children enjoyed both.

Judging from paintings, many children grew up in households where animals were pets; dogs and cats were frequent. Children took pleasure in feeding their pets. Sometimes they even danced with the family dog or cat. Birds, especially exotic imported parrots, amused some youngsters just as they delighted their elders. A few wealthy families kept imported monkeys that they trained as pets. Some boys played with (or teased) mice. Some wealthy folk also kept horses and falcons used for hunting, and rich boys learned to hunt.

Rural youngsters, especially those living on farms, befriended the horses and colts, cows and calves, pigs and piglets, sheep and lambs, ducks and ducklings, chickens with their chicks, and geese and goslings in their care. But while they took pleasure in these animals, they were fully aware that these animals were not pets being raised for amusement; ultimately they were work animals, breeders, or sources of food.

Children enjoyed watching the antics of swans and downy gray cygnets paddling about in the ponds, canals, and ditches whether they were in the city or in the Dutch countryside. Rural youngsters caught frogs or napping turtles and then raced them. Occasionally youngsters tormented the frogs or threw pebbles and stones at ducklings and waterfowl.

On frosty cold winter days, boys in rural villages accompanied their fathers, grandfathers, and uncles on spear-fishing expeditions to catch eels through the ice. The boys learned to chop holes in the ice and patiently await their quarry. In warmer weather, boys visited estuaries to collect mussels. Older boys sometimes built a fire and roasted the mussels in their shells for a succulent feast. Did they taste any better than the mussels brought home for mother or kitchen servants to cook with onions, herbs, and wine?

At the beach, children trapped crabs. They chased seagulls and terns at the water's edge. They also built sand castles and forts. They fished with rods or nets from the shoreline or they fished from rowboats or sailboats on the rivers and ponds. They waded in the water when the summer weather was sunny and warm, and sometimes boys swam in the nude (as there were no special swimsuits). Youngsters collected seashells; little girls used the shells as "pretend dishware" with their dolls.

In the countryside, especially near the dunes, children enjoyed chasing rabbits and hares, who quickly disappeared down the holes into their warrens. Youngsters sometimes robbed birds' nests of their eggs, especially true when the migratory birds (such as heron, wild geese and ducks, and woodcock) came to the dune area. They might slurp the raw eggs right from the shell, sell the eggs, take them home to be boiled for tasty snacks, or toss the raw ones at each other. Boys also enjoyed hunting thrushes, partridges, swallows, and lapwings along the river banks. Using grains of wheat and rye to attract birds, boys used nets or sticks coated with glue to ensnare them.

Children picked wildflowers; girls often wove them into daisy chains or garlands. They collected colorful bird feathers. Children searched for sweet wild strawberries or blackberries growing along country lanes. They enjoyed looking for the footprints of hares in the snow or listening to the honking sounds of migrating geese. Autumn, winter, spring and summer all offered pleasurable outdoor experiences for Dutch children in the countryside.

Boys more so than their sisters enjoyed snowball fights or mud-ball fights. Girls were more likely to make mud pies. Many children, to the dismay of their mothers, enjoyed splashing in puddles whether on country lanes or city streets.

Children played tag. They ran races against each other or they ran for the sheer joy of it. Boys balanced on fences and stiles. They leaped across water-filled ditches, often using a long stick to vault the distance. Accepting a dare, occasionally a boy fell into the ditch, emerging soaked to the mocking laughter of his challenger. Youngsters skipped flat stones across the surfaces of lakes and ponds. Children enjoyed boat and barge rides.

When canals or lakes froze in the winter, Dutch youngsters took to the ice on skates. Those who didn't own skates simply slid along the ice surface in their shoes, leather boots, or socks. Some straddled overturned three-legged stools pulled by a friend who gave them a ride. Boys, like their fathers, enjoyed playing *kolf* (an early form of ice hockey) on the ice. Frequently older boys and girls skated in pairs, with their arms around each others' waists. Snap-the-whip was even more fun if played on the ice.

Little children might have small wooden sleds (*priksleeën*) which they could move by using hand-held sticks with pointed goads to push the sled along. Others enjoyed having a ride, organized by adults, in a horse-drawn sleigh. The horses were frequently festooned with brass bells on their harnesses that jingled merrily as the sleigh sped over the slick icy surface. Rarer, but far more exciting, were rides in a wind-driven ice boat.

Dutch youngsters enjoyed listening to jokes and stories told by adults or older siblings. *Jack and the Beanstalk* had been translated into Dutch, and his feats, frequently related with coarse humor, amused children, as did tales of heroic knights, the Wandering Jew, and picaresque heroes like Til Uilenspiegel. These tales were also printed in cheap pamphlets and sold at the marketplace by the peddlers who also sold lyrics to songs and almanacs. Mocking ballads and comic rhymes were recited at market squares for the amusement of adults and children alike. Girls and boys quickly latched onto these and repeated them for their own delight.

Children might have been exposed to works of art in their homes. Wealthy families could afford to decorate their houses with paintings—portraits, scenes of daily life, landscapes, seascapes, and still lifes. Affluent children grew up with paintings hung on the walls and from time to time were privileged to look at their fathers' collections of rarities (such as old coins or tropical seashells) or prints and drawings, often stored in a wooden chest or *prentenkabinet*. Women who collected fine embroidered linen or lace or majolica dishware or Delftware vases showed these cherished treasures to their daughters, who viewed them longingly, anticipating the day when they would possess and display these items in their own homes.

Wealthy children grew up in households where there were books, including illustrated emblem books. Roemer Visscher's *Sinnepoppen*, originally published in 1614 and reissued by his daughter Anna in 1678, was a favorite. Books by Jacob Cats were in many middle-class households, where children looked at the picture illustrations. By 1679, Johannes Amos Comenius's book, *Orbis Pictus* (originally published in both Latin and German in 1658), was published in Holland. Used by children in school as a means of language learning and for its wide-ranging information, the illustrated book was also included in some home libraries. From time to time, parents showed their children emblem books and talked about the "hidden" moralistic messages in the imagery. These parental talks were meant to be part of the children's moral instruction, but the pictures were also a source of visual pleasure.

Children from middle or working classes also saw paintings displayed in their homes or in parents' workshops (as is clear in Quiringh van Brekelenkam's images of young apprentices working with a tailor whose shop has a painting hung on the wall), but the paintings were smaller and much fewer in number. Children might also see prints tacked onto a wall.

Poor children had relatively few encounters with artworks. None were displayed in their homes. They might have seen artworks—paintings or prints—displayed at outdoor fairs. They might have seen prints tacked to the wall in a tavern, and they might even have seen some paintings displayed in the regents' chambers of orphanages or alms houses if they were recipients of charity.

Children were not likely to see many artworks in Protestant churches because Protestants had removed art (both paintings and sculptures) and whitewashed the walls of former Catholic churches in the late sixteenth century during a period of iconoclasm. Some "hidden" Catholic churches (*schuilkerken*) displayed paintings religious in theme. These might have provided visual interest and pleasure for affluent and middle-class Catholic youngsters who attended with their families. However, some clandestine Catholic churches did not welcome exceedingly poor families and their children.

Most Protestant children heard Bible stories at church, read some at school, and perhaps listened to those stories at home when their father read the family Bible, often a daily occurrence. Youngsters knew of Cain and Abel, Adam and Eve's expulsion from the Garden of Eden, the sacrifice of Isaac by his father Abraham, Jonah and the whale, Joseph and his coat of many colors, and, of course, the story of Christ's miraculous birth and his crucifixion.

Children did not have many books to read, but they sometimes brought popular humorous novels to school, to the dismay of their teachers and preachers of all denominations. Children who could read took pride and pleasure in doing so. The Dutch had the highest rate of literacy in all of Europe during the seventeenth century. In part, that can be attributed not only to the provision of basic schooling for boys and girls, but also to the firmly-held Protestant conviction that everyone ought to be able to read the Bible in the vernacular Dutch language.

School learning was not completely enjoyable. Teachers used wooden ferules or bundles of birch switches to hit the hands or strike the backsides of youngsters who were not paying careful attention or whose recited lessons were "wrong." Occasionally students misbehaved (as illustrated later by Jan Steen) and turned their schoolroom into theaters for mischief.

Childhood pleasures were a function of the youngsters' family social status and economic level. Children from well-to-do families had more leisure time, more expensive toys, more exposure to art works, more sweets and treats, more money to spend, more access to books, and more opportunities for entertainment than did children from peasant or working-class families.

Peasant farm children and the sons and daughters of fishermen, cobblers, porters, weavers, carpenters, broom makers, potters, bakers, and tailors frequently had to help out in the family enterprise. They were often put to work at an early age. Their schooling was minimal, especially so for the girls.

Children of poorly paid manual workers were expected to work at home-based tasks and had limited leisure time. Children of fishermen learned to mend nets. Broom makers' children helped gather straw together so it could be bound onto broomsticks. Weavers' children learned to spin wool or flax into threads and reel threads onto bobbins. The thread could later be loaded into shuttles or stretched onto the looms operated by their fathers.

Street peddlers' children accompanied their mothers or fathers to the markets to help in sales; they helped load up wheelbarrows or peddlers' baskets. Sons and daughters of wood turners helped sweep up wood particles and sawdust from the workshop; their labor made it possible for the father to work with fewer interruptions. The wood particles could be sold to local brewers, who used them to heat malted barley for beer, or bakers, who used the wood chips to heat their ovens prior to baking breads, rolls, or pastries. Working children took pleasure in parents' praise for chores done well and quickly. Their play time was limited but thoroughly enjoyed.

Children who were apprenticed at an early age to master tailors, hatters, bakers, carpenters, coopers, pewterers, pastry bakers, or blacksmiths learned a trade. They, too, took pleasure in praise from their masters for the acquisition and display of skills, but their free time for playing games was very limited.

Children of poor families had precious little time for play. They worked when work could be found; they begged from door to door with their families. No funds were available to buy toys: it was enough to try to obtain food and clothing. No doubt some poor youngsters enjoyed listening to street singers and itinerant hurdy-gurdy players or watching jugglers if they were in a market or begging at a *kermis*, but few attended school to learn to read. Books were not part of their experience.

By the same token, children of exceedingly poor families who were placed in charitably run poor houses or those youngsters who had been orphaned and were housed in municipal or church-related orphanages were also expected to work at an early age. There was not much time for play, and few toys.

⚘

For children who had play time, what toys and games did Dutch youngsters enjoy?

Babies and infants might play with tinkle-bell rattles or teething rings. Children of wealthy families frequently had rattles made of silver with a piece of coral attached for rubbing against sore gums while the baby was teething. Infants often sat enclosed in a special wooden chair, a *speelstoel*, that had a table surface on which could be placed spoons and bowls of food, cookies, or small toys. Older siblings invented nonsense rhymes or recited familiar poems to baby sisters and brothers while tickling their toes. Babies gurgled in pleasure at these improvised games.

Learning to stand and walk—initially with, and later without, a wooden walking cart (*loopwagen*)—was the beginning stage of mobility-based games. A toddler could enjoy riding on a wooden horse (*stokpaardje*)—a stick adorned with a wooden or stuffed fabric horse head. The youngster, straddling the stick, could play at galloping and imaginary deeds of derring-do. Toddlers also delighted in running with little wooden windmills and seeing the "sails" turn.

Little girls enjoyed playing with dolls, talking with them, dressing them, having their dolls imaginatively interact and converse with the dolls belonging to their sisters, cousins, or friends. On warm, sunny days, girls took their dolls outdoors to play with them. During cold, snowy, or rainy weather, they confined their doll play indoors, close to the warmth of the family fireplace. Miniature pots and pans, made of metal or baked clay, and small-sized wooden cradles and chairs were used by girls playing with their dolls.

Girls also enjoyed playing *bikkel*, a knucklebones game that could be played indoors on a household floor or outdoors while seated on the stoop. No doubt girls also played "dress up" with adult women's garments, temporarily "borrowed" from their mothers or grandmothers.

In some households, boys and girls learned to play a peg-board game of fox and geese, while others learned to play cards, roll dice or play *tric trac* (a form of backgammon). Often gambling games involved wagers, which was part of their appeal not only for children but also for adults. The Dutch were inveterate gamblers! Other children learned to play checkers and chess. These games of chance and/or strategy were also enjoyed by adults.

Boys shot bows and arrows, used slings to fire pebbles at targets, jumped or skipped rope, spun tops either by hurling them or whipping them, and played several versions of marbles. Boys also bowled balls toward wooden pins or erect animal bones, played mumblety-peg with knives, and inflated pigs' bladders by blowing air through a hollow straw into the expandable organ (after the animal had been freshly slaughtered). The filled bladder was used to make rude noises or was tossed like a ball.

Both boys and girls enjoyed blowing bubbles, using a hollow straw and a shallow bowl or large seashell to hold soapy water. Others used a Gouda clay pipe (meant for smoking tobacco). The iridescent appearance of the evanescent bubble produced quiet pleasure when blown by a single child. If two or more youngsters were blowing bubbles and chasing them together, there were shouts of pleasure and much laughter as the bubbles burst on the hands or faces of the bubblers.

Boys and girls in cities and in country villages enjoyed making music, sometimes with real musical instruments and other times with improvised sound-making devices (banging on a metal cooking pot with a wooden spoon). Children enjoyed playing or listening to a *rommelpot* (where a pig's bladder had been drawn tightly across the mouth of an earthenware jug and a stick inserted through it could be moved up and down to produce rumbling noises). Most youngsters amused themselves by singing. Song lyrics were learned by heart. Songbooks and sheet music were also available in the marketplace. Youngsters, like adults, often improvised lyrics to familiar tunes.

Children of all social classes and religious backgrounds enjoyed making noise—whether turning rattles or banging on metal pots designed to awaken "lazy bones" from their sleep for *luilak* (a Saturday holiday of children's mischief occurring just before Pentecost); banging on toy drums; thumping on discarded beer kegs; singing on or off-key; shaking rattles with rinklebells;

stamping their feet; mimicking the neighing of horses, bleating of sheep, or clucking of hens; or mocking one another or mocking adults.

Boys especially enjoyed tooting on horns or banging on small drums, not infrequently organizing themselves in quasi-military formations to parade about pretending to be *schutters* (members of the local civic militia) or soldiers. In certain families, providing children with music lessons—perhaps on the violin, flute, recorder, harpsichord, lute, or cello—was a sign of "refinement." Families often had "musical entertainments" at home, and children were expected to join in the singing and music-making events.

Many youngsters enjoyed dancing, whether to tunes played by itinerant musicians at village fairs or to the sprightly, foot-tapping music played by fiddlers and bagpipers in taverns. Little boys and girls accompanied their parents to local taverns; babysitters were unknown. Children danced when wandering violinists and hurdy-gurdy players came door to door to provide entertainment. And they danced simply to the exuberant noises, rhythms, and impulses felt by the children themselves.

Dancing, frequently quite boisterous dancing, was learned at an early age, and dancing was a habit, much condemned by moralizing ministers, that continued into adulthood and old age. Dutch youngsters knew that their elders enjoyed dancing in taverns, at weddings, and at indoor and outdoor parties. Foot-stomping country music was favored by rural folk. More elegant forms of dance were favored by city-dwelling patrician adults and their children.

Youngsters gathered together to sing holiday songs on a door-to-door basis as "star singers" during the celebration of Twelfth Night (otherwise known as Epiphany or Three Kings Day) when they would walk through the streets in the early evening on January 6 with illuminated star-shaped lanterns to perform at doorways and later to be given small coins or sweet treats. Occasionally they joined with adult star singers. (See Peter Rose's discussion of Twelfth Night celebrations.) Others went door-to-door singing on Saint Martin's Day, November 11. Then the children begged for firewood to burn in a large bonfire at night. Children also sang special "May Songs" for the celebration of Pentecost in the spring.

In windy weather, kite flying was popular. When the weather was reasonably calm, many youngsters, particularly the boys, played blind-man's-bluff, leapfrog, tug-of-war, piggyback racing, tag, hide 'n' seek, and walking on stilts outdoors. They also had foot races and did handstands. Boys wrestled with siblings, friends, and rivals.

Many outdoor games required no special equipment, and the rules could be negotiated. Girls and boys played hopscotch on flat city street surfaces, chalk-marked with a traditional pattern, and sometimes also drew the "court" (known as the *hinkelbaan*) into the flat, damp sand at the beach using a stick or shell fragment.

Not all children's games and amusements were peaceful. An especially rough game, played by older ruffian boys and loutish drunken men, involved trapping a cat in a wooden barrel, and then rolling the barrel while beating on it with cudgels. When the barrel staves broke open and the frightened cat tried to escape, it was usually beaten to death.

Children watched adults "ride for the goose," where a live goose, its neck greased (ironically probably with rendered goose fat, or else soap), was strung up by its feet and suspended on a rope strung high over a canal. A rowboat with players would pass under the squawking bird. Players, brandishing knives, would stand up in the boat and attempt to slit the goose's throat. Occasionally players fell out of the boat splashing into the canal or the goose shat upon the players, to the amusement of onlookers. Boys knew that when they got a bit older they, too, could participate. Little boys could hardly wait.

~

Where did Dutch youngsters get their toys?

Toys made by craftsmen were often purchased for children at toy stalls, perhaps at a *kermis* or during the Saint Nicholas markets prior to Saint Nicholas day in December. Imported toys might have been made by craftsmen working abroad, principally in Nürnberg (Germany). Others were made by local Dutch craftsmen. Dolls, wooden horses, tin horns and drums, and a toy soldier are depicted as items for sale in a print used to illustrate one of Jacob Cats's books, *Spiegel van den Ouden en Nieuwen Tyt*. An eager child points them out to a woman (probably the girl's mother), who has a coin purse with which to pay for toys.

Carpenters, turners, or wheelwrights made miniature wooden wagons for little children to pull. No doubt turners, who made ball-footed cabinets and tables for households and offices, also used their lathes to produce wooden balls, tops, and dolls' heads for children. Tools that produced chair rungs could also make ninepins for bowling games. Pewterers and coppersmiths could make miniaturized pots, pans, platters, spoons, and griddles for doll's play, just as potters and glassblowers could produce tiny pots, dishes, cups, and glasses for girls to use.

Dolls, with wooden heads adorned with gesso features or porcelain heads, might have been imported. Simple rag dolls, however, could be made at home from new material or worn household fabrics, perhaps table linens and napkins, torn bed sheets and pillow covers, or no-longer-fashionable clothing. Portraits and genre paintings of Dutch girls frequently show them holding dolls dressed much like the girls themselves. Mothers with needle skills fashioned clothing for their daughters' dolls. Girls learning to knit or sew might have been encouraged to make clothes for their own dolls or the dolls of their younger sisters.

Doll furnishings, such as chairs or baby cradles, might be made by chair caners, cabinet makers, turners and joiners, or basket weavers for play by girls from affluent families. (Given the perishability of wood, straw, reeds, and osiers, these items tend not to survive, but some can be seen in portraits of girls.)

Exceedingly wealthy women, such as Petronella Dunois, could commission silversmiths, glass blowers, tapestry weavers, coppersmiths, tinsmiths, cabinet makers, porcelain makers, and artists to produce elaborate furnishings, to exact scale, for their doll houses, but these were not "toys" for children to play with. These *poppenhuizen* were meant to amuse adult women, much as a wealthy man might collect rare objects and display them in his cabinet of curiosities for the amusement of his friends.

Specialists in several Dutch towns made wooden *kolf* clubs, often with lead heads, while other workers produced the horsehair-filled, leather-covered balls used for *kolf*. Long metal blades, curving upward at the front and nailed onto a wooden form, were strapped onto shoes or boots as ice skates. Skates, laced either at the ankle or calf, were produced by the specialized *schaatsemaaker* for children as well as adults.

Children could mold clay into figurines and bake them in a cast-iron-covered Dutch oven at the family's hearth. Clay might have been "begged" from the local pottery or perhaps collected on the banks of the many rivers in Holland.

Boys enjoyed playing marbles. These glazed baked clay toys could be purchased cheaply from local potters. Some specialized in making marbles and were known as a *knikker-bakker*. To the outraged dismay of preachers, boys sometimes shot marbles on the paving stones inside a church or else outdoors on the flat gravestones in the churchyard.

Children cadged used barrel hoops from the coopers to roll along the streets. They also used discarded barrels as "horses" for mock battles and jousts. Slings could easily be fashioned with a length of string or a leather thong and a small piece of canvas or leather; all that was needed then was a stone projectile, or an acorn or chestnut. Targets might include a bird's nest in a hedge, a pretty girl's window or front door, a neighbor's cat or dog, or even a circle drawn in wet sand.

Boys could also string animal intestines, obtained from a butcher, onto flexible sticks forming a bow and devise straight sticks (sharpened to a point and outfitted with bird feathers) to serve as arrows. However, in a culture where grown adult men still practiced marksmanship with both cross-bows and guns at the local community's *doelen*, miniaturized bows and arrows might also have been purchased for children from archery suppliers.

Makers of leather whips, bridles, and saddles for use with horses no doubt also produced miniature whips for children. Boys especially enjoyed wielding whips.

Lengths of cord or rope were quickly put to use by youngsters skipping rope. Cordage was produced in immense quantities at the local rope-walk (*lijnbaan*) in many Dutch cities where rope was primarily used in ships' rigging. Cord or string reeled onto a stick could be attached to a kite, fashioned by youngsters from thin strips of wood for the spars and lightweight fabric sails. (Paper was too expensive to use for kite-making in much of the seventeenth century.)

Market vendors transported fruits, vegetables, and mussels on market day in wheelbarrows. Farmers, gardeners, and porters also used wheelbarrows. Youngsters who had access to their parents' wooden wheelbarrows occasionally used them to push around their siblings and friends. Unceremoniously dumping their "passengers" produced chortles of laughter for the barrow pusher and shrieks of surprised indignation for the riders.

Children no doubt fashioned little boats and rafts for themselves from discarded pieces of lumber and perhaps rigged some with fabric sails; boys have made these toys all over the world in times past.

Boys also carved miniature animal figures, such as rabbits or sheep, for their own amusement or that of their younger brothers and sisters. Knife skills were acquired at an early age. Unfortunately knife skills were not limited to carving and mumblety-peg; some boys fought each other with knives in very rough-and-tumble forms of play.

Whether purchased from craftsmen or peddlers, booksellers and stationers, or made by doting parents and grandparents, or put together by the children themselves, Dutch youngsters enjoyed toys and they enjoyed games.

Play, sometimes quiet and sometimes boisterous, mischievous, or violent, was certainly among children's pleasures in the seventeenth century. Children not only amused themselves through play, they also learned many physical and mental skills, attitudes, and values.

Edible Pleasures

PETER G. ROSE

Childhood pleasures extended from the joys of play with or without toys to the edible delights of various sweets and treats. In order to gain a better understanding of what children four hundred years ago might have enjoyed, we need to know what regular foodstuffs were available in the seventeenth-century Dutch Republic and what special treats were associated with the customary holidays of Christmas, Easter, Pentecost, as well as Epiphany, Shrove Tuesday, Saint Martin, and, above all for children, the Saint Nicholas celebration.

During the Republic's "Golden Age," with a growing middle class, the difference between rich and poor remained. For working-class or poor children in the seventeenth century a treat might have been merely more food, while for the upper class or more affluent children a sweet morsel of candied fruit or a cookie were readily available. From pictorial and documentary evidence we conclude that there were special foodstuffs associated with specific holidays; churches and civic organizations made sure that extra food was given to the poor during that time.

The Daily Meal for the Poor and Working Class

We are fortunate that menus from orphanages, such as the Amsterdam Municipal Orphanage, were carefully overseen by their board of regents and kept in archives until this day. As early as 1639 the city of Amsterdam required that the regents compile annual account books. Anne McCants used these books to evaluate the caloric and nutrient value of the daily meals served to the young orphans in her article "Monotonous but Not Meager: The Diet of Burgher Orphans in Early Modern Amsterdam."[1] These seasonal lists and

---

1. *Research in Economic History* 14 (1992): 69–116.

menus give us a good indication of the foods eaten by the poor (the orphans) and working class (the staff), who received more or less the same rations but in larger quantity. Her evaluations agree with Burema's assessment of seventeenth-century working-class food in his doctoral thesis regarding Dutch food from the Middle Ages to the Twentieth Century.[2] The menus given are for the noon and evening meals only. Breakfast habitually consisted of bread and butter. McCants lists a menu for the year 1640. For fifty-two weeks of the year, the orphans ate the following:

Sunday noon: beans with a piece of bread; salted or smoked meat with a piece of bread. *Evening:* porridge of whole milk and rice.

Monday noon: gray peas with melted fat and bread; sausage with barley and raisins and a piece of bread. *Evening:* porridge of barley and buttermilk.

Tuesday noon: white beans with butter and a piece of bread; smoked or salted bacon with carrots, turnip, or cabbage and bread. *Evening:* buttermilk with rye bread.

Wednesday noon: green peas with a piece of bread; salt cod or herring and bread, or instead of fish, porridge of whole milk with rice for the small children. *Evening:* in summer, a cold meal; in winter, bread cooked with syrup.

Thursday noon: beans with a piece of bread; salted or smoked meat and bread. *Evening:* porridge of buttermilk and bread.

Friday noon: gray peas with fat and a piece of bread; sausage with barley and raisins, or cabbage, and bread. *Evening:* porridge of buttermilk and barley.

Saturday noon: white peas and a piece of bread; stockfish and a piece of bread; instead of fish, whole milk with meal for the small children. *Evening:* in summer, a cold meal; in winter, porridge of bread and syrup.

As the title of her article indicates, McCants concludes that the diet of the orphans was monotonous but not meager. In her study of Dutch cultural history, Jozien Jobse-van Putten comes to the same conclusion about Dutch food and gives her book the title *Eenvoudig maar voedzaam,* or *Simple but Nutritious.*[3]

In addition to rye and wheat for bread, the orphanage purchased barley, meal, and rice for porridges. Various kinds of beans and peas, milk, buttermilk, butter, and cheese were purchased, as well as beef, pork, and three kinds

2. Lambertus Burema, *De Voeding in Nederland van de Middeleeuwen tot de Twintigste Eeuw* (Assen: Van Gorcum, 1953).

3. Jozien Jobse-van Putten, *Eenvoudig maar voedzaam: cultuurgeschiedenis van de dagelijkse maaltijd in Nederland* (Nijmegen: SUN, 1995).

of fish: stockfish (split and dried cod), herring, and salted cod; syrup/molasses; and dried fruits, mainly prunes, currants, and regular raisins. While the orphans only had three meals, workers often had a "second breakfast"—we might call it a snack—of bread and butter or cheese in the midafternoon.

The Daily Meal for the Middle and Affluent Classes

The orphanage menus might be used as an example of the meals eaten by the poor and working class. The only remaining Dutch cookbook of the seventeenth century, *De Verstandige Kock* (The Sensible Cook), first printed in 1667, gives insight into the diet of the more affluent classes and their children. The book includes recipes for vegetables, served raw as salads or cooked by themselves or as part of other dishes. After the section on vegetables, it goes on to talk about "all sorts of meats," including mutton, veal, beef, poultry, rabbit, hare, and venison, followed by "all sorts of fish," such as sturgeon, bream, pike, eel, salmon, cod, oysters, mussels, lobster, and crab. We might note that the common herring, the pillar of Dutch wealth, was eaten by all classes. The next section discusses "all sorts of baked and cooked items," puddings, custards and porridges, fritters, pancakes, waffles, and wafers. The book's last section is devoted to "all sorts of *taerten*," which are savory or sweet raised pies. Throughout the book, the author suggests the use of spices such as nutmeg, cloves, mace, or cinnamon that Dutch seafarers brought from faraway shores. It concludes with two appendixes, one for preserving meat for winter, the other for preserving fruits. The latter offers recipes that use large quantities of sugar, which was a luxury item that had become more readily available (though it was still expensive) during the seventeenth century.

As is clear from the orphanage menus, bread was an important part of the diet. Like other European countries in that period, Dutch people were heavily dependent on bread grains (rye and wheat). White bread, often referred to as *"herenbrood"* or gentlemen's bread, was the regular bread of the wealthy. The poor mostly ate dark rye bread and for them white bread was a treat for special occasions. Because white flour is bolted or carefully sifted to remove husks, it took more grain to produce and was therefore more expensive. Amsterdam physician Stefanus Blankaart concluded in *De Borgelijke Tafel: om lang gesond sonder ziekten te leven* (The bourgeois table: to live a long [life] healthfully without illness) of 1683 that rye bread is better for workers than for those who study or have little exercise, which might explain the term "gentlemen's bread" for white bread. Blankaart adds that children who eat too many regular pancakes or puffed pancakes, waffles, biscuits, white bread, and pudding will get worms and bloated bellies, but, in spite of his warnings, as we will see later, baked goods formed a major portion of children's treats.

Beverages

The common drink for every meal was beer. The poor and children generally drank a weak beer with an alcohol content of 0.5 to 2.0 percent. Beer, for which the water is boiled, was safer than water, which was very polluted, particularly in the cities. In a painting by Jan Victor that still hangs in the Amsterdam Municipal Orphanage building (now the Amsterdam Museum), we see the orphans at their evening meal, and one of them is drawing a pitcher of beer from a barrel. On the farm, buttermilk was drunk as well (the buttermilk the orphanage purchased was probably used for porridge). More affluent folks would drink heavier beer and wine imported from France, the Mediterranean countries, or Germany. Children might have been given some wine with water on occasion. Paintings of the wealthier class, as well as the accounts of herbalist Petrus Hondius and others who wrote poems praising the pleasures of the country life, show how with good weather an afternoon repast of wine and fruit was enjoyed in the garden; later in the century tea would be served.

Chocolate (hot cocoa), tea, and coffee gradually made inroads during the course of the century. Chocolate as a drink arrived in Europe through the explorations of Columbus in the late fifteenth and early sixteenth centuries, first in Spain and gradually in France and the rest of Europe. The Dutch were the first to bring a shipment of tea to Europe in 1610, but it took until the 1660s for it to became a popular drink, especially with women. Italian traders introduced coffee to the West. The drink caught on first in England, where by the 1650s coffeehouses (forerunners of gentlemen's clubs) sprang up and later, toward the last quarter of the century, in the Dutch Republic. When parents started drinking tea or coffee, cups of a weak version of the beverage were given to the children.

Holidays and Special Occasions

Period art, particularly Jan Steen's genre paintings, depict children and parents at the table together at everyday meals, but also at feasts such as Epiphany or Three Kings Day and interacting in joyous celebration on Saint Nicholas day (see illustrations).

The Synod of Dordt, a church council called in 1618 to the city of Dordrecht by the Dutch Reformed church, had eliminated Saint's Days as cause for celebration and declared only four official Protestant holidays: Christmas, Easter, Ascension Day, and Pentecost. However, some of the Catholic festivities such as Epiphany or Three Kings Day, Shrove Tuesday, Saint Martin, and Saint Nicholas continued to be happily celebrated at home, or in some cases even publicly, as the illustrations will show. These holidays had their own culinary or celebratory customs attached to them, all involving children. Despite the protestations of church ministers and government and town officials, the celebrations remained. Even government ordinances and admonitions from the pulpit could not stop the celebration of Three Kings Day and the most important one, the feast of Saint Nicholas (still celebrated to this day). They simply moved inside into the family circle and if special meals or dishes were connected with the old (Roman Catholic) celebrations, they would continue to be served.

Christmas: The Celebration of the Birth of Jesus Christ

Just as we might think that candies have always been part of everyday life, we might think a tree always has been part of the Christmas celebration, but it was not until the 1850s that Christmas trees were seen in Dutch households. Germany and England were ahead in incorporating trees into their festivities, and this German custom might have had its origin in the early seventeenth century. Before 1850, Christmas in the Netherlands was a solemn celebration. Before and after that date, it was sometimes marked regionally by bells ringing or, in the eastern part of the country, with the traditional blowing of large horns at midwinter. In general, in the seventeenth century it was marked by church services and was celebrated with a festive (or perhaps larger) meal. Gift-giving to children was reserved for Saint Nicholas day.

Easter: The Celebration of the Resurrection of Jesus Christ

Easter was marked by large fires, thought to bring fertility to people, animals, and land. Palm Sunday, the Sunday before Easter, marks the celebrated entry of Jesus into the city of Jerusalem. A custom that still prevails on that day is for the children to parade with a wooden cross decorated with greens and strings of sweets, either candies or dried fruits, and topped with a rooster made from bread dough. Another symbol of Easter is the colored Easter egg, the source of new life, an ancient custom that can be traced to the fourth century and perhaps earlier. (The Easter bunny dispensing eggs came much later and is another German custom.) Traditionally, especially in agricultural areas, children would go from house to house to collect eggs, and they sang a special song (also sung on Palm Sunday) for the occasion, part of which says: "een ei is geen ei, twee ei is een half ei; drie ei is een Paasei" (one egg is no egg; two eggs are half an egg; three eggs make an Easter egg), referring perhaps to the Trinity. The eggs were dyed with natural colors such as spinach (green), onion peels (yellow/orange), and red cabbage (purple). An Easter egg hunt and a competition for who could eat the most eggs were often part of the festivities.

Ascension Day: The Church Celebration of the Ascension of Jesus Christ into Heaven.

Ascension Day falls forty days after Easter and commemorates that Jesus Christ in the presence of his apostles ascended bodily into Heaven. It is only included here to be complete. This Christian holiday does not seem to be connected to celebrations outside the church.

Pentecost: The Commemoration of the Emanation of the Holy Spirit to the Apostles

Pentecost, *Pinxter*, present-day *Pinksteren* in Dutch, is celebrated fifty days after Easter, hence its English name, Pentecost, which means fiftieth. It is an important day in the Christian calendar and commemorates the time when the Holy Ghost came to the apostles and they spoke in tongues. It is considered to represent the day of the founding of the Church.

The *Pinxterblom* or Pinkster flower, in some areas *Pinxterbruid* or Pinkster bride, as portrayed by Dusart was an ode to spring and a symbol of sexuality and fertility. As is seen in that drawing, children participated in the celebration and were given coins for buying treats. Because Pentecost is celebrated in either late May or early June, it coincides with May celebrations of awakening fields and upcoming early harvests.

Dutch cultural historian Dr. Catharina van de Graft mentions in her book about holiday customs[4] that because it is often still quite chilly and therefore not quite time for agricultural activities during Easter, all sorts of old spring customs are also associated with Pentecost.

The following holidays continued to be celebrated in the home in spite of the Protestant Church's admonishment against such festivities.

---

4. Dr. C. Catherina van de Graft and Dr. Tjaard W. R. de Haan, *Nederlandse Volksgebruiken bij hoogtijdagen* (Prisma-reeks, 1978).

Twelfth Night, The Epiphany, or Three Kings Day: January 6

Three Kings Day, or *Driekoningen* in Dutch, occurring twelve days after Christmas and considered the end of the Christmas season, celebrates the revelation of God to man and commemorates the visitation of the Three Magi to the Christ Child.

The Epiphany festivities changed little over the centuries. Fourteenth-century documents illustrate the manner by which a king for the day (or at least the feast) is chosen. It could actually occur in two different ways: by way of a king's bread that would contain a bean; the person who received a slice with the bean was king. Lots were another way of deciding. Paper "king's letters" were sold in the streets and, when cut apart, provided the lots that assigned the roles those present would play: not only the king (for whom a paper crown was part of the "letter"), but also a jester, musician, and others, as seen in Jan Steen's painting in which a small child has been chosen king.

According to Dr. Schotel,[5] a cultural historian, who was the first to discuss in depth seventeenth-century family life, the game seen in Steen's painting—the children jumping or skipping over three candles (representing the three Magi)—often led to house fires, and the ministers from their pulpits as well as local officials tried to stop the practice. In 1661, the City of Dordrecht issued an ordinance forbidding candle makers to make and distribute such "superstitious candles."

Adults, and sometimes children, too, played another game: they dressed up as the three kings (two dressed in white and one in black), and carried paper stars lit by candles. Others (children and adults) would accompany them through the streets as they knocked on doors while singing special songs for the occasion.

Shrove Tuesday: The Day before Ash Wednesday

Ash Wednesday, the beginning of Lent, occurs forty days, not counting Sundays, before Easter. The meaning of the word to "shrove" someone in Old English, according to the dictionary, is to hear someone's acknowledgment of sins, assure him of God's forgiveness, and give him spiritual advice.

In the seventeenth-century Dutch Republic, part of the festivities of Shrove Tuesday was the sound of the *rommelpot* (rumbling pot), as previously

---

5. Dr. G. D. J. Schotel, *Het Oud-Hollandsch Huisgezin der Zeventiende Eeuw.* Rogge, H. C. Dr. 2d improved and illustrated ed. (Leiden: A. W. Sijthoff, n.d.).

described by Donna Barnes. The sound was the accompaniment to various songs, which differed from region to region. As on other holidays described above, children would go from house to house to collect coins with which to purchase treats. At home, pancakes were made on Shrove Tuesday, as we know from Gerbrand Adriaenszoon Bredero's play *Moortje* (1615), where characters talk about enjoying both thick rice pudding, another dish served for the occasion, and pancakes.

Sint Maarten (Saint Martin): November 11

As customary with all saints, it was the day of death that was celebrated—November 11, in the case of Saint Martin. Like Saint Nicholas, he was celebrated for his generosity, illustrated by his having given half his warm cloak to a cold, ragged beggar. As with the other holidays, this celebration had its traditional songs. Just like on Easter Sunday, fires were lit in the market square in the evening and the special treats for children on this day were the chestnuts that were roasted in the fire. These fires had their dangers and were often forbidden by local authorities.

Another part of the festivities was an evening parade of the town's children, who would hollow out turnips or beets and fit them with candle stubs to be lit and carried through the streets. Nowadays those have been replaced by paper Chinese lanterns, which make for a colorful procession.

Sint Nikolaas (Saint Nicholas): December 5–6

The most beloved celebration of all for children was the feast of Saint Nicholas. The Dutch had made this bishop of the Eastern Orthodox Church and patron saint of sailors, students, children, and many others their very own and celebrate him to this day. Records, as early as 1363, show that school children (who had the day off) were given money for treats on Saint Nicholas Day. Prior to Saint Nicholas Eve, December 5, stands were erected at the market squares, where toys and treats were sold. In orphanages and old-age homes, the evening meal for Saint Nicholas day was *wittebroodssop*, a porridge made of white bread and milk, which was served at other feast days as well.

Edible Pleasures

There were many places where a child could go to buy something edible. In the early decades of the seventeenth century, the apothecary shop, where medicines were prepared, also made and sold sweetmeats. To illustrate what these might consist of: an early account of an order of sweetmeats for a wedding included marzipan, sugar hearts, and candied fruits such as apricots and candied orange peel. Toward the end of the century grocery shops sold dried fruits, nuts, even candied almonds; bakeries could supply freshly baked cookies or rolls with "sweetmeats" (raisins, prunes, or currants); street vendors were around to provide pancakes, waffles, wafers, or even hot shrimp, as we see in the illustrations. And let's not forget the regular markets where vegetables, fruits, meats, and fish were available, some already cooked. The illustrations demonstrate that children bought and enjoyed these various food treats.

Sweets were mostly sweetmeats, which in the seventeenth century were dried fruits such as raisins, currants, or prunes, or fruits preserved with sugar or honey. This process of preserving is illustrated in the appendix of *The Sensible Cook*. It lists candying of green (young) walnuts, apples, pears, quince, and preserves of apricots, peaches, plums, cherries, and red currants. A perfect example of how such fruits were used can be deduced from the recipe for quince "cookies": peeled and cored quince are cooked down with sugar to make a paste that congeals when cooled and that is then rolled in sugar and cut into squares and served after the meal.

The closest we can come to today's candies are the sugar-covered *kapittelstokken:* cinnamon sticks, anise, or other seeds and almonds. In English, sugar-covered almonds are now called "Jordan almonds," and sugared seeds are referred to as comfits. *Kapittelstokken* were named for the small stick inserted at a page to indicate where one had left off reading the *kapittel* (chapter) in the Bible. When purchasing such treats at a local market, they were carefully counted the way coins are. For company, a hundred might be bought at a time, as we learn from the play *Moortje* by contemporary writer G. A. Bredero. The sugar-covered anise seeds or comfits are still part of the celebration of a birth in the Netherlands today, when they are served on a buttered rusk as *beschuit met muisjes.* Annie van 't Veer quotes a recipe in the eighteenth-century *Hollandse Keuken-meid* (Dutch kitchen maid) for making sugared almonds. It says to first make thick sugar syrup and then stir the almonds in it over a low fire until dry.

Sweetmeats of fruits preserved with honey were initially used mostly medicinally to cure various ailments; after the twelfth century sugar was used in the preparation. Under Arabic influence in the countries around the Mediterranean, the use of sugar in sweetmeats spread and reached Western Europe. Contemporary (seventeenth-century) doctors agitated against using too much sugar, as do their counterparts today. Amsterdam physician Stefanus

Blankaart argued that all items made from sugar are harmful when eaten in too large quantities. He urged moderation in all things. He enumerated items made with sugar: marzipan, macaroons, letters (see illustrations and recipe), cakes, pastries, sugared almonds, *kapittelstokken*, and confections such as candied fruit. He found that dried figs, or other dried fruits, were not bad to use but considered candied fruits to be harmful because of their sugar content, and he assured his readers that these were no longer prescribed by physicians.[6]

Other treats would include baked goods of various kinds prepared by the baker, at home, or in the street. The town's baker prepared the daily bread, rolls, pretzels, and cookies as well as specialty breads for the holidays, as we see in the Berckheyde painting. In the Netherlands, bakers were organized in guilds (associations of artisans), and their recipes were trade secrets, so it was not until 1753 that the first baking recipes were published. In the painting the children have come into the shop to buy a cookie, or perhaps a pretzel. A pretzel recipe in that first baking book shows that the Dutch version was sweet rather than salty. It calls for a pound each of flour and sugar, potash (baking soda), cinnamon, butter, and eggs. This quantity of dough makes eight *krakelingen* (pretzels; the old English word for them is *cracknels*).

In the Berckheyde painting and in the Steen Saint Nicholas painting, as well as in the Dusart watercolor, we see *duivekaters*. The meaning of the word is not clear but seems to refer to *duivel* (devil) and *kater* (tomcat). These often lemon-flavored white breads were shaped differently in various towns; for instance the kind shaped as a Chinese diamond seen in Dusart's work is typical for the *duivekaters* of the town of Broek op Waterland. Other towns known for their *duivekaters* are Delft, Nieuwendam, and Zaandam. They were made during the holiday season from the beginning of December through Epiphany on January 6. They were charitably dispensed to the poor during that period and were considered a treat by all.

The *duivekater* in the Berckheyde bakery shop is decorated with *patacons*; here they seemed to have been made from bread dough, but generally they were earthenware disks colorfully painted with either biblical or worldly images, prebaked, and baked again onto the bread as decorations. Small and larger *patacons* were used between the sixteenth and eighteenth centuries in the Netherlands (mostly in the south) and far longer in Flanders. Recently some were archeologically excavated from the garden of a house in Deventer

---

6. Stephanus Blankaart, *De Borgerlijke Tafel: om lang Sonder Ziekten Gesond te Leven.* 1683; reprint 1967.

in the northeastern Netherlands. One might think of them as little gifts in the way a ring or toy is placed in a Cracker Jack box, or a paper parasol garnishes a drink in a restaurant. They remain after the treat is consumed.

In the Dusart watercolor, which shows the Saint Nicholas celebration, the girl on the right has a basket on her arm that contains a long *koek*, a spiced molded gingerbread. We see the same baked good in Jan Steen's painting of the same celebration (see recipes). The Jb. Bussink bakery in the old Hanseatic town of Deventer has been long known for this *koek*. (The Hanseatic League was an economic alliance of trading cities and their guilds, stretching from the Baltic to the North Seas and inland, during the thirteenth through seventeenth centuries.) The company celebrated its quadricentennial anniversary in 1993, but that kind of spiced *koek* made with honey and potash (baking soda) was already known in the early Middle Ages.

In both the Steen and Dusart depictions we notice *klaeskoek*. This flat gingerbread, originally chewy dough made with honey, later a crisper baked good because of the use of sugar, was formed in wooden molds. Schilstra asserts in his book on wooden *koek* molds (cake boards) that while the traditional depiction would be Saint Nicholas in bishop's regalia, during the seventeenth century authorities tried to get rid of this "popish" celebration and the images were changed to hide their religious implication.[7] Because Saint Nicholas was frequently referred to as *hylickmaker* or "wedding maker," *klaeskoeck* could also have the shape of a male or female figure, and young men would give young women such cakes, and vice versa. Acceptance of such a gift indicated an interest for the person. Nowadays we know those spiced molded cookies as "windmill cookies," a shape frequently found in their modern version. In Dutch they are called *speculaas* (probably from the Latin word *speculum*, or mirror [image]).

On Epiphany, star singers, as depicted in another Steen painting, might receive some food or coins and would end up in the tavern, where they would treat each other to beer and *olie-koecken*, deep-fried dough ball containing apples, raisins, and almonds. *Olie-koecken* now are an integral part of New Year's in the Netherlands but are called *oliebollen*. During Rembrandt's time they were made in taverns, as street food, and at home. It is hard to improve on the recipe in *The Sensible Cook*, which calls for two pounds each of flour and raisins, and chopped apples, almonds, butter, and yeast. The dough is spiced with cinnamon, ginger, and cloves. The risen dough is scooped up with two

7. J. J. Schilstra, *Prenten in hout: Speculaas-, taai-, en dragantvormen in Nederland* (Lochem: Uitgeversmaatschappij De Tijdstroom bv, 1985).

spoons and shaped into a ball, which is dropped in hot fat or oil; originally rapeseed oil was used.

Pancakes, waffles, and wafers also were made both at home and on the street. Both the Steen painting and the Rembrandt etching show pancakes sold as street food. Pancakes and waffles are listed together in *The Sensible Cook*. The book gives recipes for three kinds of pancakes. The first recipe, which comes from the northeastern town of Groningen, calls for flour, eggs, currants, and cinnamon; the second is for "common pancakes" and lists flour, milk, and eggs and says "some add some sugar to it." The last one tells how "to fry the best kind of pancakes" and is made with water, eggs, and flour and is flavored with cloves, cinnamon, mace, nutmeg, and salt. After frying they are sprinkled with sugar. Because none of these employs baking powder the way today's American pancakes do, they were less pliable. They were commonly eaten out of hand, as is demonstrated by the boy in Rembrandt's etching.

To make waffles and wafers requires the use of special irons, which were often given as wedding gifts and were adorned with the couple's initials. Dutch museums have such irons, once belonging to local families, in their collections. The waffles were very similar to the ones we know today, although perhaps a little sturdier and more breadlike. Hot waffles were often served at home, as seen in Steen's depiction of the Epiphany celebration, but were also hawked at fairs or festivals or sold on the street, as Bramer depicts. They were usually spread with butter and no further topping.

The history of wafers is most interesting. Since the early Middle Ages monks would carefully make the "hostia oblata" (sacred consecrated wafers) used in Catholic mass in wafer irons, engraved with religious images. In around 1400 this manufacture gradually came into the hands of lay people, first in Paris, where these kinds of bakers (*oublieurs* in French) would deliver them to the church but simultaneously peddle them on the street. Van de Graft explains that these secular wafers became associated with New Year's in the Netherlands but retained their religious imprints.[8] Bramer also portrayed a wafer seller peddling her wares, akin to the waffle seller shown in the illustrations. The drawing is entitled "cinnamon wafers." The saleswoman sells them from a shallow basket, and two boys are each buying one from her.

Some vegetables and various fruits made excellent snacks. In both depictions of the Saint Nicholas celebration we see winter fruits like apples, pears,

8. Dr. C. Catherina Van de Graft and Dr. Tjaard W. R. de Haan. *Nederlandse Volksgebruiken bij hoogtijdagen* (Prisma-reeks, 1978).

and nuts as part of the baskets of treats. Apples particularly were used for a variety of dishes such as pancakes, custard, *olie-koecken*, and fritters and in many different apple-*taerten* (tarts or raised pies), as five recipes in *The Sensible Cook* demonstrate. Oranges were also associated with the feast; some believe this is in honor of the beloved house of Orange and the "Father of the Fatherland," Prince William of Orange (1533–1584). Others think the oranges represent the balls of gold that Saint Nicholas gave to three young women who needed dowries. He is frequently depicted with three balls of gold as attributes. Any fruit and vegetables such as carrots or radishes would make treats for children. They were fun to pull up in a garden; from the dirt would seemingly magically appear an orange root or a white-and-red radish (the variety most seen during the period), both deliciously crunchy and slightly sweet. Stefanus Blankaart warned children not to eat peapods, as they liked to do, because it caused bad breath. Strawberries and other fruits, he suggested, were best eaten with a slice of bread.

One can easily imagine a group of kids sneaking into a garden and grabbing an apple, pear, a handful of cherries, or some berries, or jostling a market stall and running off with whatever fell on the ground.

Other treats might come at slaughtering time in November, when sausage or head cheese was made, hams were smoked, and meat was pickled with salt to preserve it for winter. On the celebration of Saint Maarten on November 11, a roasted goose was a traditional part of the festivities.

In a country that borders the sea and has three major rivers running through, it comes as no surprise that fish and seafood are part of the menu. In Bramer's drawing of the shrimp seller we see how hot shrimp are sold on the street. Shrimp were generally boiled in sea water either onboard ship or on the shore, and this scene was probably drawn in a nearby village. Fish markets were divided into two sections, one for freshwater fish such as pike, eel, perch, bass, or bream and one for saltwater fish, such as salmon, cod, turbot, haddock, flounder, plaice, thornback (ray), herring, of course, and lobster, crab, and shrimp. For shrimp prepared at home we turn to Gheeraert Vorselman, who explained in his *Eenen Nieuwen Coock Boeck* (A new cookbook) of 1560 how to prepare shrimp: "Take lively shrimp; salt the water and allow it to come to a rolling boil, add some vinegar to the water, and throw in the shrimp, make sure they boil as if it were a sea and allow the wave to pass over them three or four times. Remove them to a colander and sprinkle with salt, is good to eat cold, peeled with vinegar, pepper and chopped parsley."

Four hundred years ago, children did not have the variety of hundreds of candies and chocolates that a modern child can enjoy. Their choices were limited to cookies from the bakery shop, comfits from the apothecary or itinerant market seller, fruits and vegetables from the garden or a market stall, or items such as cooked shrimp, waffles, wafers, or pancakes from street vendors. Yet there were enough places and occasions to add something tasty to their monotonous fare. Parents and various institutions or governmental entities made sure there were special, extra items as rewards for good behavior, or for holidays and festive occasions.

Images of Childhood Pleasures

MATTHIJS NAIVEU (1647–1726)

The Newborn Baby

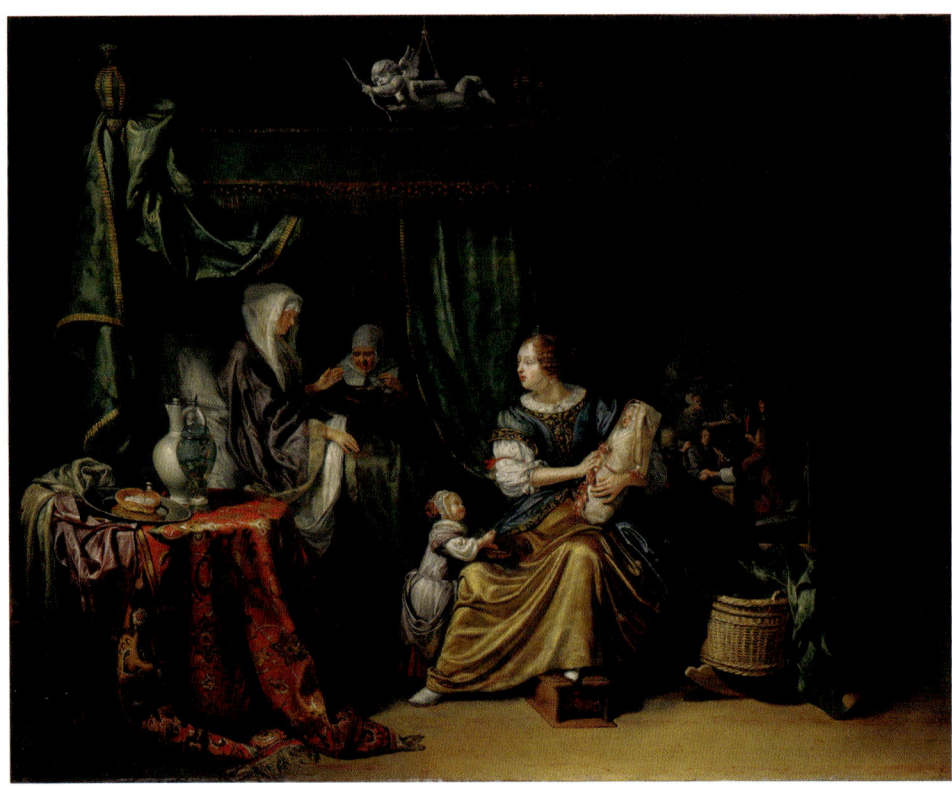

Matthijs Naiveu (Dutch, 1647–1726), *The Newborn Baby*. Oil on canvas, 25 1/4 x 31 1/2 in. (64.1 x 80 cm). The Metropolitan Museum of Art, Purchase, 1871 (71.160). Image © The Metropolitan Museum of Art.

In the seventeenth century, children were born at home with the assistance of a midwife. Custom dictated that new mothers remain in bed for nine days after the birth of their babies, although family and friends were allowed to visit and celebrate the birth. In well-to-do families the bed was hung with rich draperies for the occasion, as portrayed here by Naiveu. In the foreground on the right, the female visitor is holding the swaddled baby. In the background, according to custom, the men have been provided with pipes and wine and are seen smoking and toasting the father. The Dutch imported tobacco from Virginia by way of New Amsterdam and even grew some themselves, predominantly around the city of Amersfoort.

On the table on the left are the traditional refreshments for the occasion. In the glass pitcher is a drink, named *kandeel,* made from white wine, eggs, sugar, mace, nutmeg, cinnamon, and cloves; the accompaniments are so-called *suikertjes* (little sugars) or comfits, sugar-covered cinnamon sticks, almonds, or sugar-covered anise seed (still served nowadays). Anise probably flavors the mother's porridge as well because it was thought to encourage the flow of her milk. The *suikertjes* are served in a bowl-shaped baked good akin to a rusk. The little girl impatiently pulling the visitor's gown seems to be holding a comfit to draw her attention to the delicious treats that are waiting. (PGR)

LUDOLF DE JONGH (1616–1679)

Portrait of a Couple with Two Children, ca. 1673

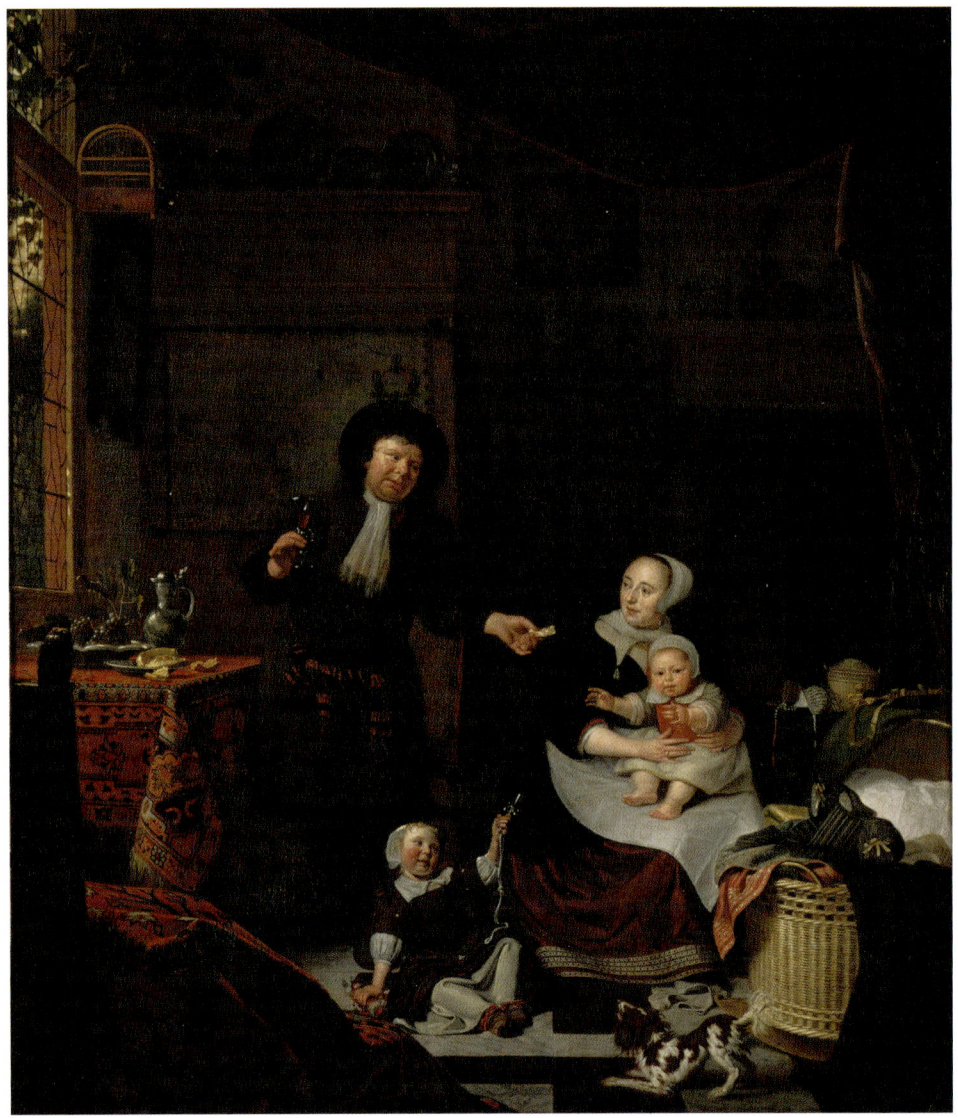

Ludolf de Jongh, *Portrait of a Couple with Two Children*, ca. 1673. Oil on canvas, 72.5 x 63.5 cm. Collection Amsterdam Museum (SA 7525).

Inside a cozy sun-drenched interior room, a small child seated on the floor offers a rattle to a baby sibling who is perched on the mother's lap. The father, standing near a table topped with a Turkish rug, pauses from drinking his wine to offer a broken rusk to the baby. The family's brown-and-white spaniel dog watches carefully, prepared to snatch the rusk if the infant doesn't want it.

The mother had removed the baby from the beautifully woven wicker cradle: nap time was over. Pudgy little hands outstretched, the baby is ready to receive whichever treat—toy or munchy-crunchy rusk—gets there first. If the baby is teething, either treat will help divert attention from aching gums.

The child seated on the floor seems to have a toy clutched in the other hand. No matter what parents might say, that toy is not for sharing!

The identity of this family is unknown. At one time, the painting was thought to have been painted by Michiel van Musscher, and it was assumed to be a portrait of his own family. Now it is attributed to Ludolf de Jongh. But whoever the artist, it is a visual celebration of the intimacy of family life.

Babies in affluent families were often depicted with rattles, some with jingling bells and some with a stick of coral or polished rock crystal attached. If rubbed against irritated gums by a teething baby, the smooth cool stone would be soothing. Rattles were often an infant's very first toy. Christian children sometimes received rattles as baptismal gifts. (DRB)

J AN L UYKEN (1649–1712)

De Speelstoel (The play chair)

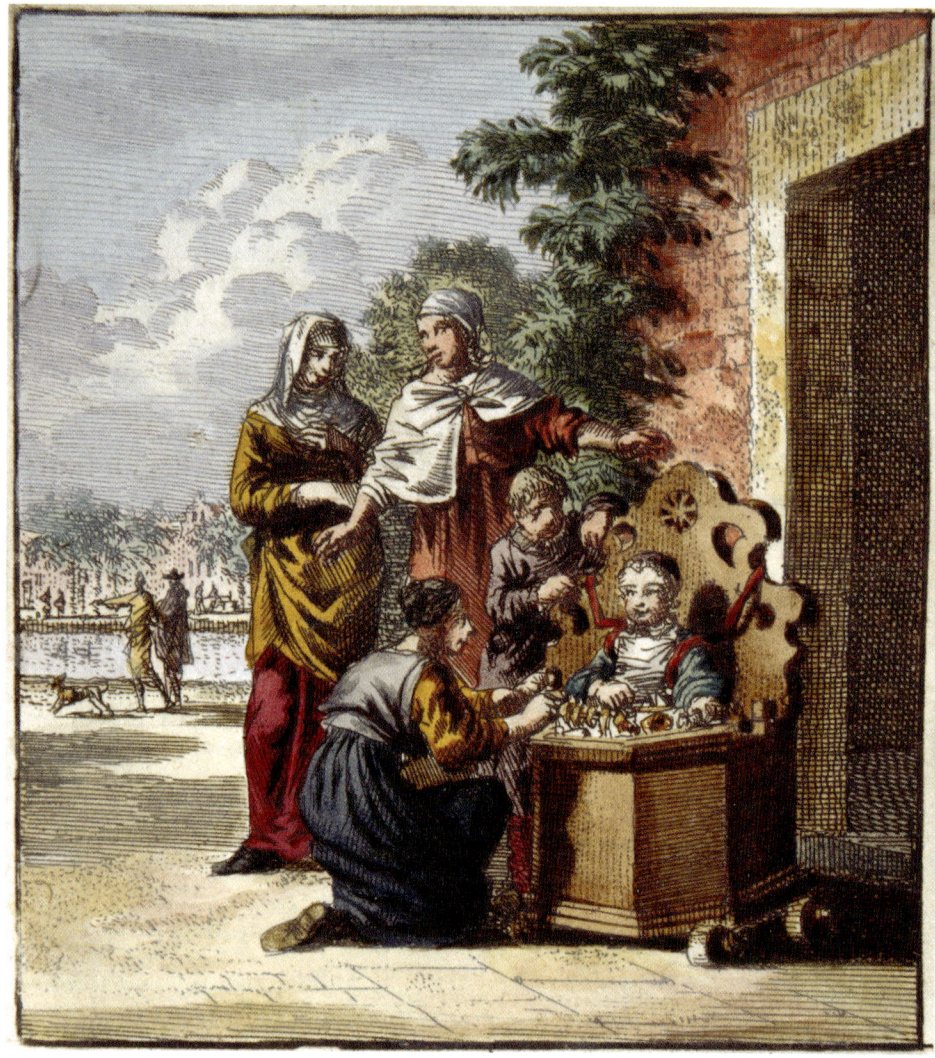

Jan Luyken, *De Speelstoel* (The play chair). Print (hand colored), *Des Menschen Begin, Midden en Einde,* 1712. Collection Amsterdam Museum (P 4397; A 18942).

Little children sit enclosed in wooden chairs with an attached tray used either for treats and food bowls when eating or for small toys when playing. Sometimes a small metal or ceramic chamber pot was placed under the child's seat or an earthenware brazier of warming coals beneath the child's feet. If the *speelstoel* had wheels, it was possible for mother or other older siblings to roll the youngster about. This young tot is enthroned like a ruling monarch, attended by supplicating older children trying to get the toddler interested in toys.

Artists frequently depicted young children seated in their *speelstoelen* or *kinderstoelen*. Elsewhere in this volume, Govert Flinck portrays a small girl standing near her *kinderstoel*, her hand stretched toward some sweets, and Cornelis Dusart also shows an infant child seated in a chair with toys.

One of Jan Steen's paintings, now located in Vienna at the Kunsthistorisches Museum, shows a seated child who does not blink an eye at the surrounding family chaos, where even the dog misbehaves.

In Johan de Brune's *Emblemata of Sinnewerck* (1624), an angry child is shown seated in a *speelstoel* having a temper tantrum. Toys are tossed haphazardly on the floor; an image of the devil lurks in the background. In a painting by Quiringh Gerritsz. van Brekelenkam, now located at the Allen Memorial Museum of Oberlin College in Ohio, a child sits in a *speelstoel* in a kitchen area. A wire with small balls is stretched across the table surface, functioning as an abacus so the child can learn to count.

A few Dutch artists created "dummy boards" of youngsters sitting or dozing in a *speelstoel*. These painted objects were cut out from wood and had a standing back support. Dummy boards were used to fill a fireplace opening during the heat of summer, when fires were not lit for general heating. Some were also found in corners in country homes. In 1654, the Haarlem artist Johannes Verspronk made at least two depicting a tabby cat guarding a pudgy-faced little boy in his *speelstoel* who had fallen asleep, porridge dripping from his spoon.

Dutch ceramicists created three-dimensional decorative glazed porcelain objects for table or sideboard display in both the seventeenth and eighteenth centuries; often a child in a *kinderstoel* was featured. Similarly, Dutch silversmiths occasionally fashioned a small silver replica of a child seated in its chair. These were luxury items collected by wealthy women and were then known as "toys."

All these art works and decorative objects—prints, paintings, dummy boards, figurines, and miniature silver "toys"—provide evidence of the fond way Dutch adults thought about little children and their childhood pleasures. Dutch children were cherished. (DRB)

GOVERT FLINCK (1615–1660)

Girl by a High Chair

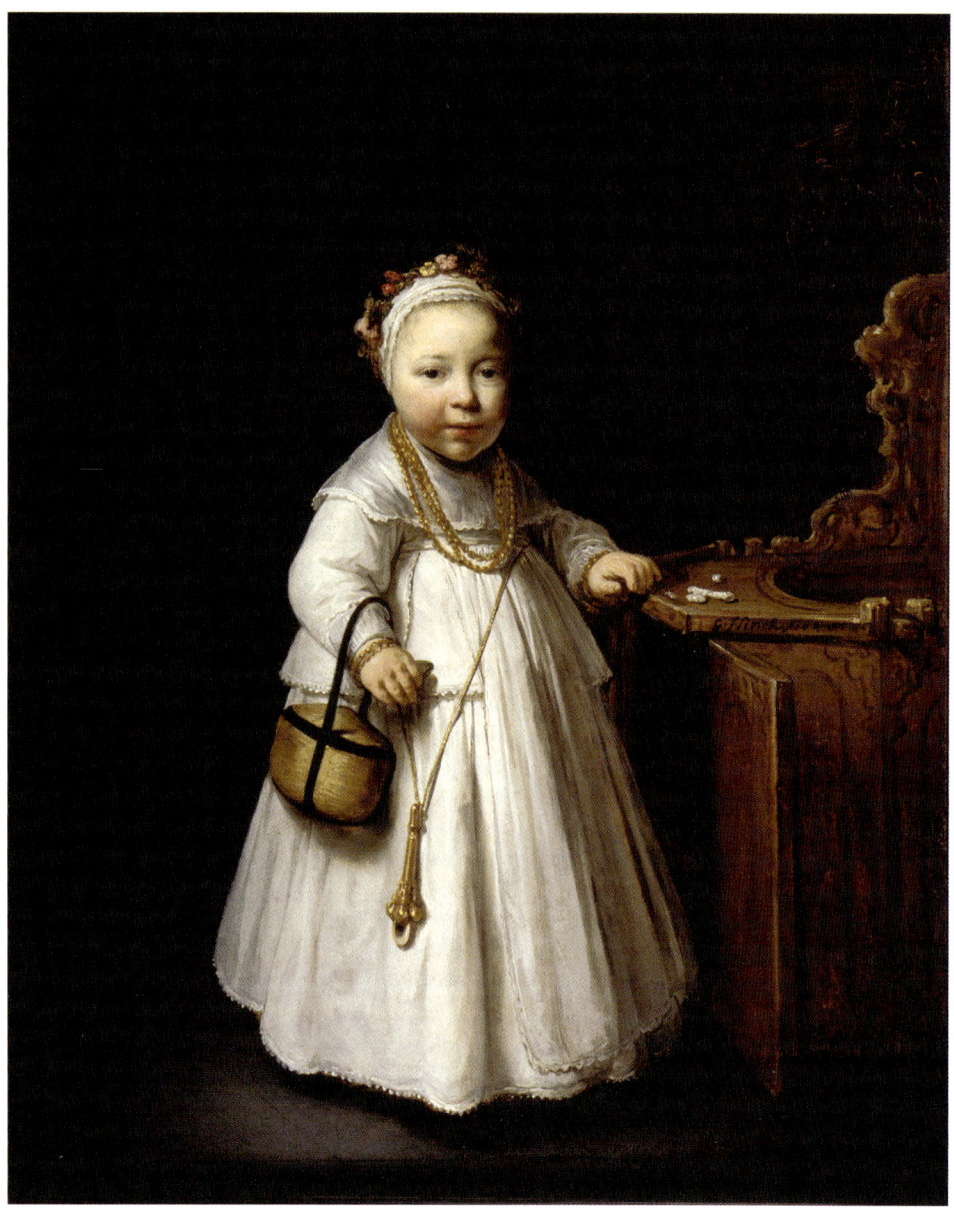

Govert Flinck, *Girl by a High Chair.* Oil on canvas. Royal Picture Gallery Mauritshuis, The Hague.

The sweet child with her soft, chubby, kissable cheeks stands by her carved high chair. Her cap is adorned with a ring of cloth flowers, and she is wearing gold chains and bracelets. A long gold chain has a *rinkelbel* attached; it is a rattle with a protruding piece of bone, crystal, or coral with the additional function of supposedly keeping away evil spirits, and it was used for teething. Some of her jewelry and her little basket seem to point to her future job as the person in charge of the household. The only childlike items are the candies on the tabletop of her high chair. They are the sugared comfits we see in other paintings in this book as well: an almond, a cinnamon stick, and a sugared anise seed.

To the modern eye such treats seem dangerous for a small child, but maybe she has been taught to suck carefully on them in the way one sucks on a present-day lollipop. Dressed in such seemingly adult garb the way she is, it is hard to tell how old she might be. The painting seems to indicate that such sweets were given to children as well as adults, but also to imply a certain social status and wealth. As we have seen in the Naiveu painting, people bought these treats for special occasions, such as births. The working class or poor probably could not afford them at all. (PGR)

CORNELIS DUSART (1660–1704)

L'Enfance (Childhood), from *Les Quatres Ages de la vie humaine* (The four ages of man)

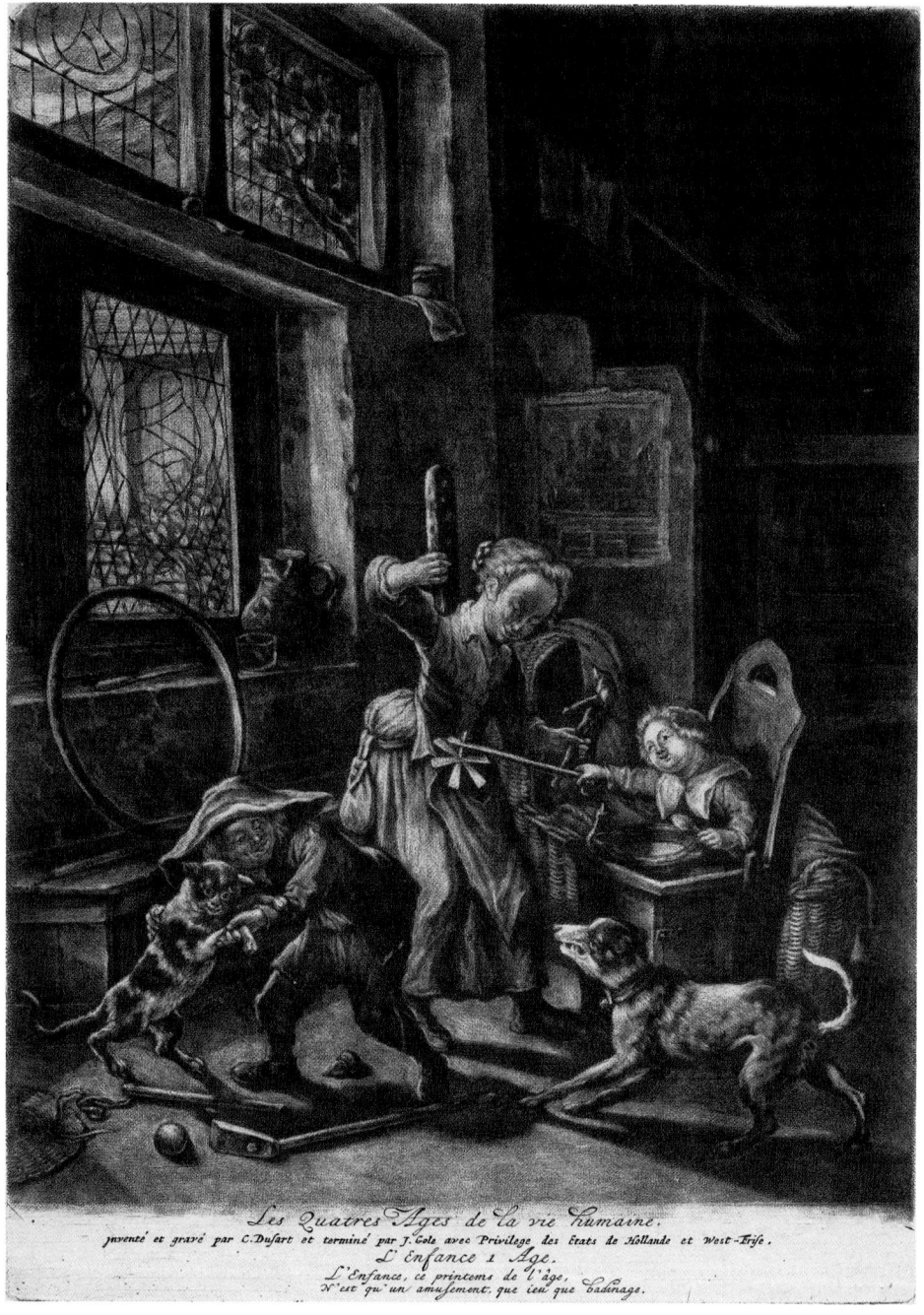

Les Quatres Ages de la vie humaine.
jnventé et gravé par C.Dusart et terminé par J.Gole avec Privilege des Etats de Hollande et West-Frise.
L'Enfance 1 Age.
L'Enfance, ce printems de l'âge,
N'est qu'un amusement que ieu que badinage.

Cornelis Dusart, *L'Enfance* (Childhood), from *Les Quatres Ages de la vie humaine*
(The four ages of man). Print. Atlas van Stolk, Rotterdam.

A young child sits in a *speelstoel*, pinwheel in hand. Other toys have been arranged for the child's pleasure. An older girl and boy attempt to divert and entertain the youngster; even the dog gets in the act. Older brothers and sisters were frequently expected to amuse the younger children in the family so that mother's attention could be focused on cooking, sewing, or her other household tasks.

Not only did youngsters need to be enclosed in the chairs for their own safety so that they wouldn't toddle into the fire burning in the fireplace hearth while meals were prepared, but sitting restricted in the chair also allowed the youngest one freedom to "rule" his or her siblings. Older sisters and brothers, who might bring toys to the infant, make grimacing faces to prompt laughter, or jingle tambourines and sing nursery songs, could disappear when they tired of playing with the little one. But so long as siblings were present, the little child wanted to be the center of attention. Baby might smile and laugh and gurgle with pleasure when happy, but could whine, cry, fling food from a spoon, or toss toys away from the *speelstoel* when unhappy.

Dusart, like many of his contemporaries, created a series of images devoted to the four stages of human life, moving from infancy with its focus on children of varying ages through maturity and ending in old age. That the youngest child is shown in a special chair simply marks the way this piece of household furniture was a familiar emblem for infancy. (DRB)

JAN LUYKEN (1649–1712)

De Loopwagen (The walker)

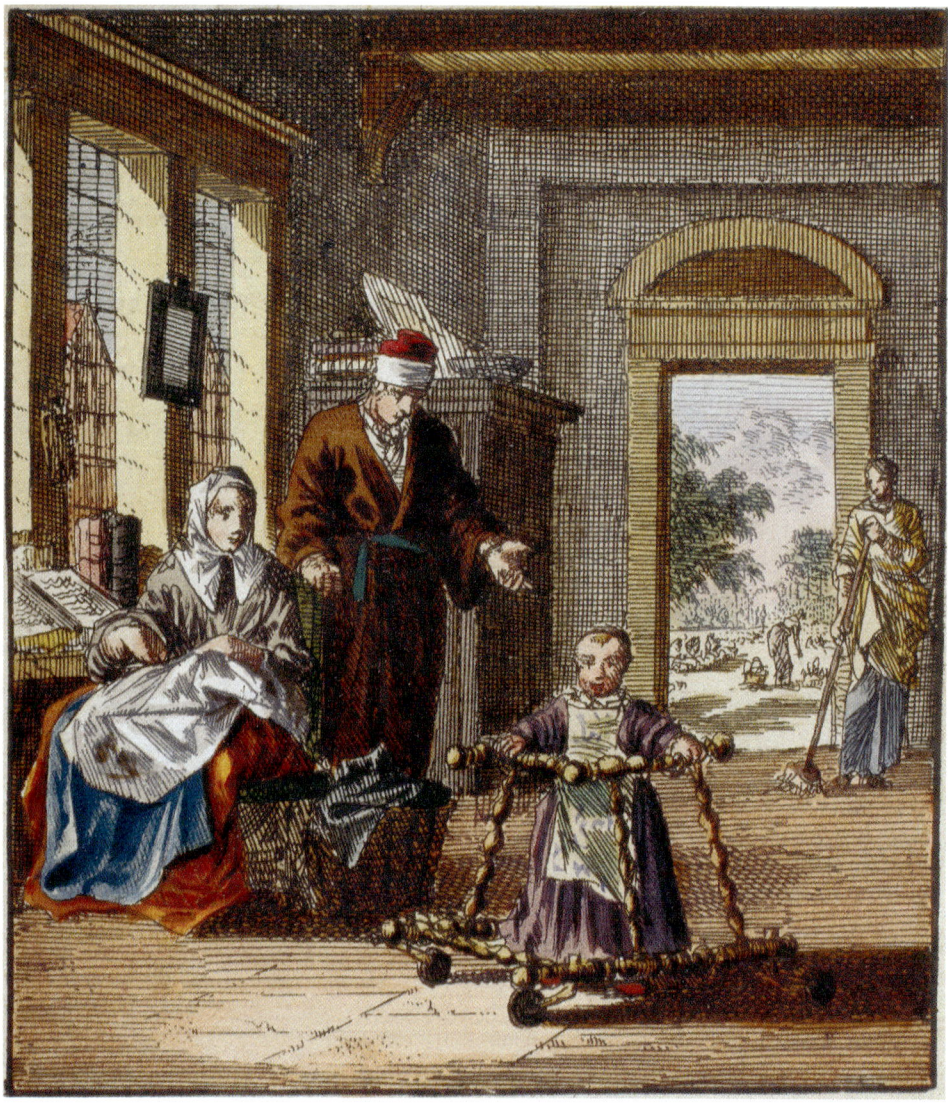

Jan Luyken, *De Loopwagen* (The walker). Print (hand colored), *Des Menschen Begin, Midden en Einde*, 1712. Collection Amsterdam Museum (P 4394; A 18939).

Learning to walk is always an important task for a little child. Parents often offer encouragement. Standing upright requires both balance and courage. A child learns initially indoors by standing in a wooden walker with wheels attached. Grasping the side support pieces, the child can walk—or toddle—rolling the walker along the floor. Uncertain at first, eventually the child gains confidence and skill.

If the youngster begins to feel uneasy, balance can be regained by firmly grasping the wooden support bars and slowing down. Failing that, the child can sink down to the floor, sitting until strength and determination reappear. At that point, cranky youngsters often wail or sniffle, hoping an adult will take notice and offer comfort and help.

In this scene, the baby is urged on by father, while mother sits raising her eyes from her needlework to pay close attention to the progress made. Even the domestic serving woman in the background pauses from her mopping to take note of this little one's achievements. It will be an even prouder day when the child no longer needs the *loopwagen* but can walk alone without assistance.

Married couples who were planning or anticipating many children in their marriage frequently purchased the best *loopwagen* they could afford, knowing it would probably last and be useful for all the family's children. Understandably such couples were especially grateful if their in-laws made them a gift of the first *loopwagen*, or perhaps a cradle, at the time the couple announced the wife's pregnancy and the impending birth.

Walkers were typically made of turned wood and often had wheels. Less expensive variations were made of basket-woven willow branches. Those could be dragged along the floor but did not have quite the movability that wheeled versions offered. Often children learning to walk wore protective helmets on their heads, a *valhoedje*, that provided cushioning for the tender bones in their skulls should they fall, hitting their heads on floor or furniture indoors or hard pavements outdoors. (DRB)

CORNELIS DUSART (1660–1704)
The Saint Nicholas Celebration

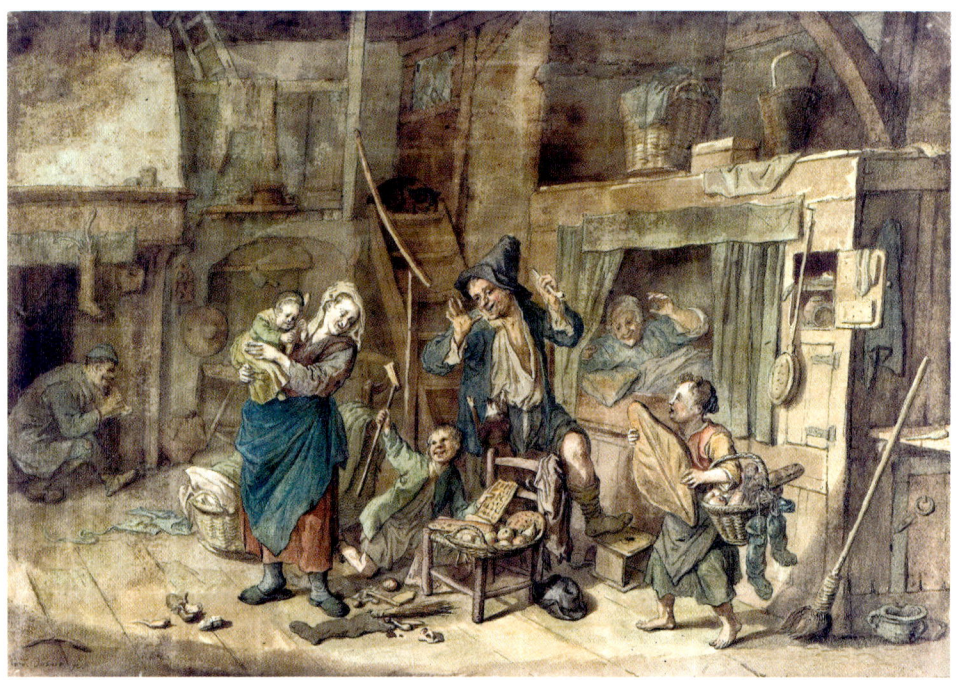

Cornelis Dusart, *The Saint Nicholas Celebration*. Colored drawing. Atlas van Stolk, Rotterdam.

The artist portrays the morning of December 6, the day of death of Saint Nicholas (saints in general are celebrated on their death days). The children have hung their stockings by the chimney, as seen here, but in other paintings of the same event, such as those by Jan Steen, they placed their shoes by the hearth. No matter what footwear is used, the children receive presents.

While the grandmother rejoices in her cupboard bed, the children show off their presents, most of which are delicious treats. The girl to the right near the well-worn broom has a basket full of baked goods including a long Deventer spiced *koek* (akin to gingerbread), but the basket also seems to hold a doll. The child proudly holds a *duivekater*, or holiday bread, made from white flour and butter, in front of her. Its shape indicates that it came for the town of Broek op Waterland. Each area had its own version.

On the chair in the middle of the room is another basket with treats. It contains apples and pears as well as more *koek*, with spiced hard gingerbread leaning against the back of the chair. The little boy by the chair is holding up a *kolf* stick (for playing a form of ice hockey) to his mother. The baby in the mother's arms holds up a long *koek*, or sweet bread called *taai taai* (the word *taai* means tough and indicates the chewy quality of the honey-flavored baked good). On the floor lies another stocking, a treat or two, but also a *roe* (bundle of switches, used for spanking), which was given to naughty children. In this heart-warming little genre scene, the parents and grandparents are clearly enjoying the merriment of the happy children with their presents and treats brought to them by Saint Nicholas during the night. (PGR)

PETER BINOIT (1690/93–1632/39)

Still Life with Letter Cookies

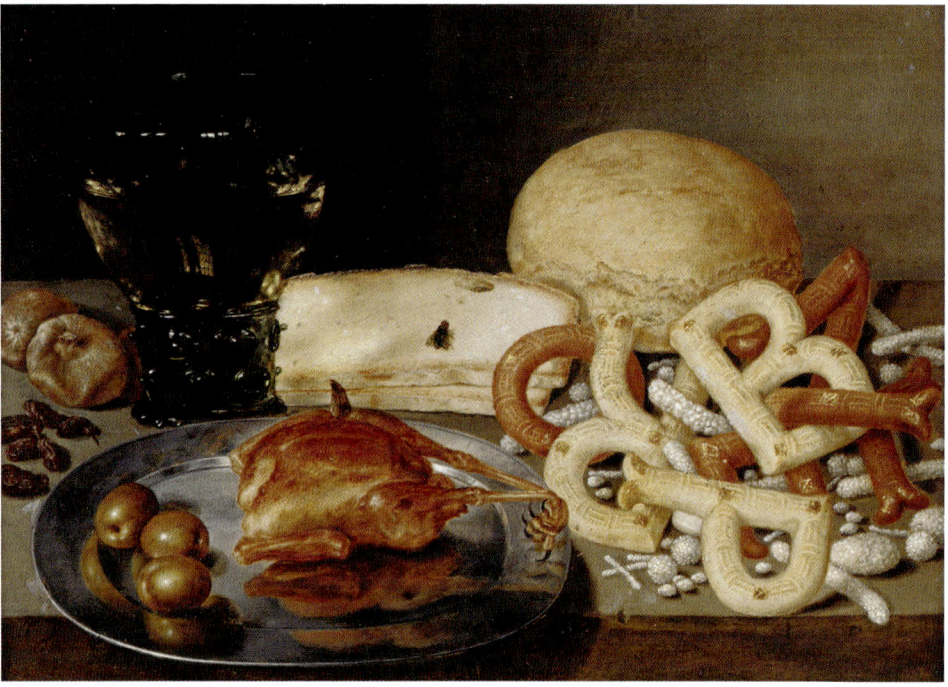

Peter Binoit, *Still Life with Letter Cookies.* Oil on canvas. Collection Groninger Museum, Photograph John Stoel.

German-born painter Peter Binoit is included because of this depiction of letter cookies, seen in the works of Dutch painters as well, but not in such profusion. The small fowl and olives on the pewter platter are surrounded by dates, what might be citron, a *berkemeyer* glass with white wine, cookies akin to biscotti, bread, and those fascinating letter cookies, some of which were made from a plain dough, others from a spiced dough. Prominent in their display are the painter's initials, but other letters can be found as well, such as R and O. Some art historians believe that when taking all into account they spell his complete name. The letters are mixed with other confectionery products, sugared comfits, in Dutch called *kapittelstokken*, also seen in the Naiveu, Flinck, and Steen paintings.

The letters depicted by Binoit were clearly molded in carved molds in the way the *koek* for the Saint Nicholas celebration was. In a painting by Willem van Mieris depicting an early–eighteenth-century grocery store, much simpler, smaller cookie letters are heaped in a tin. They would seem to be a less expensive version. This edible alphabet was an appealing way to teach children their letters, a custom apparently going back to the Middle Ages. Letters are still very much part of the Saint Nicholas celebration, but rather than molding them, they are now made from almond-paste-filled puff pastry and shaped by hand, or they are indeed molded and made from milk and dark or white chocolate. Almost all Dutch children nowadays will receive the initial of their first names in chocolate on December 5. (PGR)

JAN STEEN (1626–1679)

Het Sint Nicolaasfeest (Saint Nicholas feast), ca. 1665–1668

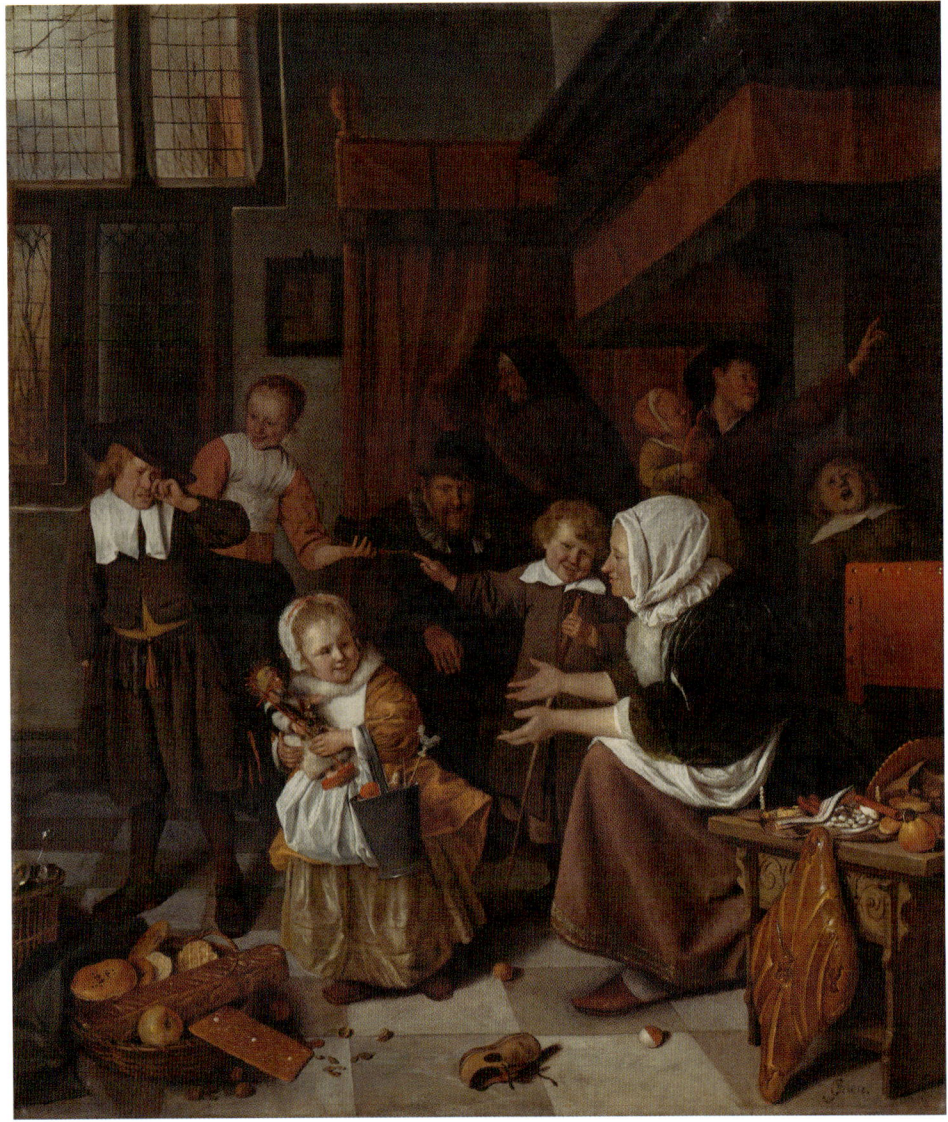

Jan Steen, *Het Sint Nicolaasfeest* (St. Nicholas feast), ca. 1665–1668. Oil on canvas, 32¼ x 27¾ inches. Rijksmuseum Amsterdam (SK-A-385).

The disappointed boy who received birch switches in his shoe wipes a tear from his eye. Message received: Saint Nicholas was not pleased with his behavior this past year. No gifts for him; instead he deserves to be spanked.

His younger brother received a *kolf* stick and red-and-white *kolf* ball from Sinterklaas. His jubilant little sister carries a figurine of Saint John the Baptist; she will play with it like a doll. She has other small toys and treats in the metal shopping can suspended on her arm. But first there are all those wonderful sweets to enjoy!

The boy's older sister smirks at her brother's embarrassment. She doesn't seem to notice that grandmother is pulling back the bedstead curtain, gesturing to her grandson. Perhaps he will end up with a toy or treat, after all, thanks to a more forgiving grandma. His older brother holds the youngest child in his arms, pointing out the chimney that the good saint descended when he left treats for the good ones and a chastising "reminder" for the brother who had misbehaved. The youngest child has already begun to explore the delights of the chewy *taai taai* baked goodie. His other brother has burst into song.

See Peter Rose's discussion of the importance children and their families attached to the Sinterklaas celebration. It was an occasion for youngsters to receive gifts of both toys and sweets. Exceedingly staunch Protestants sometimes chose not to acknowledge the day, thinking it Popish foolishness, some going so far as to call it an "abomination." Catholic youngsters eagerly awaited the December 5–6 holiday. No doubt most of their Protestant counterparts did, too.

Jan Steen returned to this theme more than once. A similar painting is located at Museum Boijmans-van Beuningen in Rotterdam, although there the young girl doesn't have a John the Baptist doll, and the grandmother offers the naughty boy a coin. (DRB)

JAN LUYKEN (1649–1712)
De Pop (The doll)

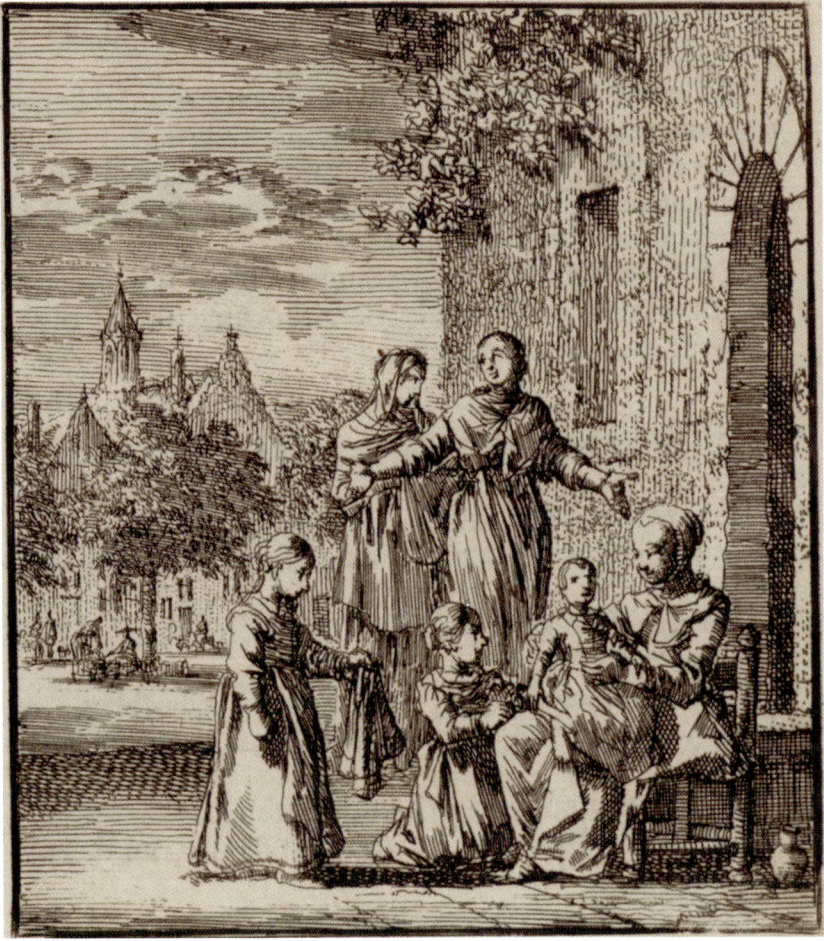

Jan Luyken, *De Pop* (The doll). Print, *Des Menschen Begin, Midden en Einde*, 1712. Collection Amsterdam Museum (P 4412; A 18957).

Just like a little mother, a girl balances her beloved doll on her knee. Other girls join her at play. These girls talk to the seated girl, but perhaps they also talk to her doll. Girls have long envisioned lives and distinct personalities for their dolls, giving them names. Two women also discuss the girls' play, perhaps recalling their own childhood dolls or commenting on the girls' mothering styles.

Dolls heads could be made from porcelain, carved wood (often covered with layers of gesso and then painted), papier mâché, or fabric. Their bodies were typically made from linen, canvas, or cotton fabric that was stuffed with horsehair or sawdust to give them firmness. Small feet and hands might have been carved from wood and attached to cloth arms and legs. Dolls were usually dressed in clothing that resembled garments worn by adult women. (Baby dolls did not exist in the seventeenth century.)

Girls whose mothers or household domestic servants possessed needlework skills often asked them to make additional garments for their dolls, building up a doll's wardrobe. Changing a doll's clothing was a fun form of play. Since sewing was valued in Dutch women of all social ranks, young girls were often encouraged to learn sewing skills by fabricating simple garments or accessories for their dolls. Fitted dresses required mature skills, time, and patience, but a simple shawl, scarf, or apron could be stitched easily by a girl.

Some girls obtained their dolls from specialized toy sellers, sold at the time of an annual *kermis* or in time for Saint Nicholas celebrations. Other girls counted on their mothers, grandmothers, or perhaps the household servant girl to fashion simple rag dolls for them.

Whether their dolls were commercially produced or homemade, the girls who owned them loved them. Playing with dolls was thought by Dutch parents to be good preparation for a girl's eventual responsibilities as a mother raising her own children. Girls usually treated their dolls lovingly, although occasionally angry girls scolded their dolls or spanked them with birch switches, repeating behaviors they themselves had experienced.

Dolls are shown in paintings and prints by other Dutch artists. Invariably the dolls are female. (DRB)

EGBERT VAN HEEMSKERK (1634/35–1704)

Jacob Fransz. Hercules (ca. 1635–1708) and His Family in the Surgeon's Work Place, 1669

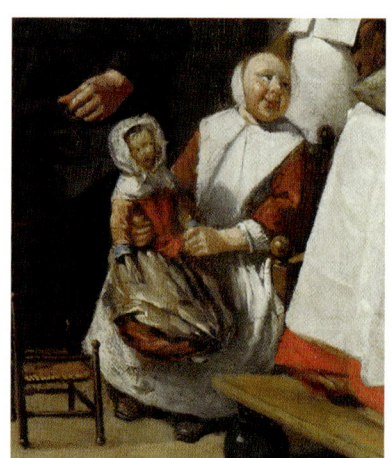
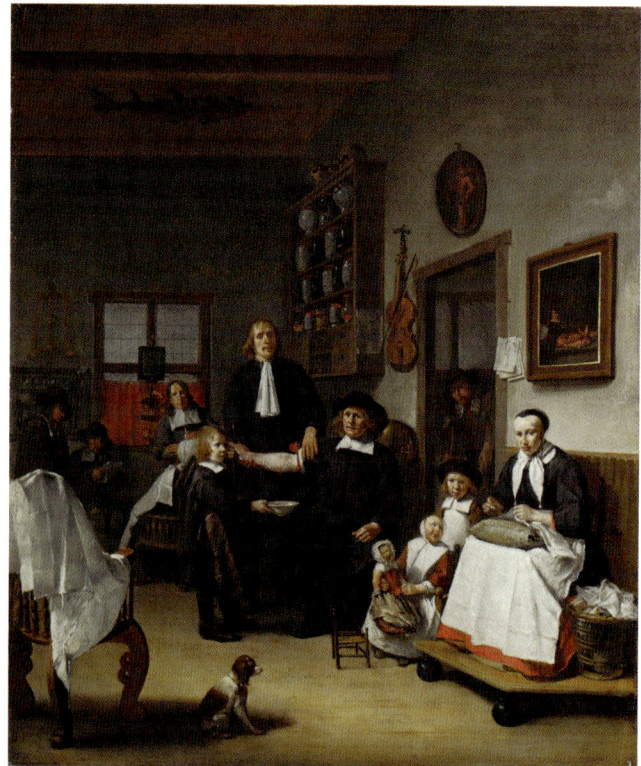

Egbert van Heemskerk, *Jacob Fransz. Hercules (ca. 1635–1708) and His Family in the Surgeon's Work Place*, 1669. Oil on canvas, 27⅝ x 23¼ inches. Collection Amsterdam Museum (SA 2121).

While the barber-surgeon bleeds a client, which was thought to be helpful in curing certain illnesses, his youngest child, a little girl, holds her large doll. A small chair for the doll is near the girl's feet. Clearly, the child enjoys her doll, which is dressed in red garments, very much like the girl and her mother. This girl probably considered the doll just as much a member of the family as her father, mother, brothers, and the brown-and-white dog. The girl sits near her mother, who is busily doing needlework on her sewing cushion, a sign of her domestic responsibility. Her slightly older brother has no time to play; he is busy assisting his father by holding the metal bowl into which the seated customer's blood will drip.

That the father conducts his business in his home was typical of the time. Merchants, lawyers, paintings dealers, and artists frequently performed their work at home, perhaps in an office, studio, or work shop. This man has achieved a measure of wealth, as can be inferred from the large painting hanging on the wall behind his wife and the oval-framed painting of the mythical god Hercules (alluding to the family name) above the doorway, as well as the mirror at the window.

This painting is unusual because it shows the father and son actually working at the tasks that financially support the household. Symbols of this man's occupation also exist in the stuffed swordfish suspended from the ceiling, and the glass and faience apothecary jars of medicinal herbs and compounds on the shelves. The violin hanging on the wall not only attests to the family's interest in music, but also alludes to the harmony existing within this family. The mother is seated on a raised platform (*vlondertje*) that keeps drafts from her feet, another reference to the family's comfort and prosperity. Not every household could afford one.

Most family portraits did not show the family at work. In this painting, it is clear that the father expects his young son to learn the skills necessary to take over the family business once he is older. Barber surgeons shaved men, trimmed their beards and mustaches, cut their hair, and also performed minor medical tasks such as setting broken bones, cleansing and suturing knife wounds, removing corns and calluses from feet, applying leeches to bad bruises to suck out accumulated blood, and opening veins with a sharp knife or scalpel to drain off a certain amount of blood. Because it was believed that people's bodily conditions were governed by four characteristic "humors," people with persistent high fevers were thought to have excessive sanguine qualities that could be relieved through blood-letting.

Evidently the little girl playing with her doll has no interest in the activities of father and son, the barber's assistant in the background shaving a man, or the other customers waiting for the barber's services. Her attention is riveted on her doll, which she might have received as a gift from Sinterklaas. No doubt her mother found that perfectly appropriate: learning now to care for her doll will equip the girl for her eventual role as a mother with her own children. Polishing, dusting, and taking proper care of the doll's chair will result in housekeeping skills needed later in life. (DRB)

JAN LUYKEN (1649–1712)
Het Poppegoed (Doll things)

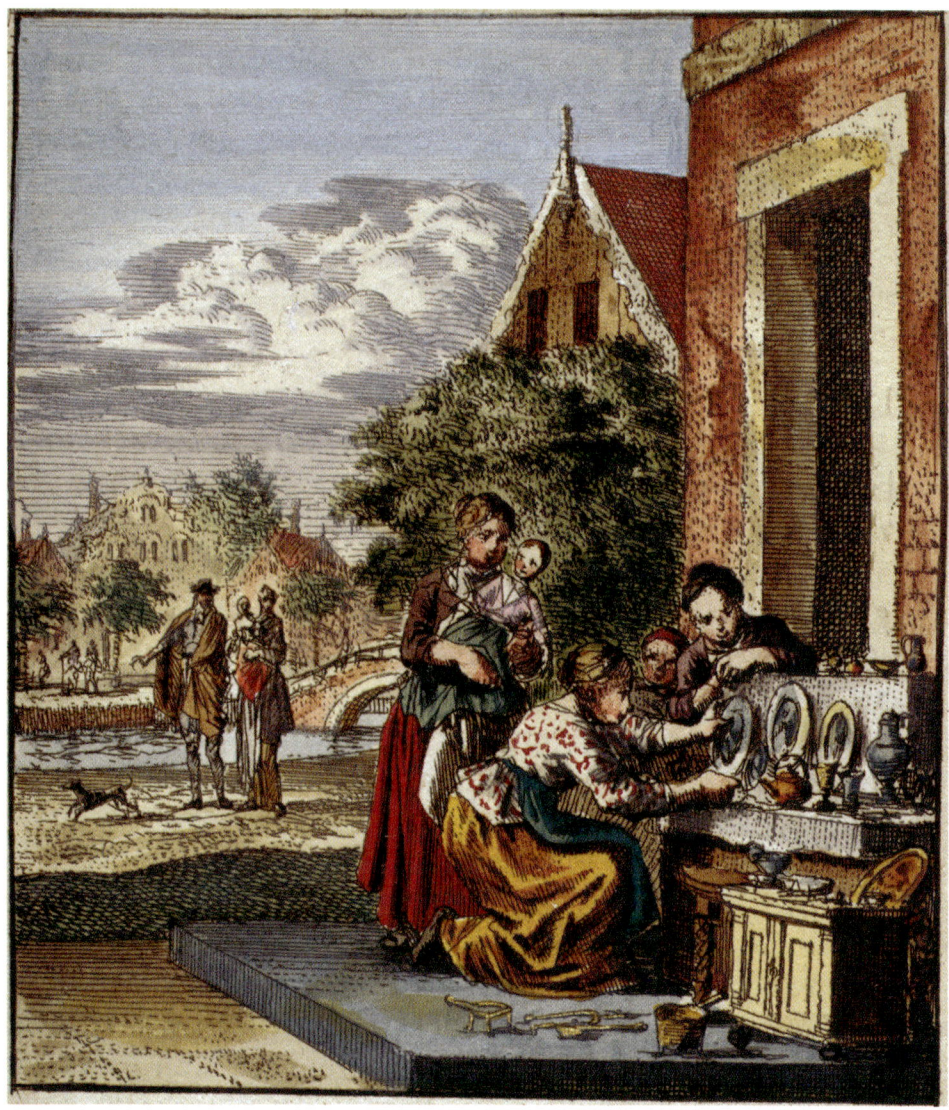

Jan Luyken, *Het Poppegoed* (Doll things). Print (hand colored), *Des Menschen Begin, Midden en Einde,* 1712. Collection Amsterdam Museum (P 4413; A 18958).

Girls play outdoors with dolls and miniature doll-sized cooking pots, platters, an iron, and a trivet. By dressing the dolls, loving them, scolding them, talking to them, and imaginatively preparing tasty meals for them, girls rehearse lessons in child care and homemaking they will eventually need as adult women. Did these girls permit their dolls more sweets than did their own mothers? Perhaps so.

Interestingly, Jan Luyken, who prepared this illustration, also wrote and illustrated an emblem book a year earlier that was focused on household furnishings. That book, *Het Leerzaam Huisraad*, depicted linen closets, mortars and pestles, roasting grid irons, racks for displaying platters, washtubs, rag mops, tables, chairs, and day beds. In most cases, women are shown using these items. The English translation of his book's title is *Instructive Household Furnishings*. Such "lessons" derived from the use and proper care of domestic objects would be ones the girls shown in this print needed to learn.

Miniature pots and pans, produced by coppersmiths, potters, and pewterers, were a source of delight to young Dutch girls. Chair caners and turners produced small chairs, tables, and beds for doll play, just as basket weavers occasionally wove tiny wicker cradles used by girls who sang lullabies as they put their dolls to sleep.

Exceedingly wealthy women in the seventeenth and eighteenth centuries had doll houses (*poppenhuizen*) created for them, which they furnished with miniaturized furnishings and small dolls. These women spent fortunes on these amusements. The doll houses conferred social cachet on their owners, who very proudly displayed their treasured "collections" to admiring family and friends. Some of these doll houses, with their miniaturized *poppengoeden*, survive at the Rijksmuseum in Amsterdam, Centraal Museum in Utrecht, Frans Halsmuseum in Haarlem, and the historical museum in Den Haag. These antique "toys" continue to fascinate today's museum visitors. (DRB)

JAN STEEN (1626–1679)

Twelfth-Night Feast

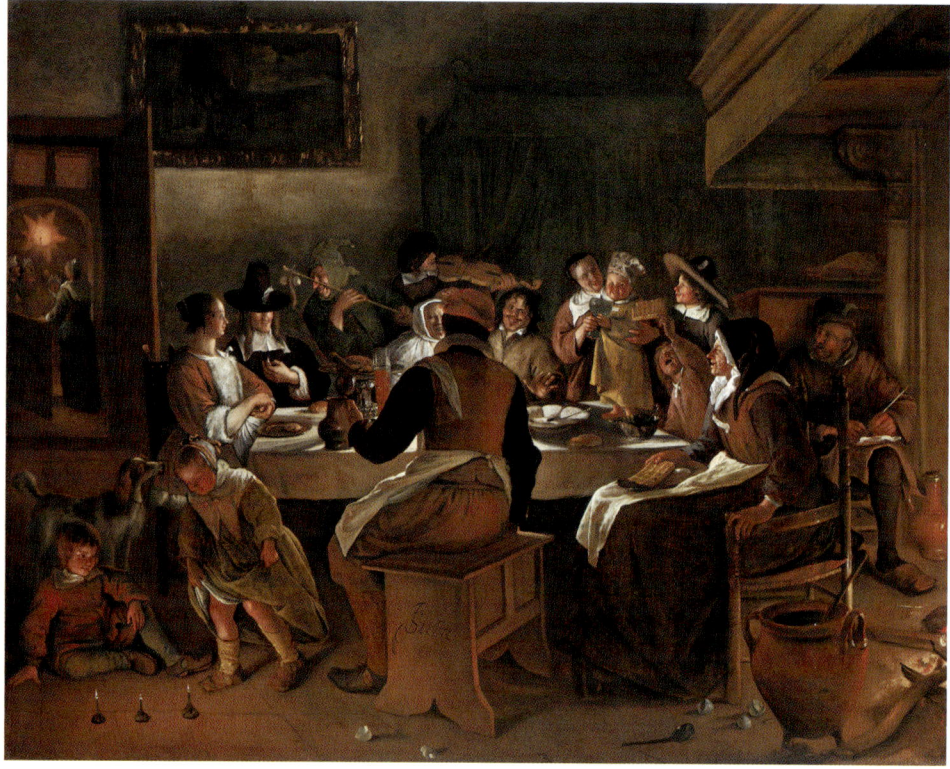

Jan Havicksz. Steen, Dutch, 1626–1679. *Twelfth-Night Feast*, 1662. Oil on canvas. 131.1 x 164.5 cm (51 5/8 x 64 3/4 in.). Museum of Fine Arts, Boston. 1951 Purchase Fund, 54.102.

It was difficult for Protestant church officials to enforce what the Synod of Dordrecht of 1618 had decreed, namely that there were only four official holidays in a church year: Christmas, Easter, Ascension Day, and Pentecost. The population continued other celebrations such as Twelfth Night or Three Kings Day and Saint Nicholas Day in their homes, and that is precisely what is shown here. Jan Steen portrays an extended family of ten adults and three children around the table in the midst of the celebration. The menu seems to consist of a fowl with a (customary) sauce, breads, and waffles, but more food-stuffs might be hidden in front of the man with his back turned to the viewer. Waffles were made in long-handled irons and were baked right over the fire.

Served often for holidays such as Twelfth Night or Easter, they were also sold by street vendors, as we will see in a drawing by Leonard Bramer.

Two small tykes are playing a game, special to Three Kings Day, of skipping over three lit candles, one of which is black, representing the three magi, who traveled to Bethlehem. In the background we see a female figure at the door greeting singers carrying the traditional star. They might be invited in to eat some food, or perhaps they are given a handout of coins to purchase their own treats. (PGR)

JAN STEEN (1626–1679)

Der Siruplecker (The syrup licker)

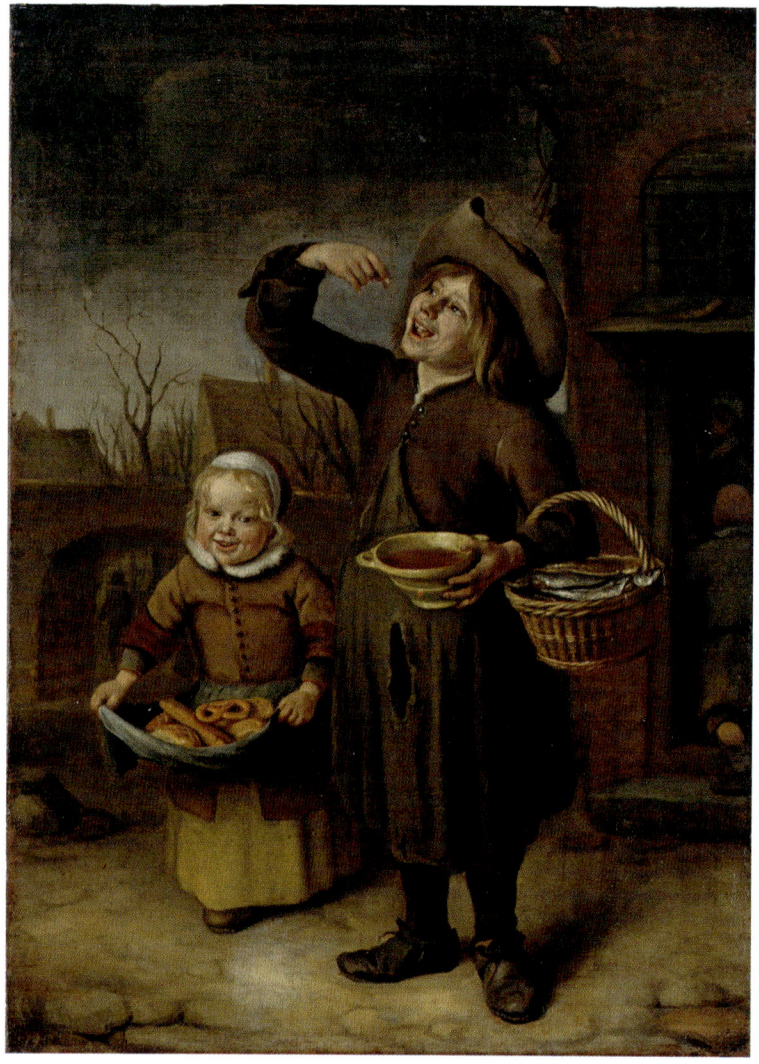

Jan Steen, *Der Siruplecker*. Oil on canvas. bpk, Berlin/Hamburger Kunsthalle, Hamburg, Germany/Elke Walford/Art Resource, NY.

On Shrove Tuesday, children have been going from door to door to collect treats and have amassed a generous store of good things to eat. There is herring in the boy's basket and syrup in the bowl. He has dipped his finger in it to get a sweet lick. The darling little girl has an apron full of baked goods, including rolls with crisscross slash marks on top; a long gingerbread called Deventer *koek* (see recipes); and a pretzel.

The syrup was made from apples, pears, or both. It was a centuries-old method of preserving the harvest. The fruits were cooked for a long time in a shallow pot over a low fire until all liquid had evaporated. The remainder was pressed and filtered. Because of its high sugar content, this syrup kept for a long time and was used as a sweetener for various foodstuffs. Today it is still eaten, smeared on buttered bread or used to top pancakes. (PGR)

CORNELIS DUSART (1660–1704)

"February" (*12 Months of the Year*)

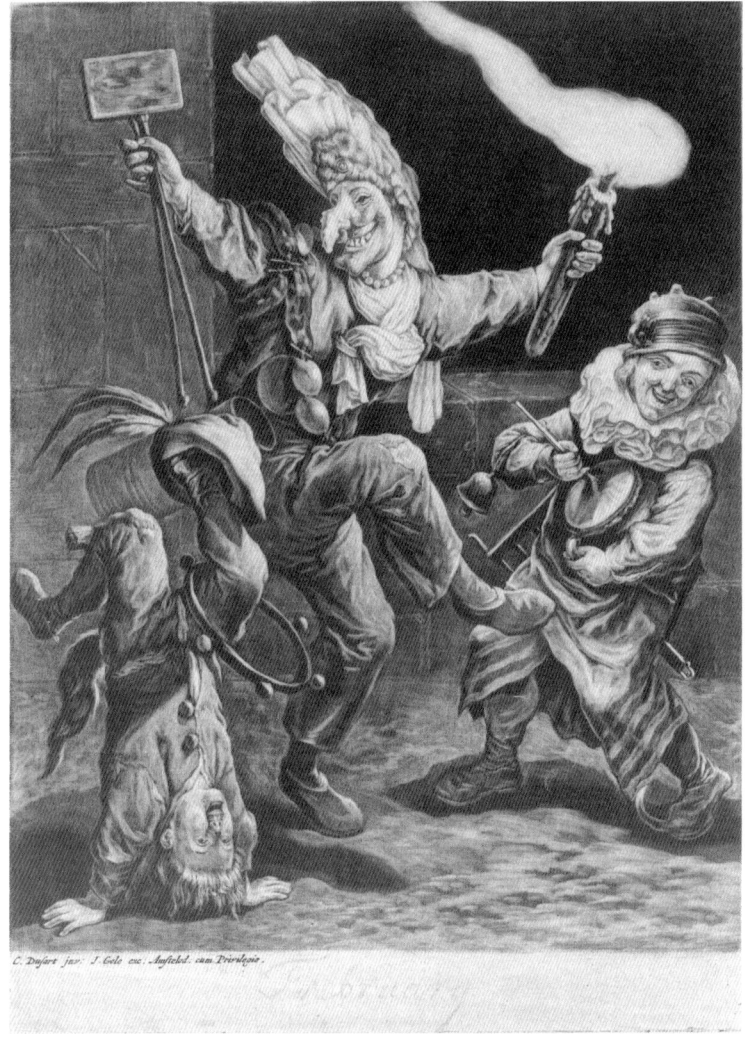

Cornelis Dusart, Dutch, 1660–1704. "February" (*12 Months of the Year*), about 1680–90. Mezzotint. 21.5 x 15.4 cm (8 7/16 x 6 1/16 in.). Museum of Fine Arts, Boston. Harvey D. Parker Collection, P3263.

Three boys are reveling in celebrations for the Shrovetide season just prior to Lent. The youngest does a handstand while twirling a jingling tambourine on his leg. Another boy works his *rommelpot*, smiling with glee at its raucous, rumbling noises. He's got an earthenware cooking pot perched on his head like a cap. Attached to his waist is a gridiron (*rooster*) used to cook sausages, fatty fish, and meats over an open fire in a hearth. The third boy, older than the others, wears a woman's necklace and an elaborate fontange headdress and wig typical of fashionable "ladies" at the end of the seventeenth century. He sports a grotesque mask with an ugly, misshapen nose and waves a waffle iron and a lit torch. He also has a garland of eggs and sausages around his neck.

Vastenavond, the night before Ash Wednesday, was celebrated by Catholic youngsters and adults primarily in the Southern Netherlands, typically with parades in cities in Brabant and Limburg and with feasts of rich, fat-laden food—like sausages, waffles, pancakes, and eggs—that would have to be given up during the Lenten fast period. Wearing costumes and masks was all part of the merriment.

These traditions had their roots in *carne vale* celebrations initially imported from Venice, where masked celebrants engaged in bawdy displays of humor. *Carne vale*, literally meaning "farewell to meat," marked the beginning of a period of dietary stringency. As early as the fourteenth century, Dutch people were celebrating in 's-Hertogenbosch. Because the Catholic Church insisted upon a penitential fast period of forty days, exclusive of Sundays, in preparation for Easter, people became accustomed to buttery rich foods for Mardi Gras, or "Fat Tuesday," knowing that Lent would be characterized by austere meatless fish days.

Usually Lent began in February; hence Dusart's use of this playful image to characterize the month of February in a series of prints devoted to the twelve months of the year.

The torch held by the oldest boy is found in other works by Dusart, specifically two print images of a man and a woman lighting a torch attached to a rocket-launching mechanism in a burst of patriotic ardor. Around 1692, Godfried Schalcken also created a painting of a young boy holding a lit torch. It is now part of the Art Gallery of Ontario collection. Dutch festivities, especially nighttime parades, often featured torchlight processions, and it is not surprising that youngsters, like moths, would be attracted to the flame. Dutch artists shared a fascination for the chiaroscuro effects of torchlight and candlelight in numerous genre paintings.

The mask worn by the oldest boy was probably made of molded leather. Tanned pigskin, horsehide, or cowhide could be soaked, molded on a cast-plaster head, with eyes and mouth carved out with a knife, a leather nose attached with skin threads, and holes punched into the side so the mask, once it hardened, could be strung and tied around the wearer's head. The mask might have been painted and varnished, but that was not always a requirement. This boy's mask was probably purchased, not self-made.

Men wearing masks and dancing with women of dubious reputations can be seen in a painting by Pieter Codde, now in the collection of the Mauritshuis in The Hague. Codde also created a painting of actors putting on masks in a changing room. That painting is in the Staatliche Museum in Berlin. Mask wearing has long been considered a device for behaving in usually forbidden ways, whether the mask was worn by children or by adult men and women.

Bells sewn onto the boy's clothing produced tinkling, jingling sounds. Small bells had a long history in the Netherlands (and elsewhere in Europe) of being associated with fools and foolishness, although some small bells were also attached to the leather bridle gear of horses pulling sleighs or carriages.

Tambourines, like the *rommelpot*, were popular folk instruments. They were easy to play; simply shaking the tambourine would make rhythmic noises. Any child older than three could produce sounds with one.

Associating Lenten revelries with sausages, eggs, drink, and music was found in a magnificent painting by Frans Hals, *Shrovetide Revelers*, now located at the Metropolitan Museum of Art. There the celebrants were grown-up adults, not children. Earlier, in 1559, the Flemish master, Pieter Brueghel the Elder, created the painting *The Battle Between Carnival and Lent*, where there were masked revelers and a tilting man astride a wine barrel brandishing a spit laden with rich meats. That painting is located in Vienna's Kunsthistorisches Museum. (DRB)

JAN LUYKEN (1649–1712)

De Trommel (The drum)

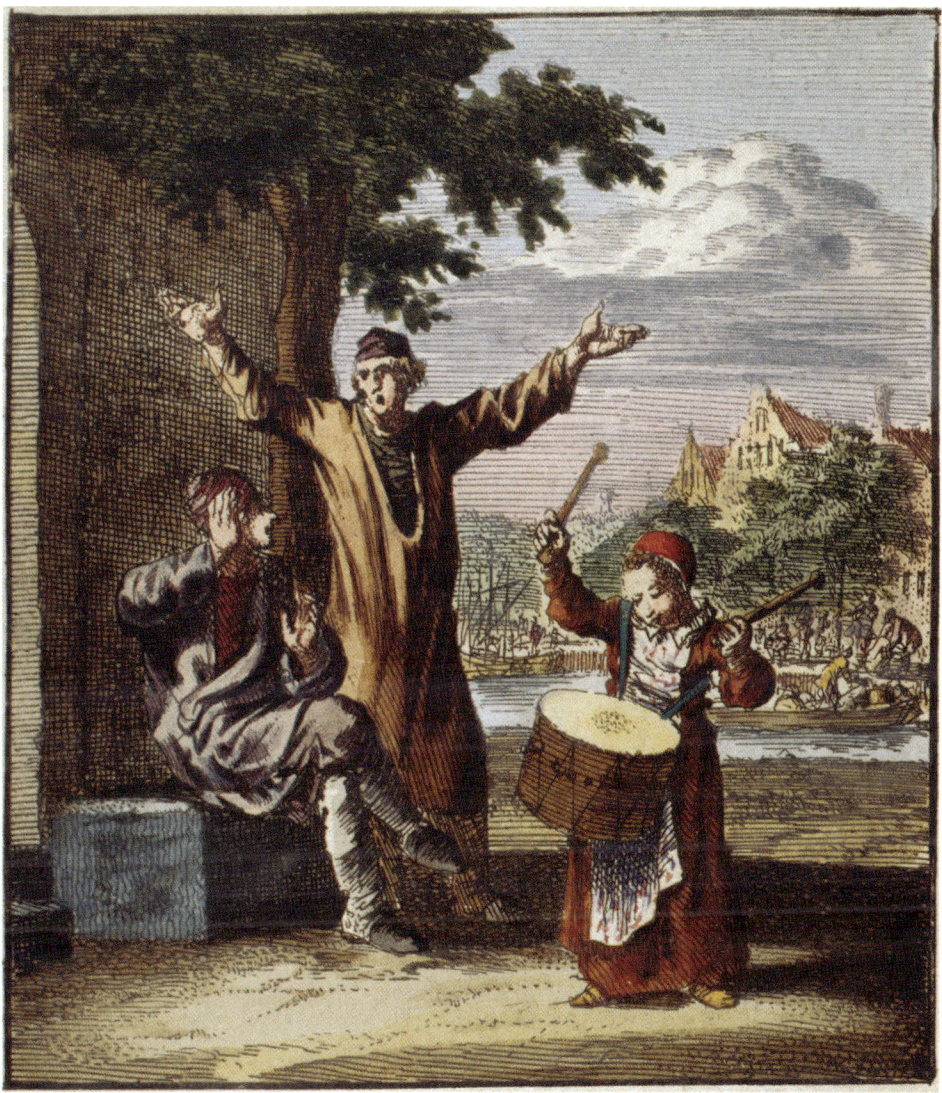

Jan Luyken, *De Trommel* (The drum). Print (hand colored), *Des Menschen Begin, Midden en Einde*, 1712. Collection Amsterdam Museum (P 4406; A 18951).

Banging on a drum is great fun for children. While the noise and rhythms might annoy adults, they are music to a child's ears. Who knows? With practice this little drummer might learn to imitate the cadences of adult male marching militia groups, the drum rolls of traveling groups of actors who summon potential audiences to their temporarily constructed stage areas, or the thumping beats of drums that get people of all ages dancing at village fairs.

In this scene, the standing adult man seems to shrug his shoulders as if to say to the seated man holding his ears "What can you do? Children are simply noisy creatures!"

Children loved to play drums. These toys were sold at outdoor stands during fairs and prior to Saint Nicholas Eve. Amsterdam youngsters banged away on drums in the streets at *Luylak*, which occurred the Saturday before Whitsunday or Pentecost (*Pinxterdag*) in an effort to torment adults in the very early morning by drumming and singing insulting songs. Then the noisy drums were also used to tease their still-sleeping friends about being lazybones.

Boys also joined together with their drums and carried small flags that imitated adult soldiers or the community's civic guard, playing those outdoor games in the streets or city squares. Drumming was such fun that any opportunity was a good excuse.

Some rich parents commissioned portrait paintings of their sons posed with drums, as an allusion to parental hopes that their sons would become valiant military leaders. (DRB)

JAN MIENSE MOLENAER (1610–1668)
Two Boys and a Girl Making Music, **1629**

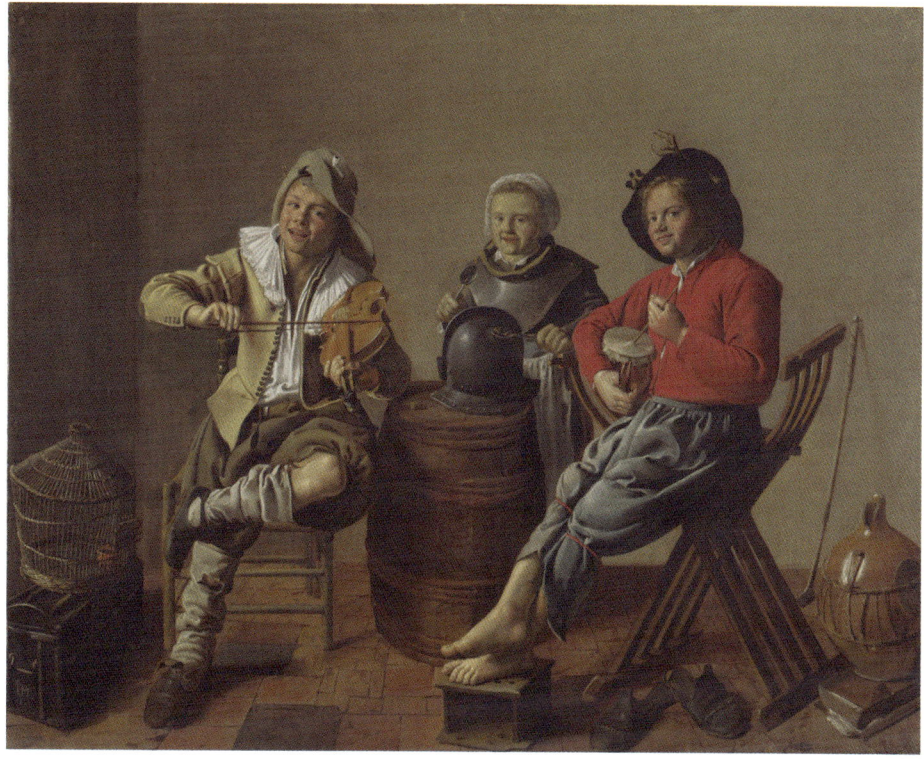

Jan Miense Molenaer, *Two Boys and a Girl Making Music,* 1629. Oil on canvas, 68.3 x 84.5 cm. © The National Gallery, London (NG5416).

No one says that music must be performed on traditional musical instruments. When it becomes necessary to improvise, this little girl puts a set of spoons and a soldier's metal helmet to good use. She beats out a martial cadence. Just to underscore the point, she also wears a soldier's breastplate around her neck. One boy scrapes away on a fiddle. The second boy "musician" plunges the stick up and down in the *rommelpot,* producing rumbling sounds. Rather than tapping his feet to the rhythms the trio produces, the *rommelpot* player has tossed aside his shoes and rests his bare feet on a foot warmer (affectionately known as a *mignon*). The children might think of their sounds as music, but it is doubtful adults would.

By depicting children who are spontaneously having fun, Molenaer has captured the spirit of childhood, when anything is possible and many things are pleasurable. An empty birdcage suggests that childhood is fleeting. It might also suggest that the bird could not bear the sonic competition provided by these carefree musicians.

When played by adult men wandering through the streets of cities or villages, the rude, rumbling sounds of the *rommelpot* attracted laughing youngsters. Occasionally stopping outside a house, the *rommelpot* player hoped to cadge a few coins from the family inside, especially if the family's young children came to the door squealing in pleasure.

Dutch artists depicted children with a *rommelpot* and adult *rommelpot* players. An engraving by Cornelis Bloemaert depicts a smiling boy wearing a feathered beret who plays his *rommelpot*, inviting the viewer's enjoyment of the sounds and the moment. Frans Hals's ruddy-faced *rommelpot* player, surrounded by five smiling children, is at the Kimbell Art Museum in Fort Worth, Texas. A very similar painting attributed to Judith Leyster, now located at the Art Institute of Chicago, depicts a bearded *rommelpot* player surrounded by joyful kids laughing at the noise.

Molenaer himself also depicted a boy playing the *rommelpot* outdoors with two other companions thumping on a small drum and jingling a tambourine as they tease a tipsy dwarf into dancing for their amusement; that painting forms part of the SØR Rusche private collection in Münster, Germany. Allegorizing the senses, Molenaer also depicted yet another laughing boy with his *rommelpot* for the sense of hearing. The painting is part of the Phoenix Art Museum's collection. Clearly the instrument was not only a favorite of Dutch youngsters, it was also a cherished studio prop for Molenaer and other Dutch artists. (DRB)

JAN LUYKEN (1649–1712)

Het Fluitje (The little horn)

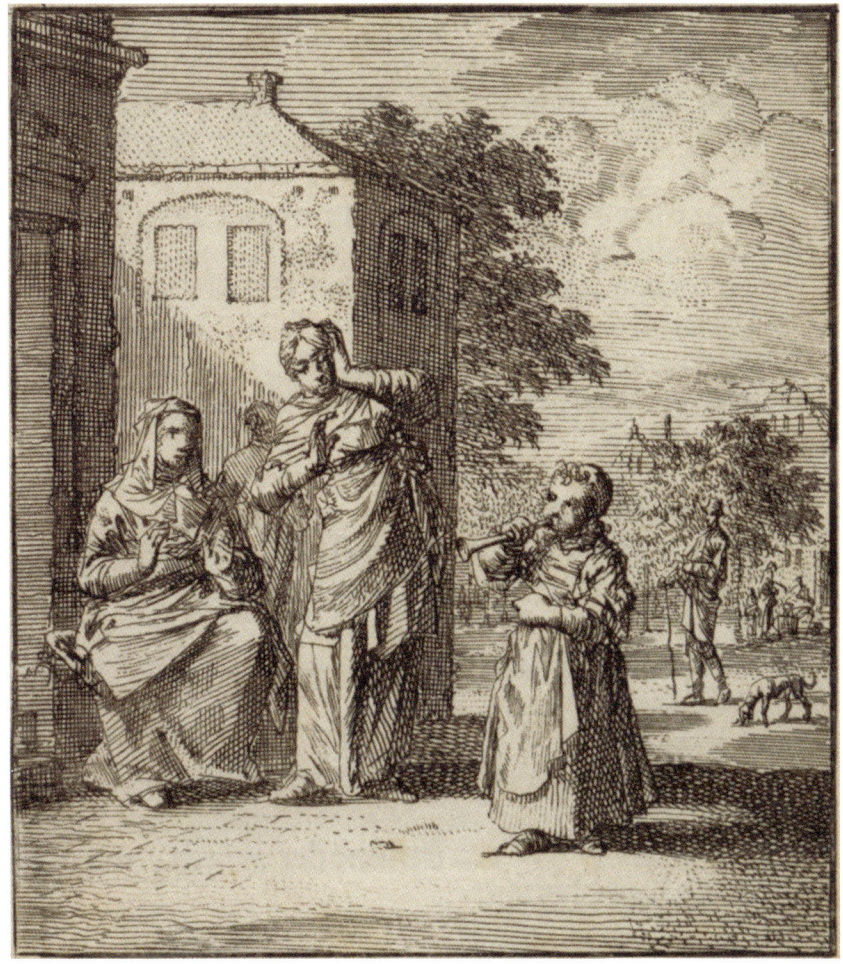

Jan Luyken, *Het Fluitje* (The little horn). Print, *Des Menschen Begin, Midden en Einde*, 1712. Collection Amsterdam Museum (P 4403; A 18950).

Music or noise? The piercing sound of the tin whistle, shaped like a little horn, may delight the child, but it does not please the adult women. Mother and grandmother doubt this child will have much of a future as a musician. No doubt, they will want the little one eventually to take music lessons, perhaps on the lute, flute, or recorder. With proper training and diligent practice, the youngster will be able to play alone or join the family in instrumental musical afternoons and evenings. But for now, the childish cacophony is earsplitting.

Many middle-class Dutch families counted among their members talented amateur performers who played the viola da gamba, lute, recorder, virginal, clavichord, theorbo, flute, cittern, guitar, zither, and violin. Musical talent was considered a sign of social grace. Families who could afford to do so owned many different musical instruments. They also had sheet music and song books. A family playing music together was taken as a sign of domestic harmony and balance. Indeed, courting couples frequently were encouraged to play, or sing, music together, as a measure of their harmonious future.

Adult horn players were associated either with hunting scenes or with military maneuvers. Hunting horns connoted the aristocracy because hunting was a privilege reserved to them. The military use of trumpets and horns had a long history for sounding the charge or waking the troops at reveille. Perhaps Luyken's little musician will later use his horn-playing skills as a hunter or soldier. But for the present, the child takes pleasure in producing loud sounds just for the joy of it.

Some adult Dutch musicians made a living as performers in urban taverns known as *musicos*, where customers came to eat and drink, to smoke pipes of tobacco, to sing, to dance, to listen to musicians, and to flirt (sometimes with whores, sometimes with tavern wenches). Those musicians often wore coin attached to their lavishly plumed hats or berets as a sign they expected to be paid for their efforts. Typically, tavern entertainers played the lute or guitar. Horn players were not in great demand. While peasants inns and country fairs frequently featured lively music played by a fiddler, bagpiper, or hurdy-gurdy man, seldom did horn players get a hearing in these settings. This raucous little musician will probably never be hired as an adult entertainer. (DRB)

JUDITH LEYSTER (1609–1660)

The Young Flute Player

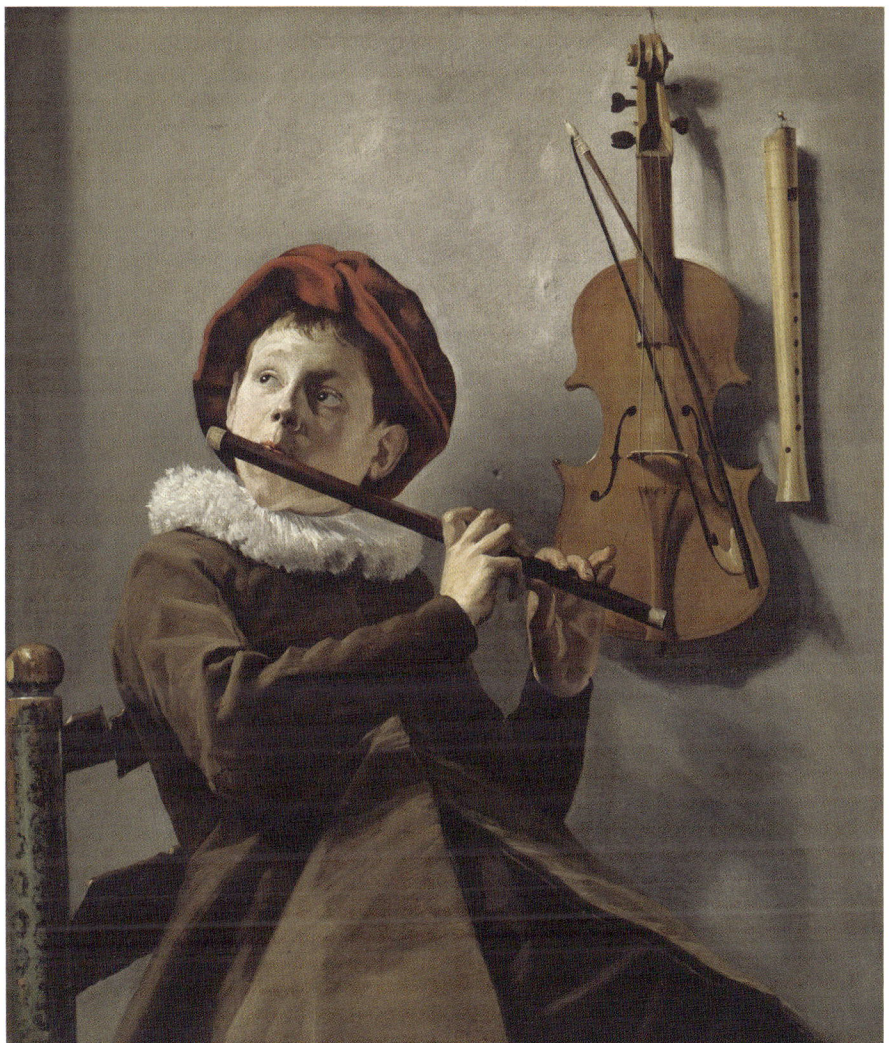

Judith Leyster, *The Young Flute Player*. Oil on canvas, 73 x 62 cm. © National-museum, Stockholm.

Seated casually in a wooden chair, a young boy looks up as though remembering the music notes for the tune he is playing on his wooden transverse flute. His fingers are gracefully arranged on the finger holes. On the wall close to him a violin with its bow and a wooden recorder (or *blokfluit*) are suspended. Perhaps the boy is looking toward unseen companions who might play those instruments? Or he might be wondering how his tune would sound if played on either one.

While children's music was often associated with festive family and holiday celebrations, some moments were devoted to improving skills through practice and to exploring the instrument's sounds.

The actual identity of the flute player is unknown. Perhaps he was a neighbor or family member who served as a model in the artist's studio. What is important is that Leyster points to making music as a source of pleasure for children.

Art historians have commented on the presence of the violin and recorder. In the seventeenth century, a theory existed that stringed instruments represented human rationality because the sounds could be carefully controlled, but that wind instruments represented emotionality (or irrationality) because the sounds were less controllable. This theory leads Pieter Biesboer and James Welu to suggest Leyster knew of this dichotomy and was underscoring the moralistic educational message for adult viewers that children needed to be taught control.

Dutch artists from Utrecht, influenced by the chiaroscuro effects achieved by the Italian painter Caravaggio, had introduced the theme of musicians playing musical instruments by candlelight in the 1620s. Works by Hendrick Terbruggen, whose *Flute Player* of 1622 is now located in the museum in Kassel, became known to Dutch artists working in other cities. Frans Hals, the leading painter of Haarlem at the time Judith Leyster painted this boy, had already painted his *Singing Boy with a Flute* around 1627. Conceivably Leyster, who might well have studied with Frans Hals, knew of the Hals painting and drew inspiration from it. (Hals's painting is now located in Berlin.)

Leyster has used a cool monochromatic palette here primarily of gray and brown tones relieved only by the boy's skin, white ruff collar, and rumpled red beret. (DRB)

CORNELIS DUSART (1660–1704)

The Pinxterblom

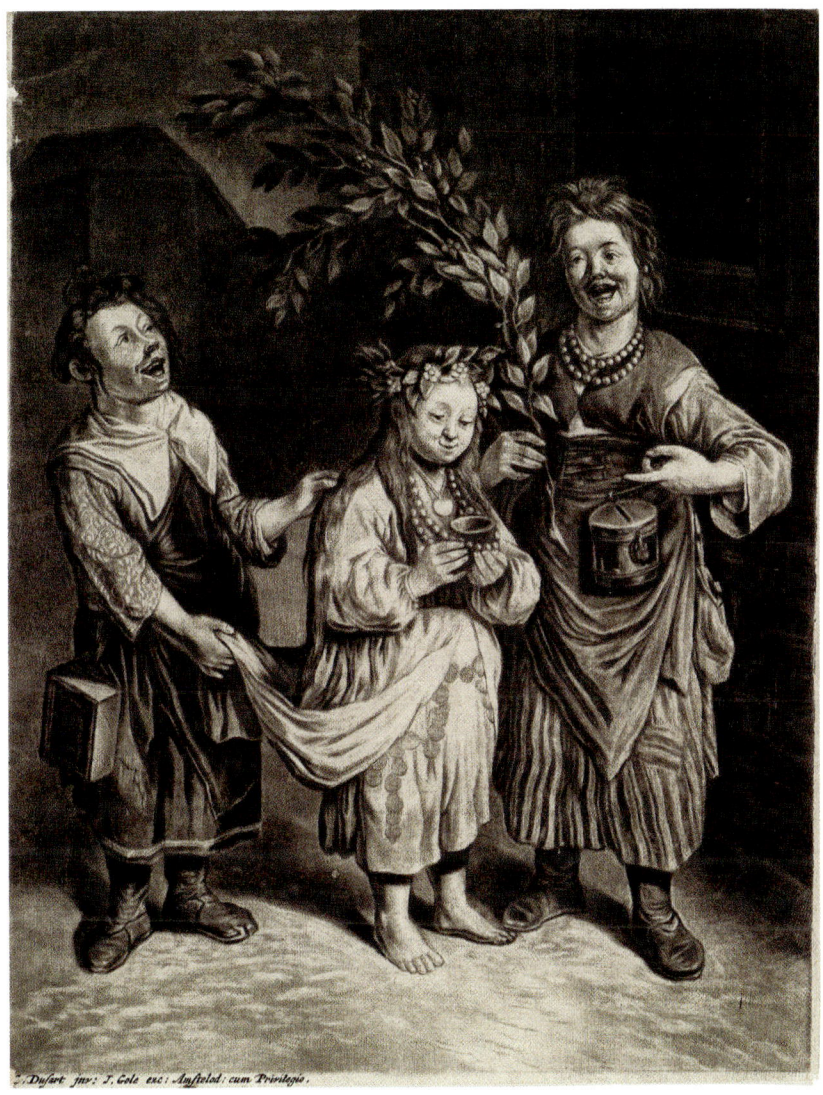

Cornelis Dusart, *The Pinxterblom*. Print. Atlas van Stolk, Rotterdam.

In Dusart's print we see a small barefoot girl wearing a flower crown and bedecked with jewelry (often lent by the women in the village) making the rounds with two older boys. One of them is holding her train, the other lifts a bough over her head, and the *Pinxterblom* (Pentecost flower) herself holds up a cup for collecting coins. With that money they will buy treats afterwards, perhaps some cookies at the bakery or a pancake or waffle from an itinerant street seller.

Pinxterblom refers to a light-lilac-colored flower (*Cardamine pratensis*) that blooms in spring around the time of the Pentecost holiday. Called Cuckoo Flower in English, it prefers a wet environment and grows in grasslands and swamps. It does not seem too far fetched to assume that a similarly colored American azalea shrub (*Rhododendron periclymenoides*) called Pinxterbloom Azalea was so named by the Dutch because it, too, prefers moist conditions and blooms in the same period. (PGR)

CASPAR NETSCHER (CA. 1639–1684)
A Child with a Top

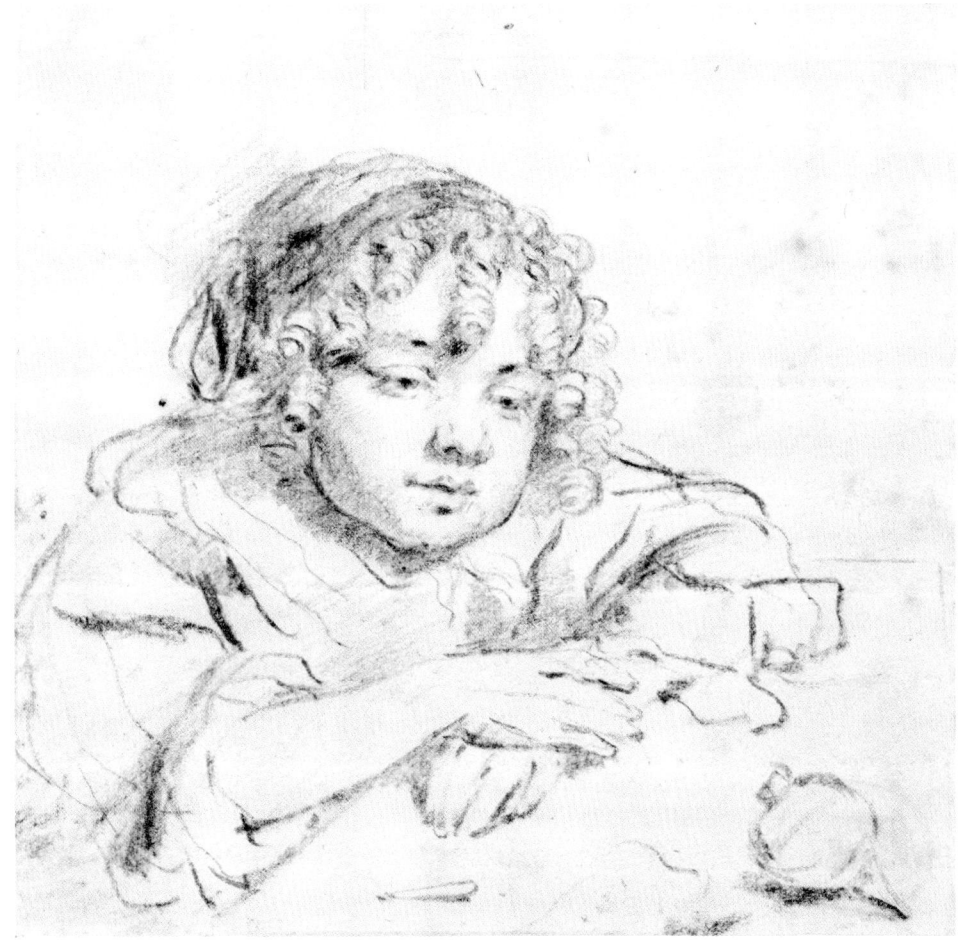

Caspar Netscher, *A Child with a Top.* Drawing. Collection Amsterdam Museum (TA 10229).

Somewhat sad-eyed, this curly haired child watches the top pensively. It has stopped spinning. Perhaps the youngster had hoped to produce a longer-lasting spin. Or perhaps the child wants to spin tops with a friend.

It is not really possible to determine whether the child is a young boy or a young girl: the curls are deceptive. But no matter, tops, while primarily associated with boys, could actually be enjoyed by all children. It was not uncommon for little girls to "borrow" their brothers' tops and try their luck at getting them to spin.

Whether this drawing was made as a preliminary study for other works by Netscher is not known. However, in his painting *A Woman Combing a Child's Hair*, now at the Rijksmuseum in Amsterdam, we see toys on the floor, including a top. (DRB)

JAN LUYKEN (1649–1712)

De Dryftol (The top)

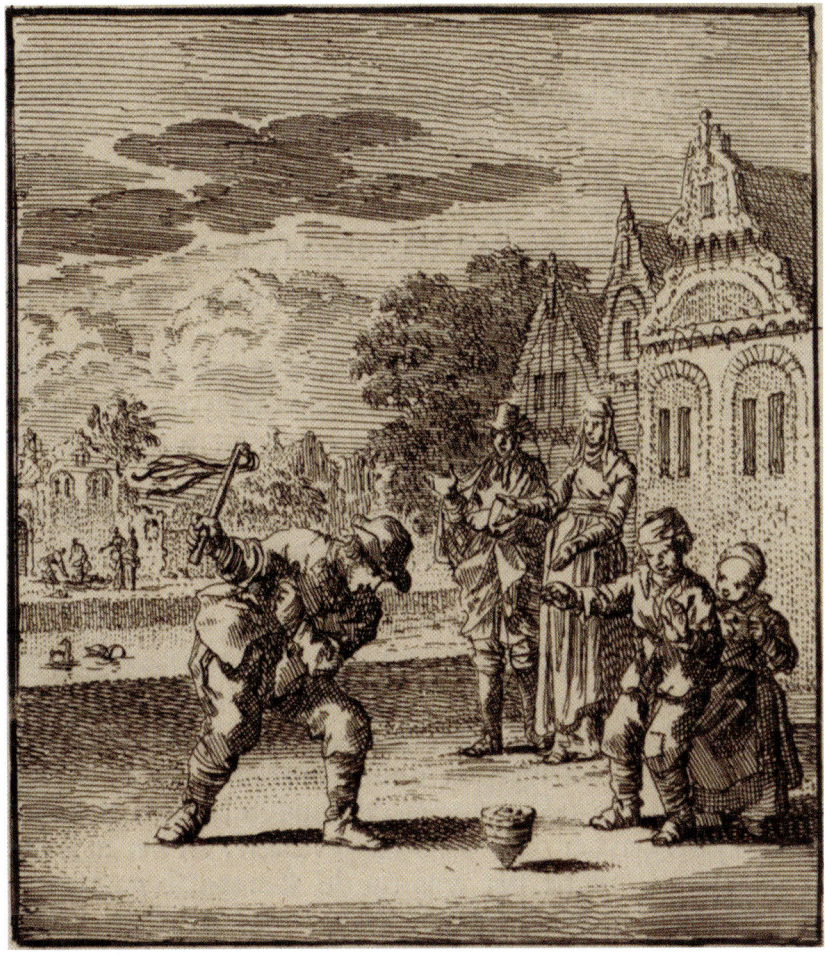

Jan Luyken, *De Dryftol* (The top). Print, *Des Menschen Begin, Midden en Einde*, 1712. Collection Amsterdam Museum (P 4424; A 18969).

Boys either whip or hurl their wooden tops to get them spinning. The boy whose top spins the longest is the winner. Sometimes boys draw a circle on the ground or pavement, and the spinning top must stay within the circle. Practicing with a whip gives a boy the competitive edge. Tops can also be spun indoors on floors or flat tabletops. No doubt, like marbles, tops can also be spun on the flat surfaces of gravestones in church floors.

So popular were tops for Dutch children that in the same book, Luyken also depicts three other boys spinning tops. One of the three is a black child.

The presence of black Africans in Amsterdam as household servants, often liveried, was a sign of status for wealthy merchant families. The Dutch were active in the African slave trade. That black and white children could play together in Amsterdam, despite differences in status, suggest that youngsters were more intent on the pleasures of the game than on social distinctions among players.

Most adults considered spinning tops examples of childish play, yet Dutch scientists and mathematicians in the seventeenth century were interested in the effects of gyroscopes for navigational instruments, the rotating balance wheels and spinning of clock mechanisms, and the spinning movement of heavenly spheres viewed through telescopes. These adults shared youngsters' fascination for the whirling movement of tops.

Roemer Visscher's early emblem book *Sinnepoppen* also shows a top spinning merrily. For adult readers of both Visscher's and Luyken's books, the top was a moralistic symbol of the frivolity of childhood and served as food for thought. As an emblem, the top was a reminder to adults that neither they, nor their children, should waste time that could be used productively. Parents might mention such ideas to their children while showing them the books, but for boys, tops were simply a source of delight. A boy could practice whipping or hurling his top alone to be better prepared to compete later in games with other boys.

Occasionally Dutch portraits of children from affluent families depict boys with whips, symbolic of their parentally envisioned futures as commanding leaders who were expected to wield both power and authority. But here the whip is simply part of the equipment needed to set the top spinning.

Tops have a long history. Dutch toy historian Lourens Bas believes they are among the world's oldest toys, having begun not as shaped wood but as conically shaped seashells (rather like small conchs) filled or weighted with mud or sand and then spun on its bottom point. In prehistoric times such spinning devices were used in divination ceremonies.

Wooden tops from the seventeenth century have been excavated from cesspits, wells, and old road beds in Amsterdam and other cities in Holland. Lost or tossed away because they were damaged or nicked, these old toys were preserved beneath the soil and unearthed by twentieth-century archaeologists. (DRB)

CASPAR NETSCHER (CA. 1639–1684)

Interieur met een Moeder die Haar Kind Kamt (A woman combing a child's hair), 1669

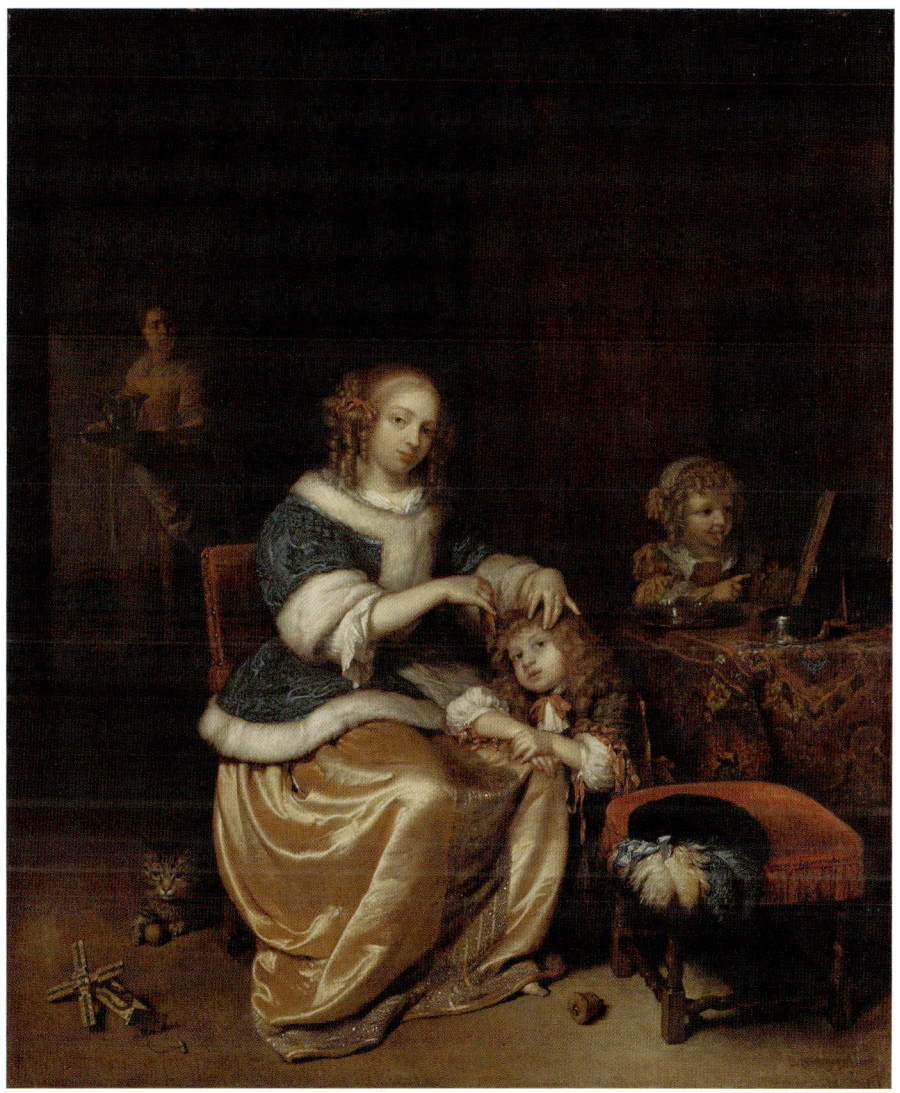

Caspar Netscher, *Interieur met een Moeder die Haar Kind Kamt* (A woman combing a child's hair), 1669. Oil on panel, 44.5 x 58 cm. Rijksmuseum Amsterdam (SK-A-293).

It is difficult to imagine that the boy whose hair is being combed takes much pleasure in this moment. Combing is not enjoyable if there are any snarls in the hair. But perhaps his mother will pull the comb gently through his wavy locks. Once this child submits to his mother's ministrations, there are toys he can play with: a top and a little mill are on the floor. Perhaps the black-and-gray tiger cat will relinquish the ball it grasps in its paws. His sister looks at her own carefully combed hair by peering into the mirror on top of the table. Once mother finishes combing, the boy can again place his feathered hat firmly on his head. Or maybe he'll expect the housemaid, standing in the doorway in the back of the room, to do it for him. The only pleasure he will experience is the ordeal being over.

Images of mothers (or grandmothers) combing children's hair, or checking their hair and scalps for head lice, are found in many paintings, notably by Pieter de Hooch, Quiringh Gerritsz. van Brekelenkam, and Michael Sweerts. At least one is entitled "Maternal Devotion" (or *Moeder Zorg*) suggesting that this was a task performed by mothers but not fathers.

Hair combing was unwelcomed by children, albeit necessary. In *Des Menschen Begin, Midden en Einde*, Jan Luyken also provides an image of a child having his hair combed, where the child is not submitting but screaming in a temper tantrum. Netscher's child is tame by comparison.

In this painting, Netscher has lavished attention on the silken sheen of the woman's yellow skirt, the soft white ermine fur trimming her blue jacket, and her own curly ringlets, tied back with a bow, that echo those of her daughter. Mother-daughter hairstyles were the fashion. (DRB)

JAN LUYKEN (1649–1712)

Het Molentje (The little windmill)

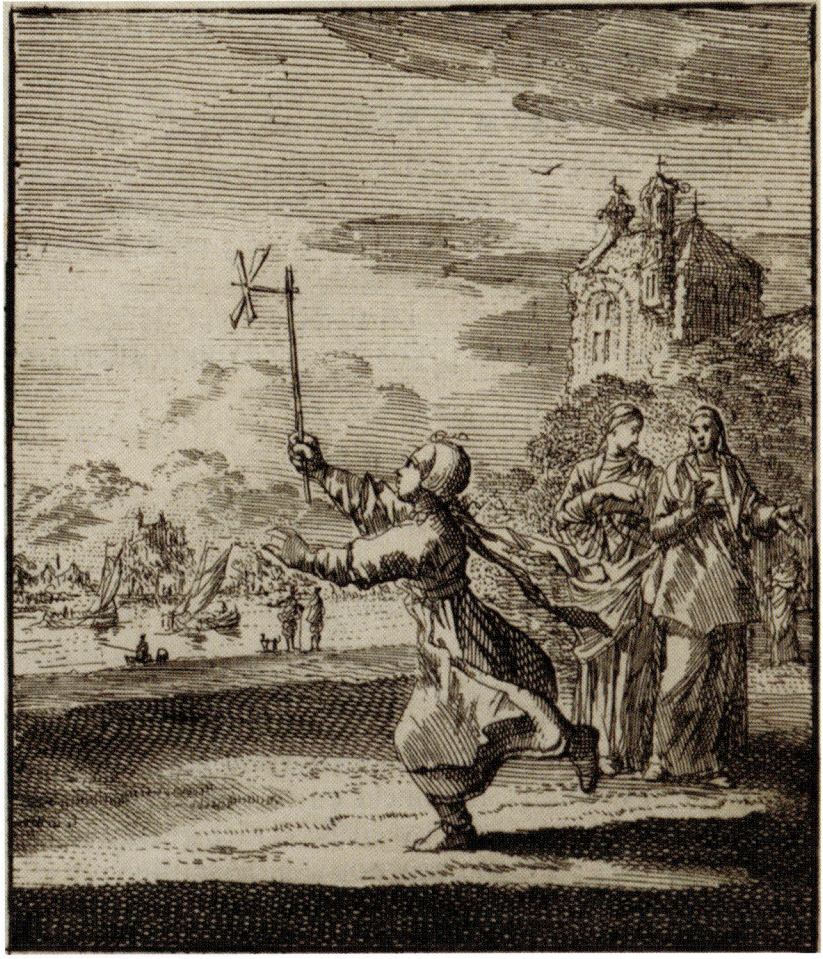

Jan Luyken, *Het Molentje* (The little windmill). Print, *Des Menschen Begin, Midden en Einde* (1712). Collection Amsterdam Museum (P 4403; A 18948).

Running with a small toy windmill is one of life's pleasures for a young Dutch child. Leading strings (*leibanden*) flutter from this youngster's shoulders. Captivated by the movement of the mill's spinning wooden blades, the carefree child does not even think about the dangerous possibility of running into another person. The adult women laugh together and comment about the child's intensity. "Why doesn't that youngster wear a protective hat [*valhoedje*]?" But the child knows running quickly spins the sails of the little wooden mill even faster.

Wind whips across the sea and lake water in Holland's terrain, propelling children's little mills. The same wind turns the sails of large industrial and agricultural windmills dotting the countryside. Windmills, ever an enchanting sight in the Dutch landscape, were built for practical purposes. Mills pumped water from the polders, channeling it into ditches, so the resulting dry farm land could be used either as pastures for cows and sheep or as growing fields for hay, grains, vegetables, fruits, or flowers and shrubs.

Mills were also used to grind rye and wheat grains into flours for baking; without windmills there could not be the delicious sweet treats enjoyed by Dutch children. Mills ground pigment colorants used in paints and dyes. Mills pulverized linen and cotton rags used in making paper. Mills ground flax seed to produce linseed oil used in the manufacture of house paint and used by artists in mixing pigments for their paintings. Mills ground rape and cole seed into oils used industrially as lubricants, pharmaceutically in medicinal salves and ointments, and in home frying. And mills ground mustard seed to produce that spicy condiment so enjoyed with sausages.

Dutch children were often given little windmills as gifts. One is shown in this volume in Cornelis Dusart's print characterizing infancy as one of the four stages of human life; another is seen on the floor in Casper Netscher's painting of a child having his hair combed. In a painting by Jacob Duck, now located at the Centraal Museum in Utrecht, a child sits in a kitchen area holding a little windmill while a woman is busy with her ironing. There the contrast between childhood playfulness and adult work responsibilities is firmly underscored.

As Luyken shows in the background, wind also filled the sails of both ships and boats, propelling them over lakes, down rivers, and across the seas and oceans. The Dutch economy depended on sailing vessels used for domestic and international trade, fishing, and transport. Wealthy Dutch families also used sailboats and fast-moving wind-driven yachts (*jachten*) for pleasure, enjoying short voyages and outings on nearby lakes or rivers. Those voyages were a source of pleasure for youngsters, too, but did not provide as much physical exercise as running with a miniature mill. (DRB)

JAN LUYKEN (1649–1712)

Het Houte Stokpaard (The wooden horse)

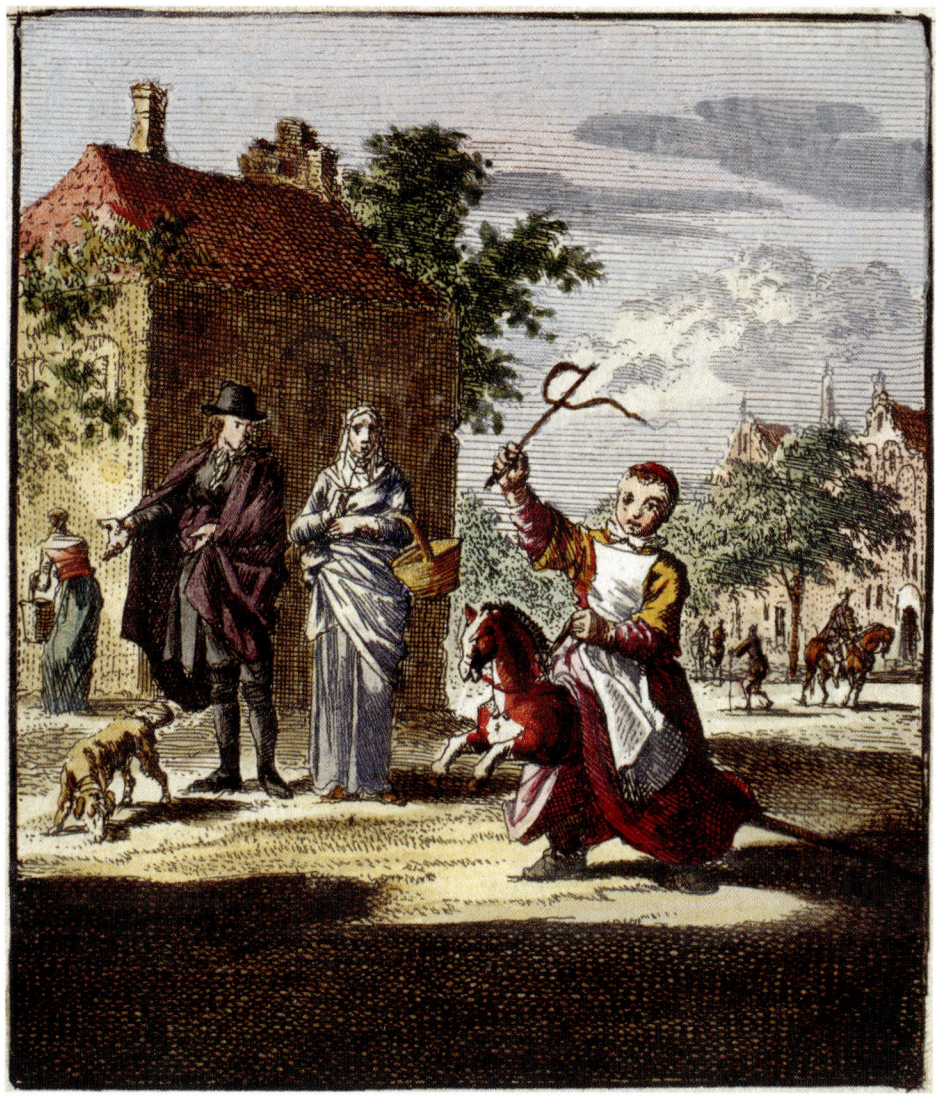

Jan Luyken, *Het Houte Stokpaard* (The wooden horse). Print (hand colored), *Des Menschen Begin, Midden en Einde*, 1712. Collection Amsterdam Museum (P 4404; A 18949).

Riding a wooden horse might prompt a young boy to dream of becoming an equestrian military officer, or a post rider, or a stable hand. Little kids loved to straddle the wooden stick with its horse head, hold the reins, raise their small whip, and spur themselves and their imagined steed onto adventures. The child could envision glorious races and battles on horseback.

This child's wooden horse is elaborate; more than a head is provided. The front legs are visible, as is the mane, and while the boy's feet are firmly on the ground, the horse seems to have a fabric covering or blanket, adding yet another "realistic" touch to the toy.

Wooden horses have a history that goes back in time. European boys training for positions as medieval squires and knights might well have initially rehearsed their dreams of chivalric horsemanship using just such wooden surrogates.

Probably little girls also rode their brothers' wooden horses in the seventeenth century, although they are not depicted in paintings or in prints doing so. We know from some genre and landscape paintings that women from privileged families learned to ride horses and occasionally accompanied their men folk hunting with falcons. So it was not at all unthinkable that a little girl would find the fantasy of a wooden horse enjoyable.

Toy sellers at stalls and itinerant peddlers sold wooden horses for children. Many of these toys were made in Germany. Often they were among the earliest gifts for children, once they had learned to walk alone. (DRB)

JAN VAN DER HEYDEN (1637–1712)
The Dam

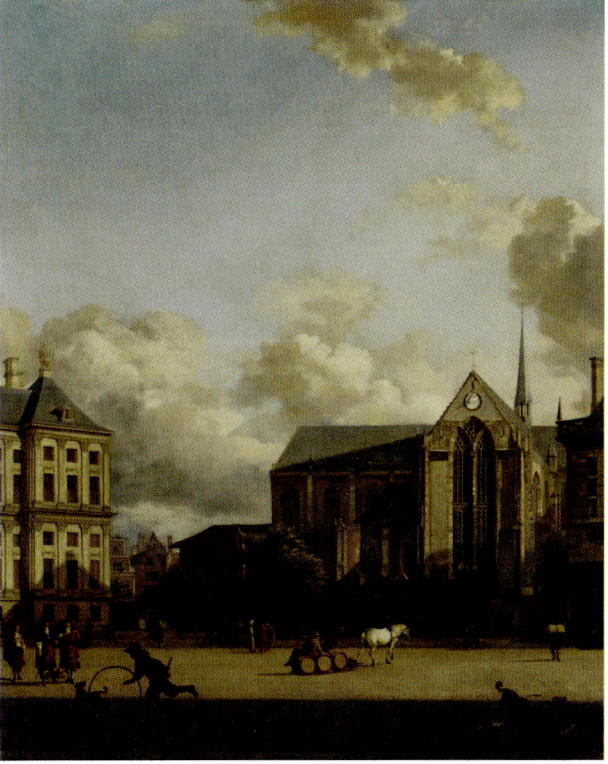

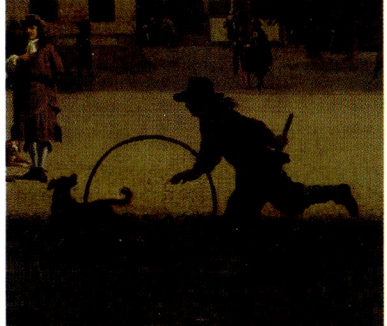

Jan van der Heyden, *The Dam*. Oil painting, ca. 1668. Collection Amsterdam Museum (SA7332).

The boy rolls his hoop across the most important square in Amsterdam, Dam Square. He is accompanied by a barking dog. The boy is intent on keeping the hoop in motion and probably gives no thought to the fact that he is playing in the place where much of the city's economic life was conducted.

The recently completed new city hall was nearby; the annual *kermis* or fair took place on the Dam; the Nieuwe Kerk was nearby; the Weigh House was on the Dam; and daily markets were often conducted outdoors during the week with people selling fruits, vegetables, and earthenware kitchen crockery.

On this morning, Dam Square is remarkably quiet, although a beer porter uses a horse-drawn sledge to deliver three large barrels of beer and a few people stroll in the sunlight. Caught up in their own pleasures, the boy and dog ignore the adults.

Jan van der Heyden and other Dutch artists found clients interested in decorating their homes with paintings of important buildings, streets, and markets in their hometown cities. It was a matter of local pride, especially if the cities were flourishing. Clients for these cityscape works could be found in Amsterdam, Haarlem, Leiden, Rotterdam, and Delft. Often the artists included images of children in these cityscape scenes, perhaps to add human interest or to suggest that the cities, like children, were growing and developing. (DRB)

JAN LUYKEN (1649–1712)

De Hoepel (The hoop)

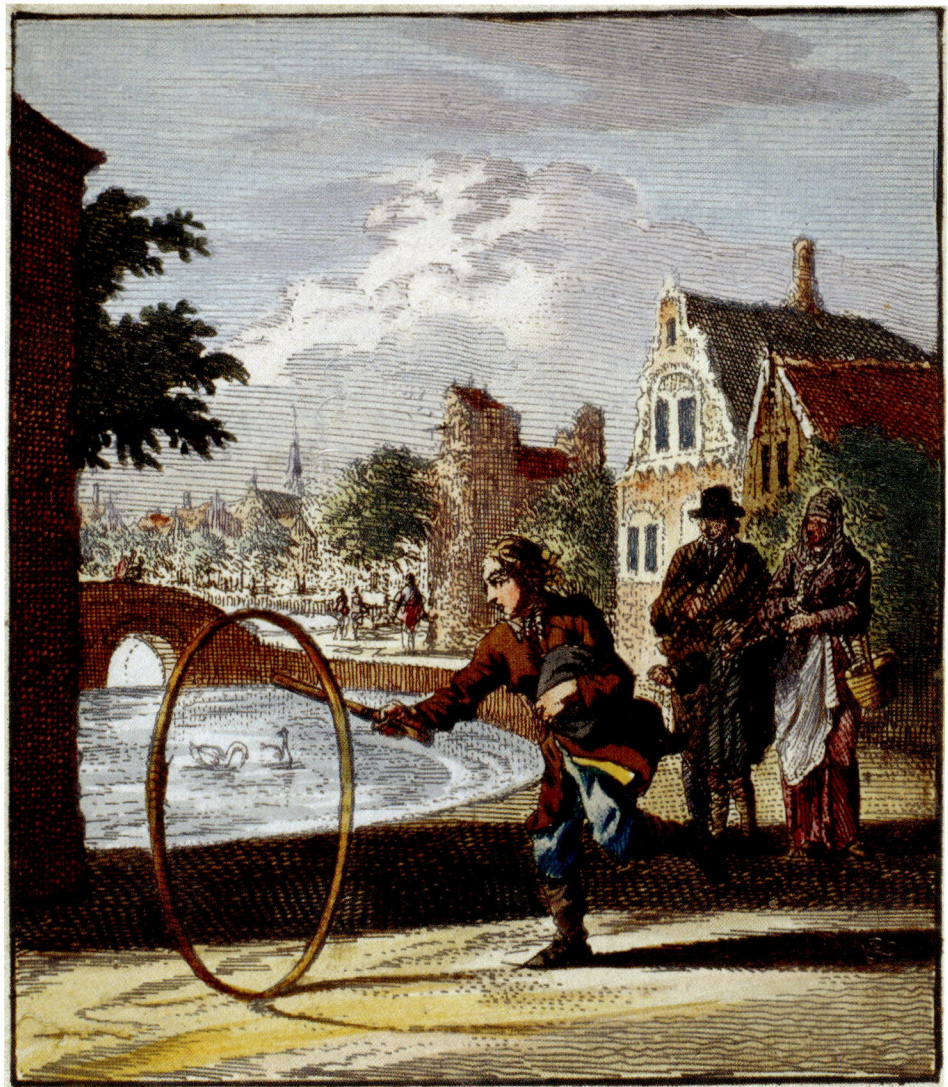

Jan Luyken, *De Hoepel* (The hoop). Print (hand colored), *Des Menschen Begin, Midden en Einde*, 1712. Collection Amsterdam Museum (P 4412; A 18963).

Rolling a wooden hoop along city streets near the canals requires a stick to keep the hoop in motion. The boy must avoid crashing into people who are walking. He must not get in the way of men with delivery carts. He also takes care so he doesn't inadvertently send the hoop over the edge of the canal into the water. Retrieving it from the water would be almost impossible. Rolling the hoop up and over bridges poses special challenges.

Just as skipping rope provided a boy with an opportunity to explore streets he had not previously known, so did rolling a hoop in unfamiliar neighborhoods. However, the hoop-roller also had to be wary of potential dangers or threats from ruffians.

Children enjoyed rolling hoops. It was a popular boys' activity. Often the hoops themselves could be cadged from a cooper who had them in supply when making wooden barrels. Youngsters often attached small metal disks to the inside of a hoop, causing it to jingle as the hoop rolled along. The clattering noise added to the fun.

Girls might have also played occasionally with hoops, but their long skirts made running much more difficult. Furthermore, girls were discouraged from running as it was not considered "lady-like," nor were young girls permitted to wander far from home. Boys, on the other hand, enjoyed much more freedom of movement.

Jan Luyken had many predecessors depicting boys with hoops. One of Roemer Visscher's emblems in *Sinnepoppen* (1614) depicted a tousle-haired boy rolling a hoop. In the print of children's games, (*Kinderspel*) in Jacob Cats's *Houwelijck* of 1628, hoop rolling is shown. Jan Steen frequently depicted a boy standing with a hoop as he observed foolish behavior on the part of gullible adults. In Pieter Brueghel the Elder's magnificent mid-sixteenth-century Flemish painting *Children's Games,* now housed in Vienna's Kunsthistorische Museum, a child rolls a hoop. All these artistic renderings point to the ongoing popularity of this toy for children in both the Northern and Southern Netherlands. (DRB)

JAN LUYKEN (1649–1712)

De Vlieger (The kite)

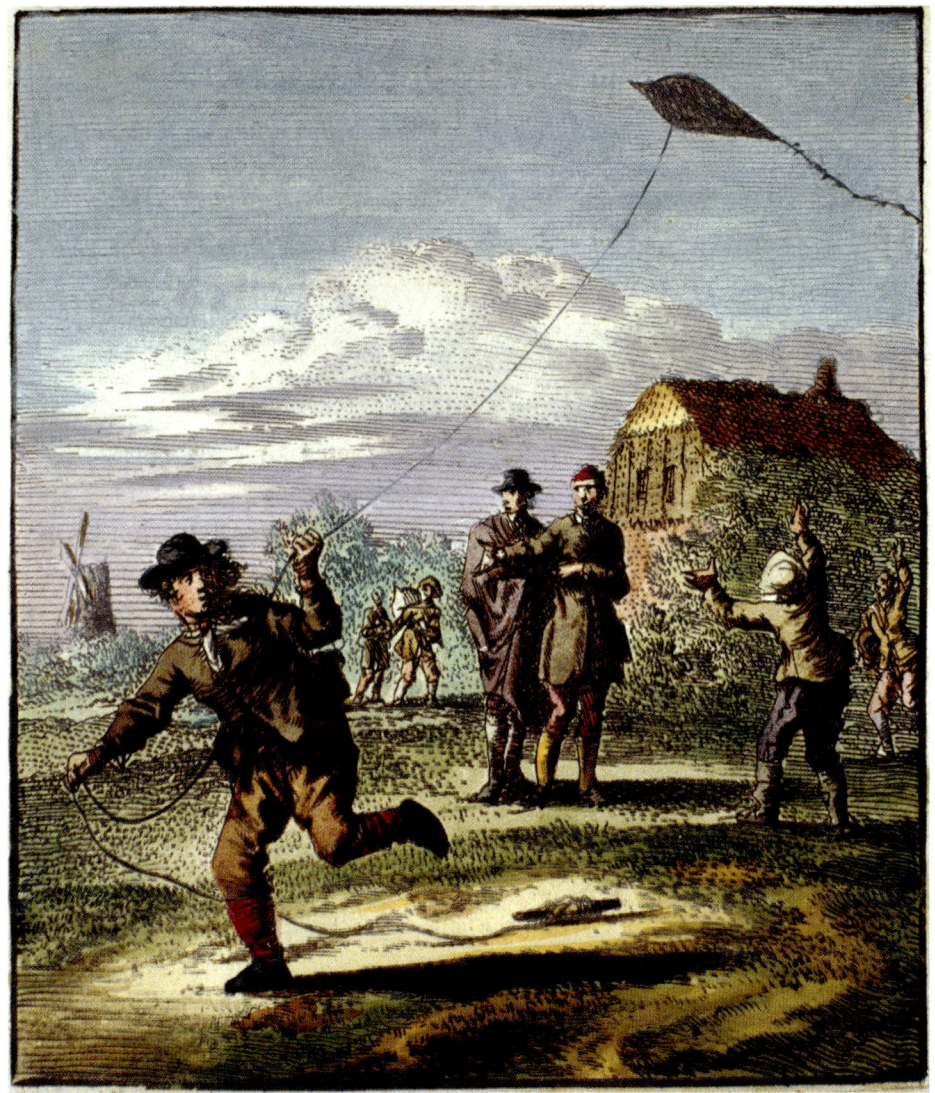

Jan Luyken, *De Vlieger* (The kite). Print (hand colored), *Des Menschen Begin, Midden en Einde*, 1712. Collection Amsterdam Museum (P 4423; A 18968).

A boy runs outdoors with a diamond-shaped kite attached to a long string. Attempting to catch the wind and lift his kite aloft, he has dropped the excess string that's been wrapped around a stick. Kite tails flutter in the stiff breeze, just as the distant windmill's sails rotate with the wind. The boy will have to calculate the direction and velocity of the wind carefully to maximize his chances of keeping his kite soaring in the air.

Some Dutch children made their own kites, using two thin narrow pieces of wood as the vertical and cross spars to form the frame over which they attached paper or thin fabric. Some daubed the paper or fabric with pigments, adding color to the toy. Kite tails could be made of fabric scraps, perhaps ripped from an old shirt or linen table cloth or household napkin that had become scorched with an iron or worn with holes. Kite tails were tied onto the kite strings and fluttered in the breeze. The kite string could be of varying lengths, but longer ones had a greater chance of helping to get the kite high into the sky. Other youngsters probably purchased their kites at fairs.

In a portrait painting now located in the Stedelijk Museum in Alkmaar, a well-dressed young boy stands holding onto a kite with an abundance of tails attached to the kite string. Regrettably, both the artist and the boy are unknown, but the viewer can identify the boy's pleasure in the white kite with its large red spots.

For many Dutch adult viewers, kites were emblematic of human folly because they tended to come crashing to the ground in relatively short order. To that extent, Dutch adults saw kites as symbolic of human ambitions and plans, tossed by the winds of fortune and frequently coming to disappointing ends. On the other hand, Dutch youngsters loved to fly kites whenever the weather permitted. They attached no such moralistic interpretation to their pleasurable activity.

Kite flying probably came to Europe from China, where it had an ancient history, but by the start of the seventeenth century it was already a popular activity for Dutch youngsters. This is clearly shown in a 1618 print used to illustrate one of Jacob Cats's books, based on a design by Adriaen van de Venne. Many youngsters are shown playing a wide variety of games in front of the town hall in Middelburg; among the favored toys is a kite. (DRB)

JAN LUYKEN (1649–1712)

Het Kind Loopt door 't Touw (The child runs with a rope)

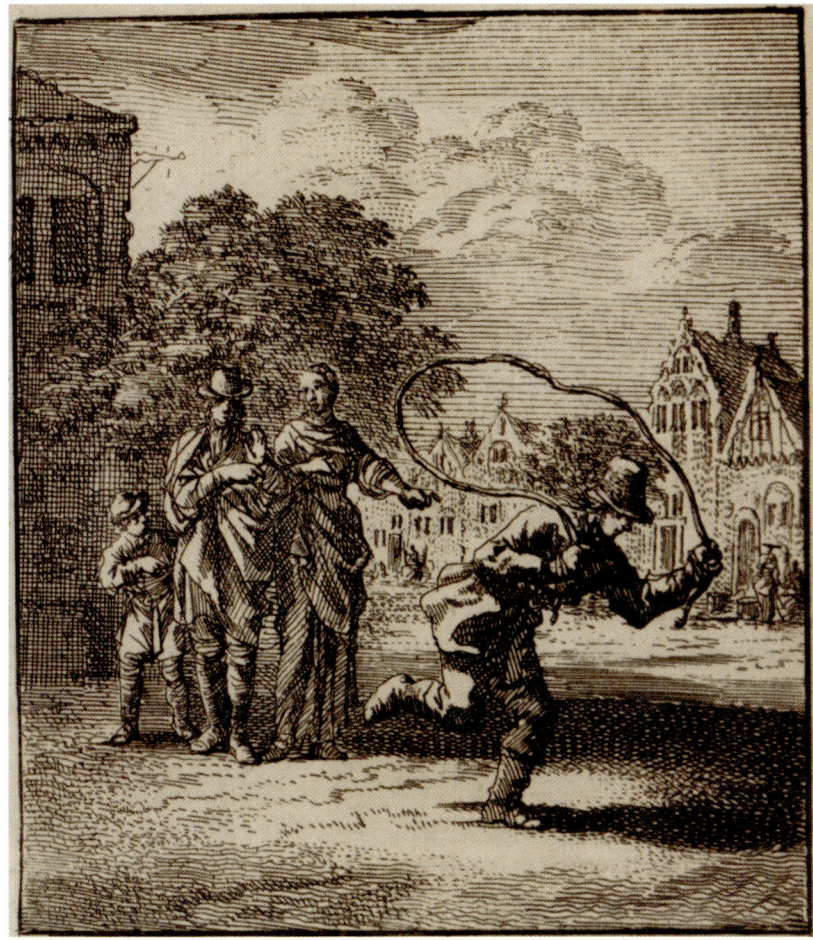

Jan Luyken, *Het Kind Loopt door 't Touw* (The child runs with a rope). Print, *Des Menschen Begin, Midden en Einde* (1712). Collection Amsterdam Museum (P 4421; A 18966).

Skipping along with a rope is a fine way to go through the city streets. You never know who you might meet along the way or what changes in the city you can observe. The boy can adjust his pace to suit himself; he can skip down whichever streets intrigue him; and he can pause and jump in place if he wants to linger for a while observing the activities of people he encounters.

With so many coastal or waterfront cities having shipyards for building and repairing boats and ropewalks for twisting lengths of fibrous hemp into strings, cords, and ropes used in the rigging of large sailing ships and small fishing boats, there was ample rope available for boys to use. The catch was to try to get a piece of rope at no cost—perhaps after new lengths had been measured for sale and there was a bit extra remaining. Other alternatives involved adapting used rope no longer strong enough for its initially intended purposes to recreational use.

Ropes had myriad uses in Holland. Ropes were used with pulleys to haul heavy, bulky items and burlap bags or wooden barrels to the upper floors of warehouses and private residences. Ropes were used to tie packages onto the wheelbarrows that porters or schleppers used to move goods from one arriving cargo barge or wagon to another location. Ropes were attached to the wooden yokes that milkmaids used to transport pails of fresh milk from the cow to the buttery and cheese works or into the nearby town for local purchasers. Ropes were strung between the side frames of bedsteads so that straw-filled or down-filled mattresses could be arranged on them. Ropes were used to lead horses, cows, or oxen from barn to field.

Most urban and rural boys knew where they could find rope for running and skipping. Girls did not often skip rope; their long skirts, reaching down to their ankles, would get in the way, causing them to trip or fall. (DRB)

JAN LUYKEN (1649–1712)

De Hinkelbaan (Hopscotch)

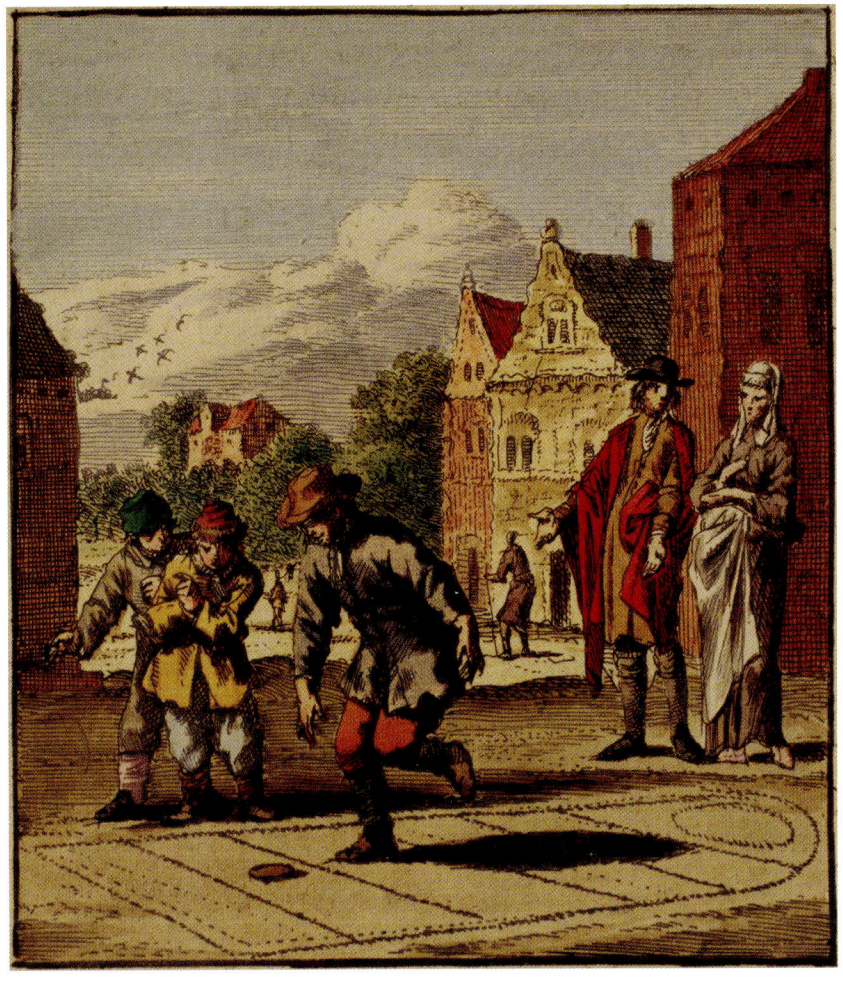

Jan Luyken, *De Hinkelbaan* (Hopscotch). Print (hand colored), *Des Menschen Begin, Midden en Einde* (1712). Collection Amsterdam Museum (P 4428; A 18793).

On the smooth surface of a city square, a boy hops on one foot following the rules for hopscotch. He is carefully monitored by two other boys who watch him intently, making sure he does not land on a line. The player will balance on one foot, bend down to pick up the flat stone, and then hop back to the top of his hopscotch court.

Youngsters could play this game alone or with companions and rivals. They could draw a court on the city street with chalk or a charred stick, scratch a court into the smoothed out dirt on a city square or a country lane, or use a stick or seashell to mark out the margins and spaces for a court in the wet sand at the edge of the sea or a lake's shoreline. A flat stone, seashell, acorn, or chestnut could serve as a marker.

The game required agility and balance but was not at all difficult. Nonetheless, skills acquired in balancing and hopping might later be put to occupational use if boys became roofers, construction workers, or seamen. Roofers needed to balance themselves carefully to carry slates, tiles, and drain pipes up onto the steeply pitched roofs of buildings; construction workers, including carpenters and bricklayers, carried wooden beams and loads of bricks up ladders and scaffolding where balance was again a consideration. Boys who went to sea at early ages found it necessary to balance themselves carefully along the booms as they rigged sails.

Luyken does not show girls playing hopscotch, but no doubt some did. Providing they modestly did not permit too much of their stockings to show, girls could toss the marker and hop in the court, too. Some of the "moves" in hopscotch were similar to steps in rustic country folk dances. (DRB)

JAN LUYKEN (1649–1712)
De Boog (The bow)

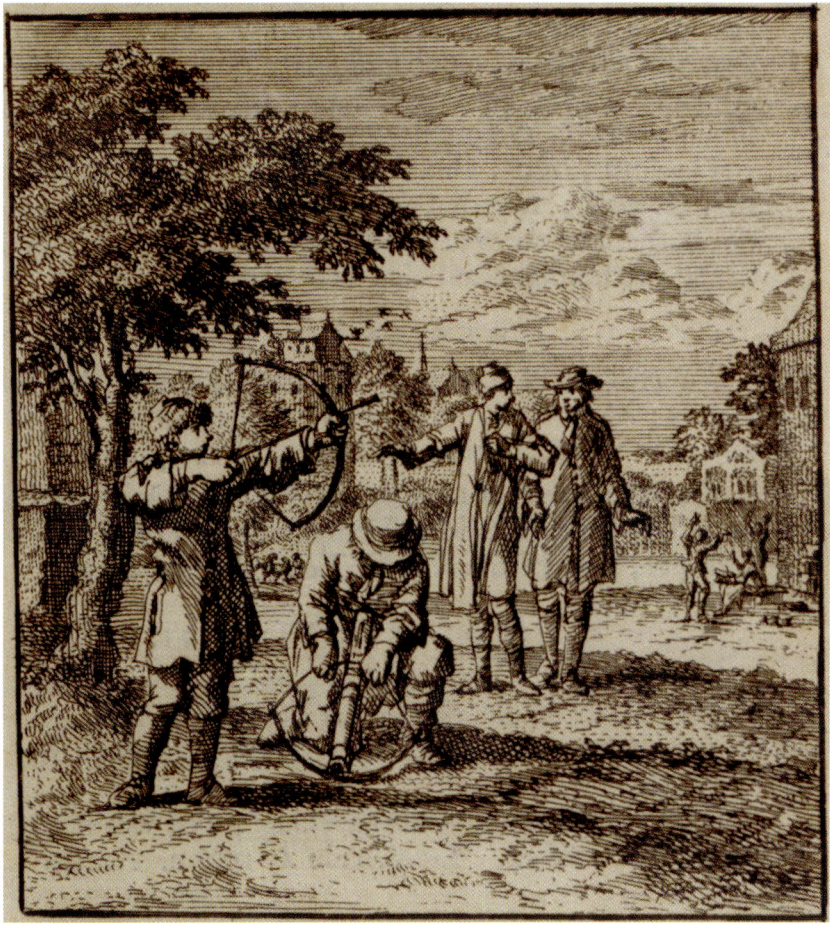

Jan Luyken, *De Boog* (The bow). Print, *Des Menschen Begin, Midden en Einde*, 1712. Collection Amsterdam Museum (P4424; A 18969).

Learning to shoot arrows from a bow is a sport for older boys. Here one is ready to let loose his arrows, while his companion is loading his crossbow. A steady hand must be joined with sharp eyes and careful aim if these boys are to shoot arrows successfully at targets.

Dutch boys knew full well that adult men in cities often served as members of the local militia, the *schutterij*, where it was thought they could come to the defense of their city in the event of an invasion or emergency, although they actually had little occasion to do so. Men were organized into quasi-military companies with officers. They practiced their marksmanship by shooting arrows from long bows and crossbows and shooting bullets from guns at targets in the city's target ranges, the *doelen*. Adolescent boys had no hopes of joining the *schutters* in these events until they became mature men, but the allure of this very masculine activity was popular.

Many of the *schutters* were socially prominent. They took pride in their abilities to handle weapons, although truth be told, they were seldom put to any actual tests beyond the target range. The men took special delight in their annual banquets, where they gathered together around a large table. Resplendent in their uniforms, wearing badges and colorful sashes, they brandished their swords and other weapons.

At their banquets, they passed around drinking horns, seated on elaborate silver or gilded mounts, which were filled with wine. They toasted each other. They toasted their city. They toasted the patron saint after whom their company took its name. They gnawed on roasted capons and ate rolls, fish, and pastries, all washed down with generous supplies of wine or beer. And they had their group banquet portraits painted by notable artists, such as Rembrandt and Frans Hals. Boys knew of these activities; rumors about the quantities of food and drink consumed were part of local community gossip.

By the time Jan Luyken created this print in 1712, Dutch people had seen printed images by other Dutch artists of Native American Indians brandishing bows and arrows when they encountered the Dutchmen who had come to trade for beaver skins and other furs in the Hudson Valley. Shooting a bow was thought to link boys not only to the Indian braves of the American colonies, but also to the glorious ancient Greek and Roman warriors and the chivalrous knights of the medieval crusades that boys had learned about in school.

While other Dutch artists and poets also connected the image of a bow-shooting boy with that of Cupid and his associations with love and lovers, Jan Luyken does not suggest such a connotation here. (DRB)

JAN LUYKEN (1649–1712)

De Slinger (The sling)

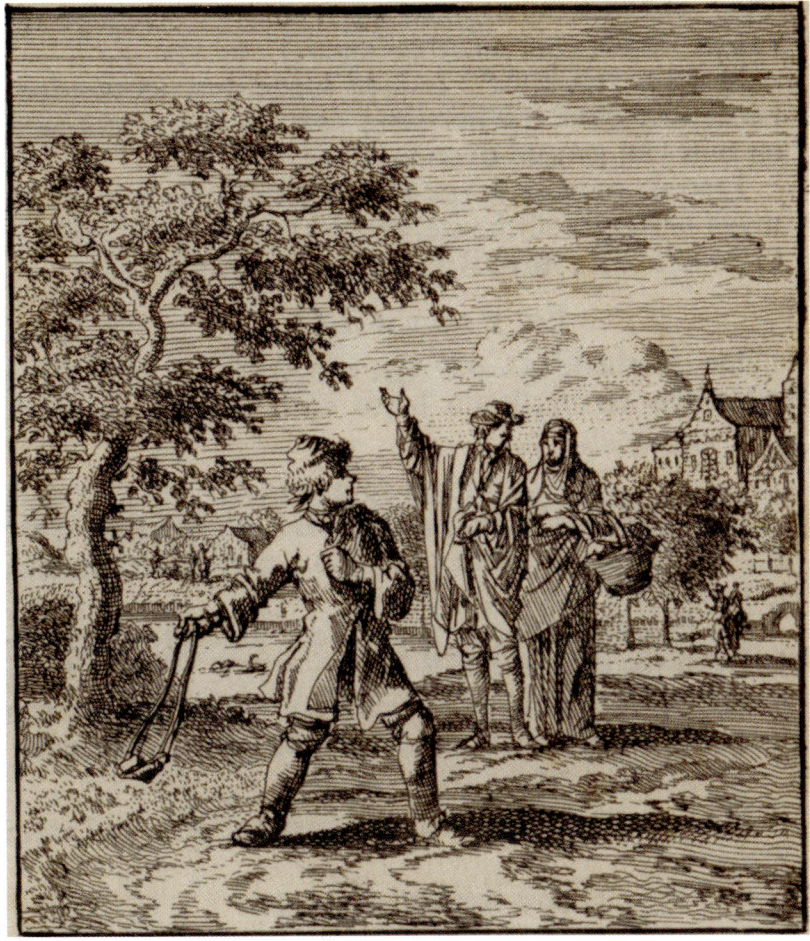

Jan Luyken, *De Slinger* (The sling). Print, *Des Menschen Begin, Midden en Einde* (1712). Collection Amsterdam Museum (P 4420 A 18971).

Slings are ancient weapons, known throughout much of the world. Perhaps this young boy thinks of himself as a Dutch David, preparing to battle an unseen Goliath. Surely he would have known that biblical story, and perhaps the fame of Benjamin among the Israelites. Or maybe he is taking aim at a bird flying by.

The armies of the ancient Persians used slings in their battles with the Greeks. Perhaps the boy is remembering this history lesson. Or maybe he recalls that ancient Greek shepherds used slings and stones to scare ferocious predators, like wolves, away from their flocks.

Boys used a variety of projectiles in their slings: pebbles, packed mud balls, knotted grasses, bones, broken pottery shards, and hardened clay balls. Country boys even used cow-dung patties. The youngsters took aim at either stationary or moving targets. Then they whirled the leather sling with its projectile-filled pouch over their heads and released one cord or strap sending the "bullet" on its way. Boys believed that if you could throw a small object, you could also sling it, but usually for a greater distance. Besides, slinging was more fun than simply throwing or tossing.

What were their targets? The door on an outhouse or privy if someone was occupying it was great fun: the thud of the projectile hitting the door startled the occupant. Boys competing with each other could designate a challenging makeshift target, such as knocking a leaf off a tree, or set a distance limit—perhaps getting their shots over a fence or wheelbarrow in the field. Taking aim at a rabbit or hare hopping over grassy fields or dunes enhanced hunting skills. Hurling pebbles at a strutting rooster in the barnyard, firing cherry pits at a neighbor's dog or cat, or slinging plum and peach pits at pigeons atop a dovecote was sure to produce a noisy protesting response, bringing a satisfied smirk of pleasure to the lad with a sling. Occasionally unsuspecting boys found themselves the targets of rival enemies: pleasure for the attackers, chagrin for the victims. (DRB)

JAN LUYKEN (1649–1712)

De Knikker (Marbles)

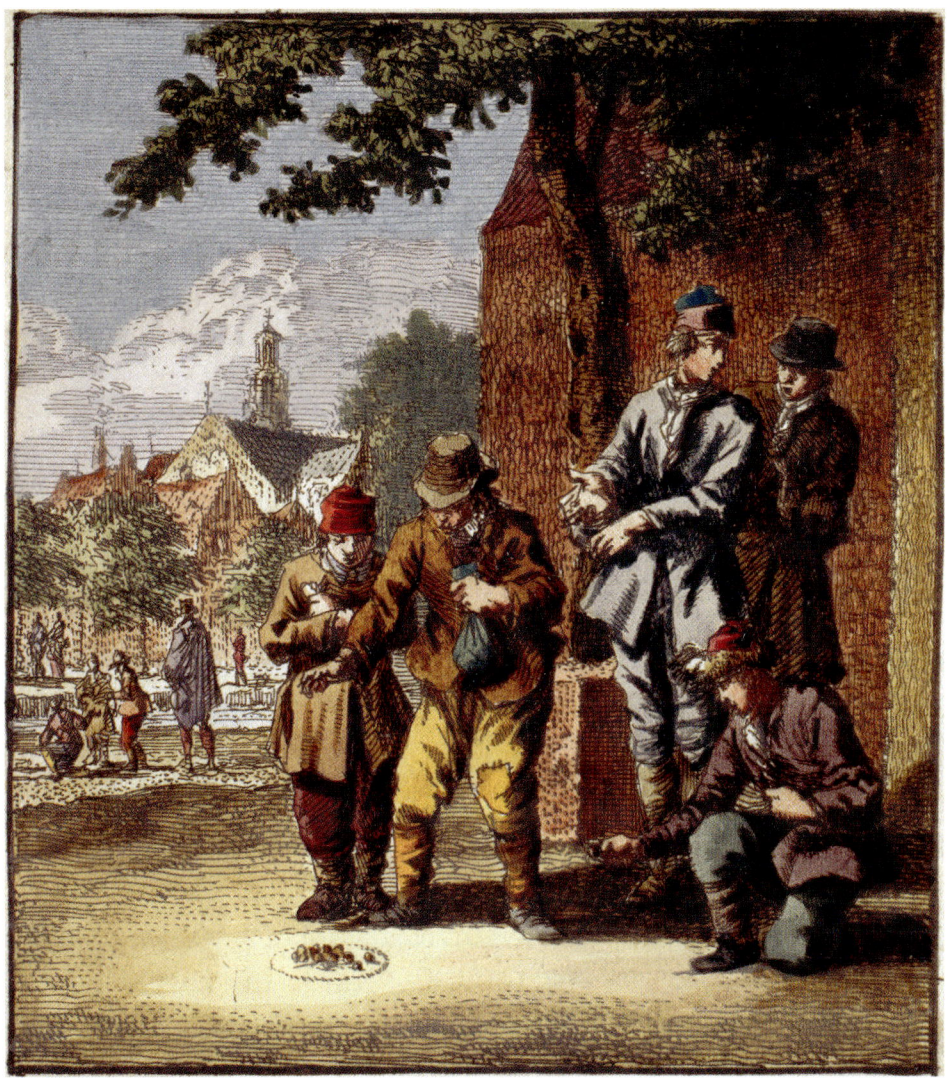

Jan Luyken, *De Knikker* (Marbles). Print (hand colored), *Des Menschen Begin, Midden en Einde* (1712). Collection Amsterdam Museum (P 4420; A 18965).

The boys are playing a game of "ringers," where players have drawn a ring on the ground and placed their marbles inside. The boy on bended knee is using his shooter (sometimes called a "taw" in English) to attempt to knock one of the other players' marbles out of the circle. It is important that the knuckles of his shooting hand remain on the ground. He is literally "knuckling down" to play. If he succeeds, he wins the marble (which, when it is a target, is known in English as a "duck").

In other versions of marbles, balls were rolled toward a hole in the ground or were knocked into a hole by a shooter. But whichever form of marble shooting boys chose, each variant game required eye-hand coordination skills, and a fiercely competitive spirit.

Because smooth surfaces were needed to roll marbles successfully, boys either smoothed a playing area for themselves on packed earth or they adapted other smooth surfaces to their purposes: perhaps using a large paving stone with a circle drawn in chalk or a gravestone inside a church or outside in a church graveyard.

Dutch boys carried their marbles in leather or cloth pouches, closed with a drawstring. These could be hand-carried or tied to a belt (interior pockets did not exist in clothing at the time). Luyken rightly observes that boys considered their marbles as "treasure."

Boys might have obtained baked clay or stoneware marbles from a potter using up excess clay as he loaded his kiln with objects that needed to be fired or from a specialized *knikker-bakker* (literally, a marble baker). Some fortunate Dutch boys in the seventeenth century owned imported marbles of ground and polished agate, alabaster, or marble produced in German water-powered stone mills located in Coburg or Oberstein. These marbles were brought to Holland by peddlers. (Glass marbles did not come into existence until 1846. They were first produced in Germany.)

Originating in Egypt, Greece, or Rome as games of skill played with acorns, cherry pits, or rounded stones, marble playing in the ancient world was not limited to children. Adults sometimes played, too, often making bets on the outcome. By the time Jan Luyken created this print, at least nine different marble games were immortalized on Dutch tiles, bespeaking the popularity of these games.

In a 1650 painting by Gerrit Houckheest, boys shoot marbles in the interior of the Nieuwe Kerk in Delft. Jan Steen, on the other hand, shows a boy so intent on playing marbles outdoors even as a bridal pair meets to marry that he ignores the couple and their entourage. In 1643, Bartholomeus van der Helst included marbles among masculine objects surrounding a nude baby boy, possibly his son, Lodewijk, in *Boy with a Spoon*. (DRB)

DIRCK HALS (1591–1656)

Children Playing Cards, 1631

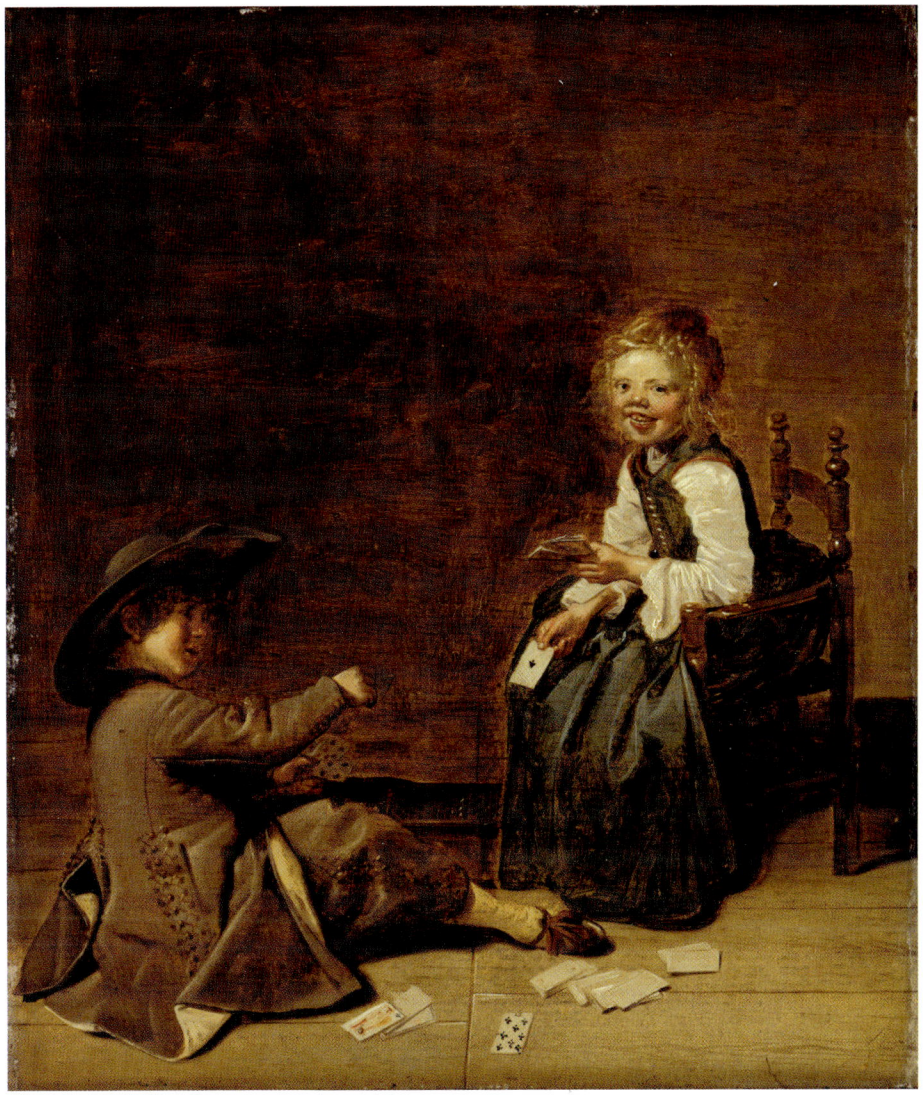

Dirck Hals, *Children Playing Cards,* 1631. Oil on panel, 12.83 x 10.91 in. (32.6 x 27.7 cm). Sterling and Francine Clark Art Institute, Williamstown, Massachusetts, USA, 1955.757. © Sterling and Francine Clark Art Institute, Williamstown, Massachusetts, USA.

Grinning with triumph, a little girl produces her winning ace from the cards held in her hand. Her opponent, seated on the floor, doesn't have a chance: he has just lost the game. Discarded playing cards, some with their point values showing, and others face down, are on the floor near the boy's slipper-covered feet. Unless he has a higher-valued ace tucked away in that wide floppy brimmed hat of his, he's finished and he knows it.

Hals has used a limited palate of colors to depict the two children. The girl's golden curls echo the golden buttons on her sleeveless dark bodice. The red trim at the armholes echoes her red lips. Her white long-sleeved blouse is the same color as her winning card. The young boy is dressed like a cavalier in his gray knee breeches and doublet. The pale-colored lining of his doublet, revealed in its folds, is echoed in his stockings. His doublet also has a series of decorative buttons on the side.

Viewers of this painting probably understood that this little girl is going to be a winning coquette as she grows older, dominating men in the game of love just as she has dominated this boy in cards. The girl looks out at the viewer, inviting us to share her victory.

Playing cards was not only a favorite activity of Dutch adults and children, but also a frequent theme in art works. Card games and backgammon (the dice-and-board game known as *tric trac*) were popular amusements, sometimes played by men in taverns, coffee houses, or at home; sometimes played by couples; and sometimes played by children.

Despite moralists' objections, card-game rules could be learned at an early age. Children could learn to count and add point values when playing cards. Some games depended on the skillfulness and strategies of the players, others were simply a matter of luck. Learning to accept defeat gracefully was another "lesson" learned through card games, although most children preferred winning. (DRB)

NICOLAES MAES (1634–1693)

Young Boy in Classical Dress in a Goat-Drawn Chariot, 1667

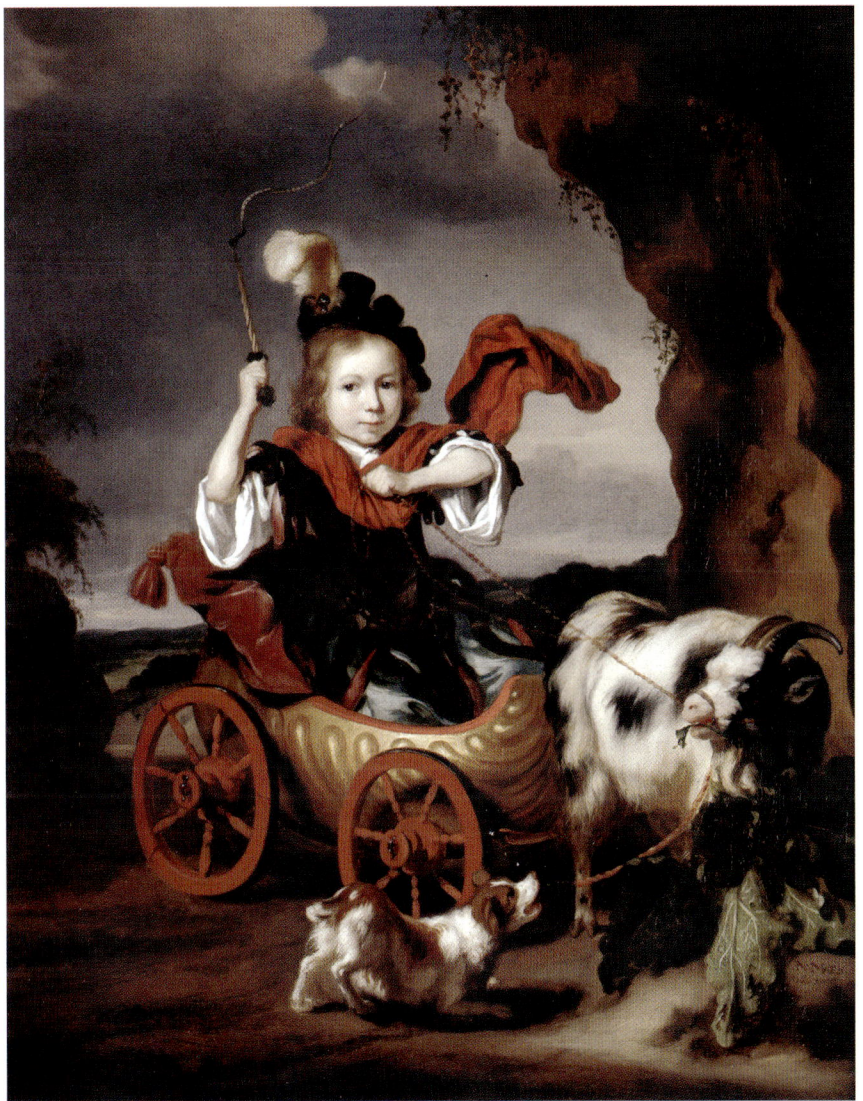

Nicolaes Maes, *Young Boy in Classical Dress in a Goat-Drawn Chariot,* 1667. Oil on canvas, 29⅛ x 24⅛ inches. Private European Collection.

Wearing a jaunty black velvet beret trimmed with a curled white feather held in place by a jewel, a red cloak across his neck and fluttering over his shoulders, a long blue skirt, white shirt, and fancifully slashed black tunic as an over-garment, this youngster has raised his whip as if to urge on the goat pulling a gilded four-wheeled chariot. He also tugs on a rope attached to the goat's muzzle. The boy is nestled against a rose-colored cushion whose colors echo the trim on the sides of the chariot and wheels. The black-and-white billy goat chomps placidly on a leaf, unmindful of either his master's command or the barking brown-and-white spaniel.

Goat carts and pony carts were used by wealthy youngsters at their families' country estates. In this painting, the chariot looks like an elaborate sea-shell, which perhaps accounts for the fanciful setting. The cloudy sky meets the river in the background; a rocky formation forms a half niche to surround the image of the boy as the chariot itself encloses him. Cleverly, the velvet beret's sculptural folds echo the rocky formation.

The sitter for this portrait is unknown. We can be sure that the parents who commissioned this portrait of their son paid dearly to have his light brown curly hair immortalized. Perhaps the painting itself hung in a country estate located along the Vecht or Amstel rivers. Whether the chariot belonged to the family or was a studio prop for Nicolaes Maes is also not known. However, it was often the case that artists used their own studio props (objects or costumes) and even scenic canvas backdrops when working on their paintings. Maes was known for his portraiture and was sought after for his portraits of wealthy children.

Unlike this serious-faced young boy, Frans Hals painted three smiling, laughing children with a goat cart; the painting is currently at the Musées Royaux des Beaux-Arts in Brussels. In 1654, Ferdinand Bol also painted an image of three wealthy children riding in a goat-drawn chariot, accompanied by nude cherubs. It is assumed that the children might belong to the wealthy Trip family. The painting is housed at the Louvre in Paris. (DRB)

PHILIPS WOUWERMAN (1619–1668)

De Schimmel (The gray), ca. 1645–47

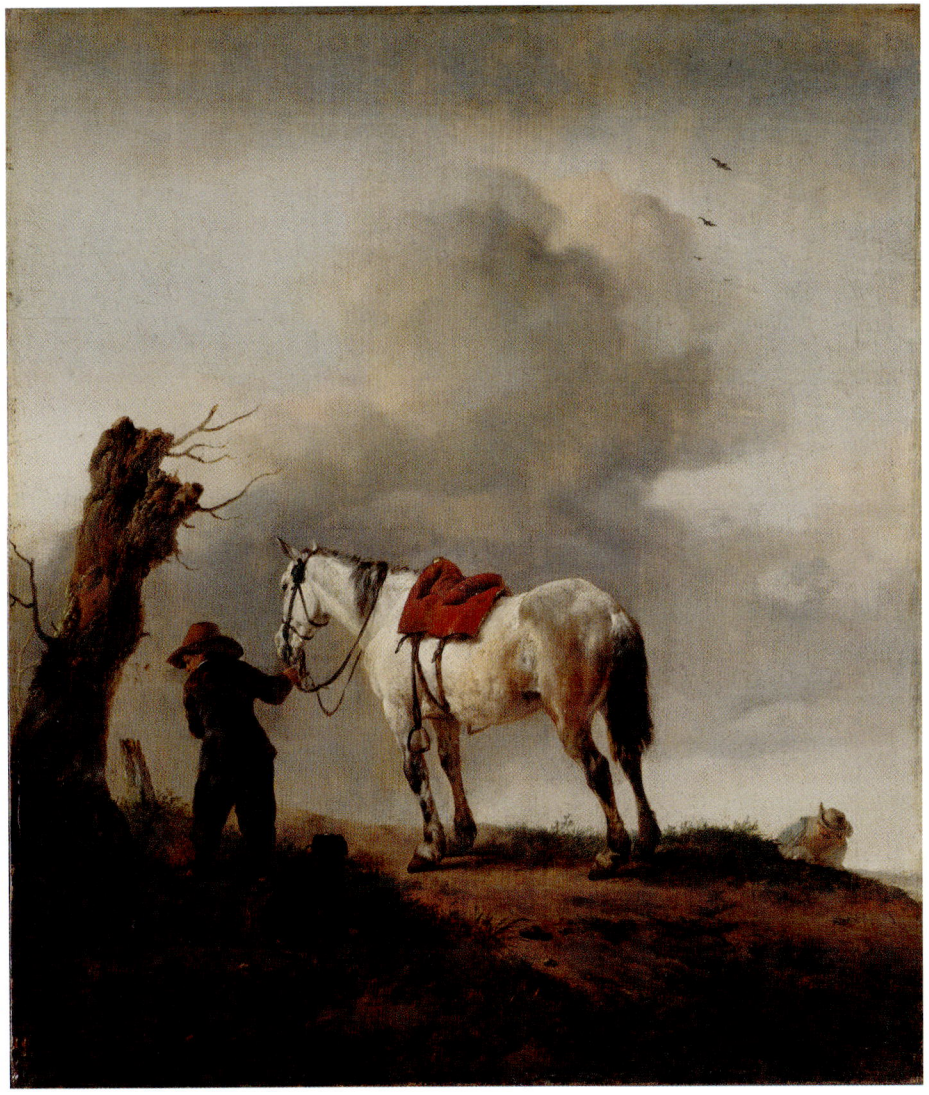

Philips Wouwerman, *De Schimmel* (The gray), ca. 1645–47. Oil on panel, 43.5 x 38 cm. Rijksmuseum Amsterdam (SK-A-1610).

A young boy walks up a hill, leading a gray horse by its bridle. The horse is saddled, ready for the boy to mount, should he decide to ride. A small black dog accompanies them. Both boy and horse seem unmindful of the gnarled dead tree at the left. Perhaps they are as exhausted as the tree. The clouds overhead offer some relief, but there is little shade or shadow for the horse and boy as they trudge along. The boy ignores the man at the right who is squatting to relieve himself. Perhaps he is the dismounted rider; if so, this boy will not get to ride the horse. He won't dare to do so.

Boys from wealthy families might have owned horses that they rode on their country estates, sometimes hunting and other times racing. Boys from farm families might have taken care of the horses used to pull plows and hay wagons. Boys whose fathers were carriage drivers probably also helped curry and groom the horses whose labors contributed to family income. Boys whose fathers were military officers might also occasionally ride on their fathers' horses. And boys who watched adult men ride on horseback as they attempted to catch live, wriggling eels or geese suspended from a cord between two buildings or two trees looked forward to the day when they, too, might join in these grown-up games. Girls rode horseback less often and usually sat sidesaddle, making racing almost impossible.

Philips Wouwerman was the foremost painter of horses among seventeenth-century Dutch artists. He painted them in fields and as part of military battle charges or hunting scenes. Here he has lavished care on the horse's gray-black mane and tail, the bridle, and the stirrups, as well as the red saddle. His skills in capturing the details of tired bony horses as well as plumper ones brimming with energy were admired by many of his wealthy patrons. Similarly, Wouwerman also admired the skills of the painter Jan Wynants in capturing landscape details. Wouwerman's tree in this painting closely resembles Wynants' *Landscape with Two Dead Trees,* now located at the National Gallery in London. (DRB)

DIRCK HALS (1591–1656)

Children with a Cat, 1631

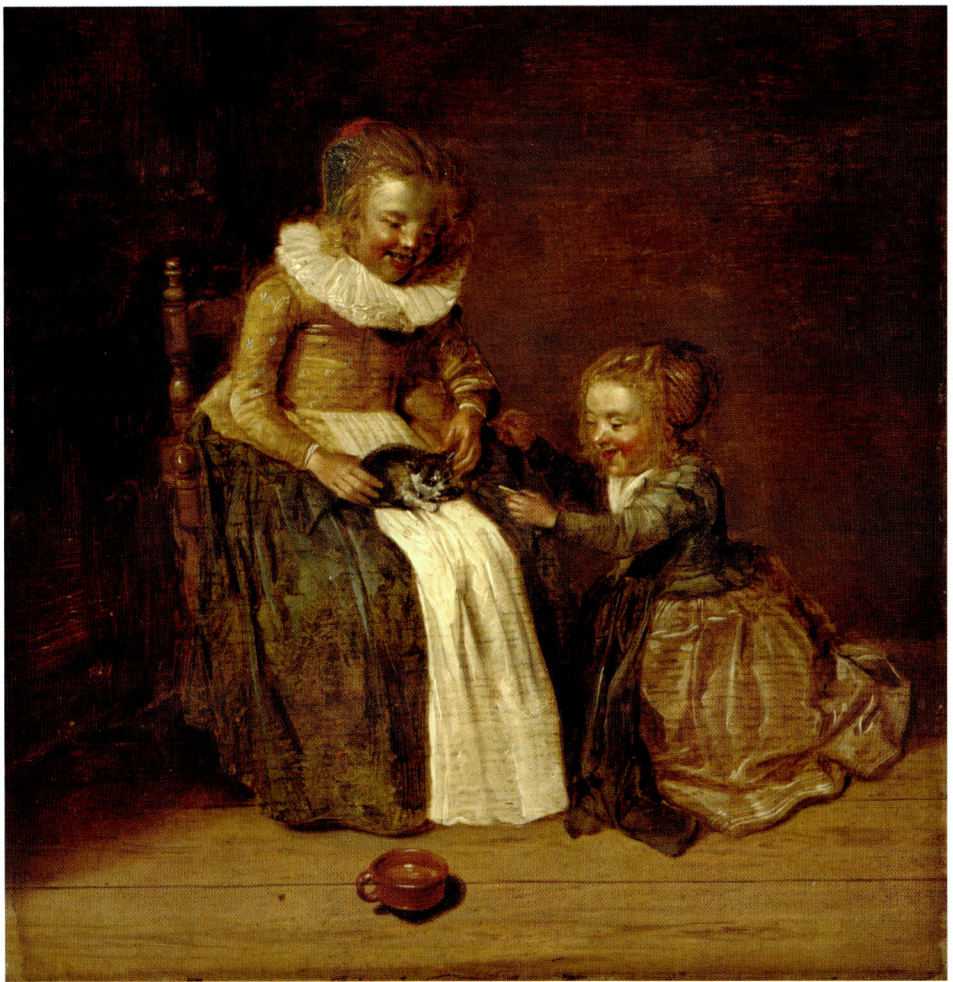

Dirck Hals, *Children with a Cat,* 1631. Oil on panel, 12.83 x 10.91 in. (32.6 x 27.7 cm). Sterling and Francine Clark Art Institute, Williamstown, Massachusetts, USA, 1955.756. © Sterling and Francine Clark Art Institute, Williamstown, Massachusetts, USA.

The older sister sits on a wooden chair holding a small gray kitten on the white apron covering her lap. Holding the kitten's back leg, she gently caresses the kitten's ear, hoping to make the little cat purr. Her younger sister kneels on the floor next to her. She extends her left arm toward the kitten, offering it a treat. Both girls are smiling with delight. Whether the kitten is equally delighted is not so clear. Perhaps the small red earthenware pipkin on the floor once had some milk in it for the little cat; it now is empty.

The older sister wears a millstone collar around her neck as a sign of her "maturity" because that was a garment accessory worn by grown women. Both girls have their skirts covered with floor-length aprons and their heads covered with small close-fitting caps, as was the custom.

With a very limited palette, Dirck Hals had captured a tender and joyful moment for his two little rosy-cheeked blondes. The image makes viewers smile today just as it did in the seventeenth century.

Cats had a mixed reputation in Holland during the seventeenth century. They were obviously useful in controlling the mice and rat population that bedeviled householders. They were often a source of amusement for children. However, cats were also viewed as sneaky and untrustworthy, perhaps because they could not be trained. Cats were frequently depicted by painters as stealing fish or poultry from the kitchen table or larder. (DRB)

JAN STEEN (1626–1679)

Kinderen Leren een Poes Dansen, bekend als 'De dansles'
(Children teaching a cat to dance, known as
"The Dancing Lesson")

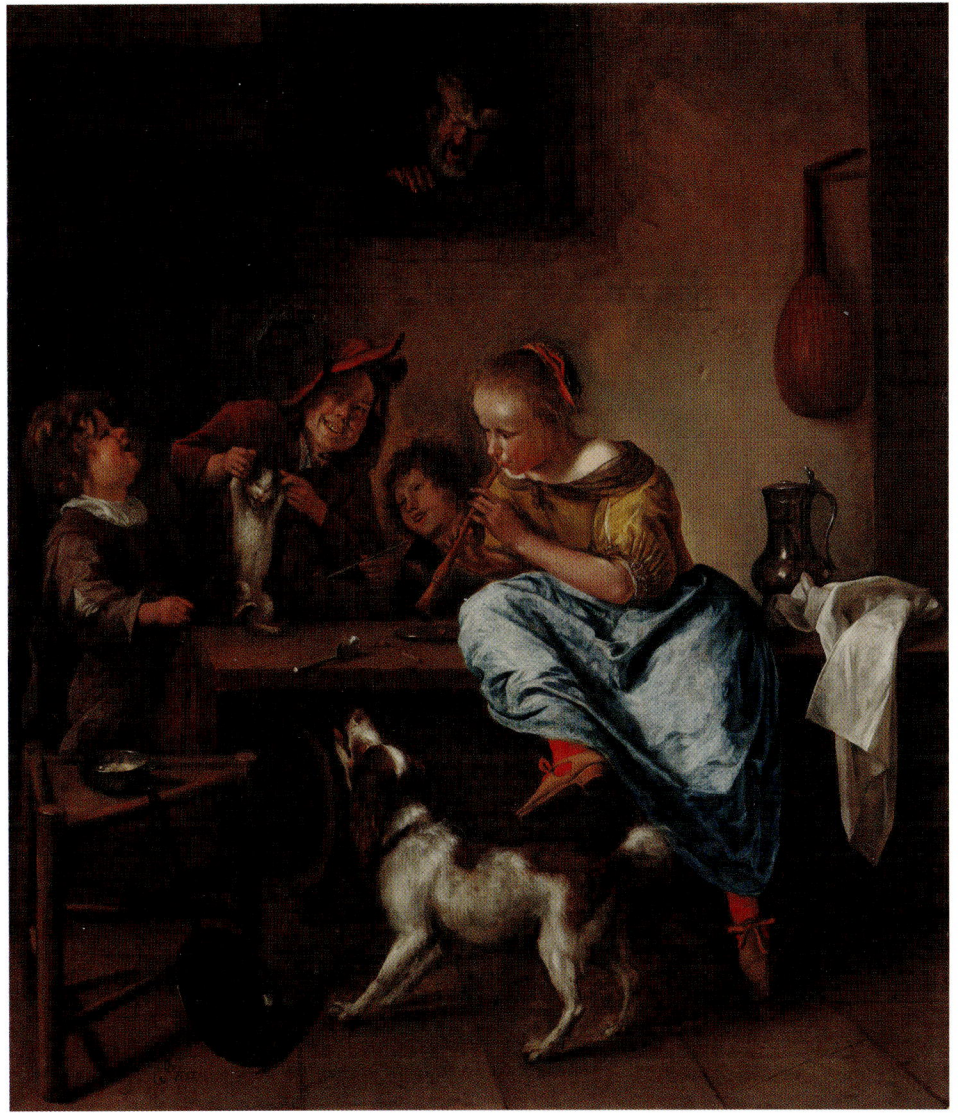

Jan Steen, *Kinderen Leren een Poes Dansen*, *bekend als 'De dansles'* (Children teaching a cat to dance, known as "The Dancing Lesson"). Oil on panel, 68.5 x 59 cm. Rijksmuseum Amsterdam SK-A-718.

Four mischievous children are intent on teaching a small, unhappy tabby cat to dance. The youngsters have gathered indoors around a wooden table. The oldest boy holds the cat's front paws, forcing the cat to stand on its rear legs. The cat's mouth is open, yowling in protest. A girl is perched on the table, playing a wooden recorder to supply the music for this dancing lesson. Two other younger boys have joined the "fun." One laughs and offers the cat a pipe of tobacco; the second boy holds onto the cat's tail while singing and laughing to the girl's music. A brown-and-white spaniel dog barks at the cat and children. An elderly man peers in through an upper window, probably objecting grumpily to the cacophony of noisy sounds.

Near the dog, a porringer of pap is resting on a three-legged stool. The spoon on the table might have been used by the boys in an attempt to feed the cat, before subjecting it to the dancing lesson. Perhaps the boys also drank beer from the pewter jug before beginning to torment the cat. Both tobacco and alcohol were considered to be intoxicating, whether used by children or by adults.

While the two younger boys are simply dressed, the "teacher" is wearing a jaunty feather in his red beret. Hats like those were often worn by professional musicians when entertaining an audience. The girl playing the recorder is more lavishly dressed, wearing her blue silken skirt, red stockings, and yellow blouse. She might have chosen to pluck the lute hanging up on the wall but instead decided the recorder would be best, perhaps because its frequently screechy sounds would prompt the dog to bark.

Dogs were considered good family pets because they were loyal, affectionate, and could be trained to be obedient. Cats, on the other hand, were often thought to be unpredictable and occasionally sneaky, although many children loved and enjoyed them. In this particular instance, it is the children who are less than affectionate toward the cat. Efforts at forcing the cat to dance will result in the tabby running away as soon as it can break free. Did Jan Steen mean to suggest that children's "pleasures" need to be closely monitored by attentive parents, lest they turn to malicious mischief? (DRB)

HENDRICK BERCKMAN (1629–1679)

A Young Boy with a Dog, 1667

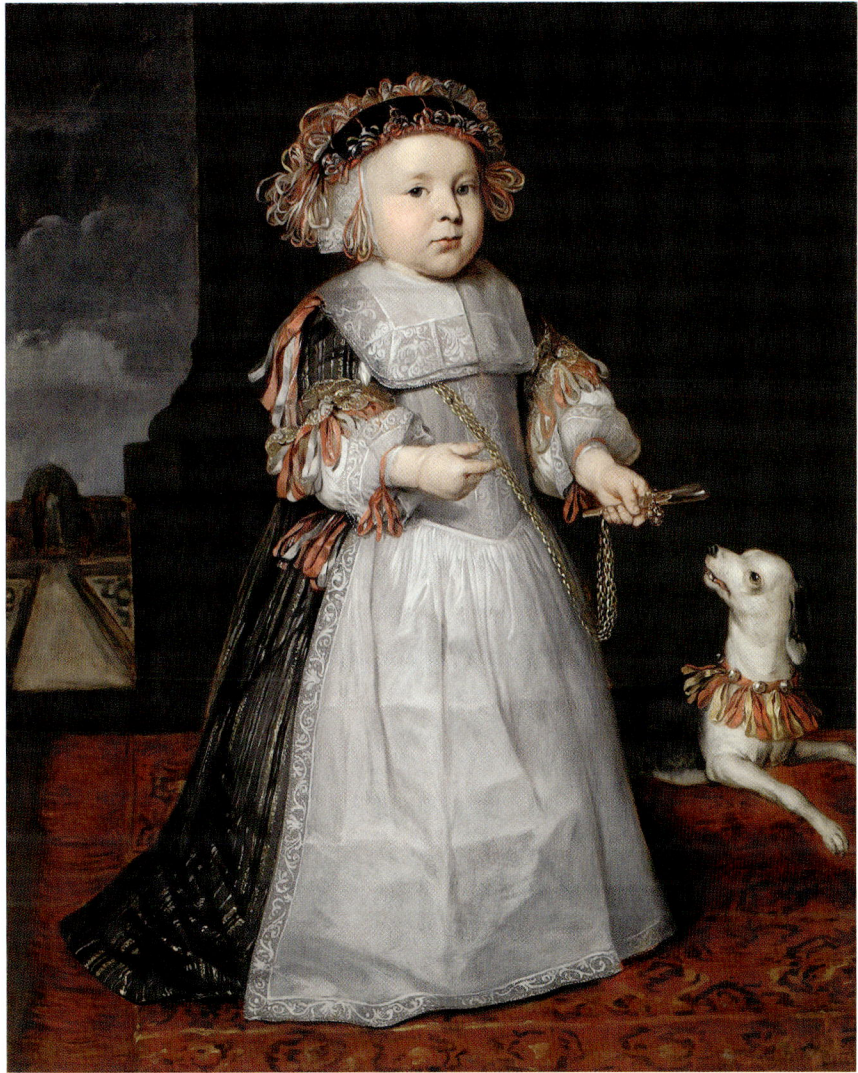

Hendrick Berckman, *A Young Boy with a Dog*, 1667. Oil on mahogany panel, 79.5 x 63 cm. Photograph courtesy Lawrence Steigrad Fine Arts.

The lavishly attired little boy is barely old enough to stand upright. He is young enough still to be wearing a dress and white lacy apron rather than breeches, and he *might* have taken pleasure in his clothing, which was surely a source of pride for his wealthy, perhaps even aristocratic, parents. But surely the pudgy-faced boy delighted in both the *rinkelbel* rattle held in his hand and the small black-and-white dog, wearing ribbons around its neck that echo the ribbons worn by the boy.

His rattle, or *rinkelbel*, is suspended from a gold chain that crosses diagonally over his chest, worn like a jeweled medal awarded to military heroes or distinguished men of culture. He holds the rattle's gold handle as though it were a scepter by which he could "rule" his dog. Whether the eager dog will accept his "master's" commands is an open question. Nothing in this image suggests the boy uses the rock crystal top to soothe aching, inflamed gums while teething.

No doubt the boy's parents, who commissioned the child's portrait, thought of him as the likely heir to their estate, hence the allusion to the country house with its large formal garden in the background and the luxurious Oriental carpet on which he stands. Wealthy enough to afford an imported Italian Greyhound used occasionally as a hunting dog, the painting hints at the boy eventually learning to hunt. Hunting was an aristocratic privilege in the Netherlands during the seventeenth century.

The boy's dark dress, consisting of skirt and doublet, is shot with silvery gray metallic threads. Such fabrics were expensive. He wears colored ribbons on his black outer cap, at his neck, on his wrists, and at his waist; ribbons were also costly. His long white linen apron is trimmed with lace; a similar lace trims the wide loose cuffs on his shirt under his doublet; and he wears a white lace undercap. Lace was also expensive. Everything about this child's clothing says "wealth"!

Boys and girls at very young ages wore dresses or petticoats and aprons. Only when the family considered the boy sufficiently mature would he be breeched, that is, attired in a doublet, shirt, and knee breeches. These garments were not his everyday clothing, but special attire meant to signify his—and his family's—status. He is *not* dressed for play; he is dressed to pose for his portrait.

Intimate portraits of family members were usually displayed at home in the more-private quarters of wealthy Dutch families rather than in the entryway where visitors were greeted. Close friends and relatives who saw this picture could not help but reflect on the parental pride that led to its creation and display.

Dutch adults believed that children's naturally exuberant dispositions needed to be trained and guided through discipline, parental admonitions and examples, and education. Advice books cautioned that unless children took well to this moral education, parents (and schoolmasters) were to use bundles of birch twigs or rods to spank disobedient youngsters on their backs, legs, hands, or buttocks.

Perhaps this boy's family thought about the need to train and discipline their child, just as a dog required careful training to be loyal and obedient. The parents might therefore have wanted their son posed with his dog, but this dog is not yet a strong example of disciplined behavior. The dog appears frisky, ready to leap and bound and bark. The faint smile on the boy's face shows how much he is amused by his pet. He can jingle the bells on his rattle, and the dog can respond by jingling the bells around his neck. Both little boy and dog could make a "game" of bell-jingling for their mutual pleasure.

Dogs were favorite pets of Dutch people. Children, especially boys, are often depicted playing with dogs or enjoying canine participation in family events. In portraits of girls, they are more often depicted with flowers or baskets of fruit. Judging from numerous paintings, spaniels were especially popular with people at all levels of society. Greyhounds, hunting dogs, lap dogs, and other breeds tended to be owned only by very wealthy families. Poor people might own mutts of mixed breed.

Dogs were considered ideal pets because they were loyal, affectionate, and could be trained to be obedient. Some dogs worked as hunters or as herders and were more than household pets. Cats, on the other hand, were often thought to be unpredictable and occasionally sneaky, although many children loved and enjoyed them. "Trained cat" was an oxymoron then . . . and now. (DRB)

JOB BERCKHEYDE (1630–1693)

The Bakery Shop

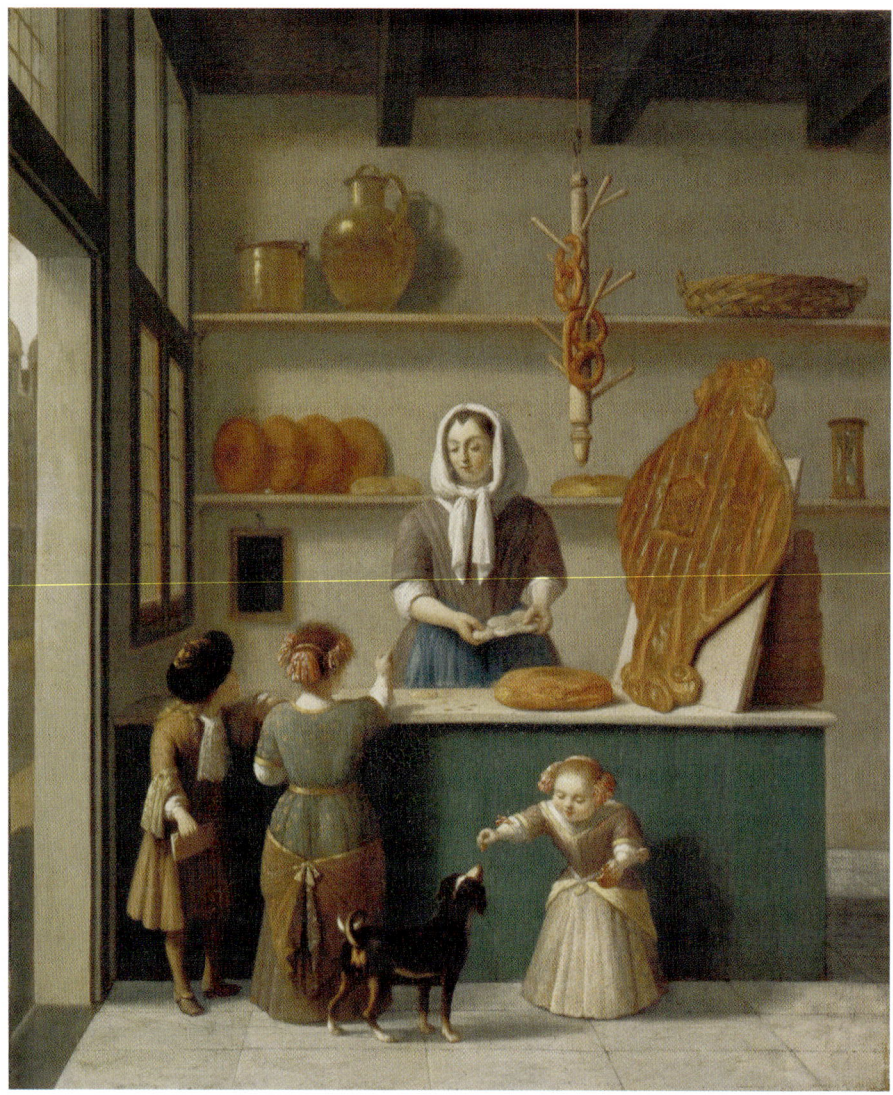

Job Berckheyde, *The Bakery Shop*. Oil on canvas. Allen Memorial Art Museum, Oberlin College, Ohio; R. T. Miller, Jr. Fund, 1956.

In the simple bakery shop a woman is attending the children who have come to purchase a cookie. A little girl seems oblivious to those around her as she is busy feeding her dog a bite from her cookie, while another girl and a boy are waiting for their treat to be broken off as the sugared cookies seem to have run together in baking. Behind the woman are shelves with a small brass cauldron, a brass milk jug, and a basket for rolls. On the shelf below, floor breads, so called because they are baked on the floor of the oven, are stacked in various sizes. A typical pretzel rack displays some very large pretzels.

In the Netherlands, bakers were organized in guilds, and their recipes were a trade secret. The first baking recipes were published in 1753 by "B.G." in *Volmaakte Onderrichtinge ten Dienste der Koek-Bakkers of hunne Leerlingen* (Perfect instructions to serve the pastry bakers, or their students [often boys in their teens]). Its recipe for pretzels calls for equal amounts of flour and sugar; butter, cinnamon, and potash (baking soda) are added. It makes a pretzel similar in shape but different in taste than the salty pretzels sold as street food nowadays.

On the counter we find another floor bread and propped up stands an enormous *duivekater*, a holiday bread generally made around Saint Nicholas Day, December 6, until Epiphany, January 6, and often given to the needy on New Year's Day.

The *duivekater* is carved with a sharp knife before baking and is decorated with *patacons*. These are usually colorfully decorated earthenware disks that are baked onto the bread; here they seemed to have been made of bread dough. The earthenware disks would remain after the holiday bread was consumed in the way a ring or toy remains in a Cracker Jack box. (PGR)

Inventing Fun, Games, and Mischief

MICHIEL VAN MUSSCHER (1645–1705)

A Pig on a Ladder / The Vegetable Market Woman, **1668**

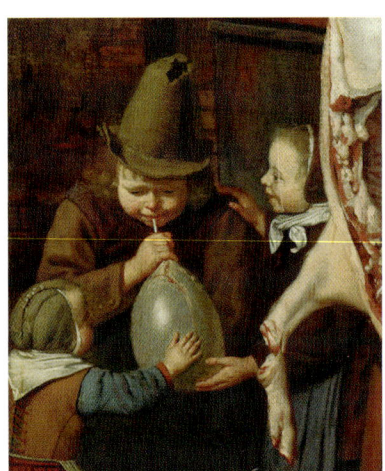
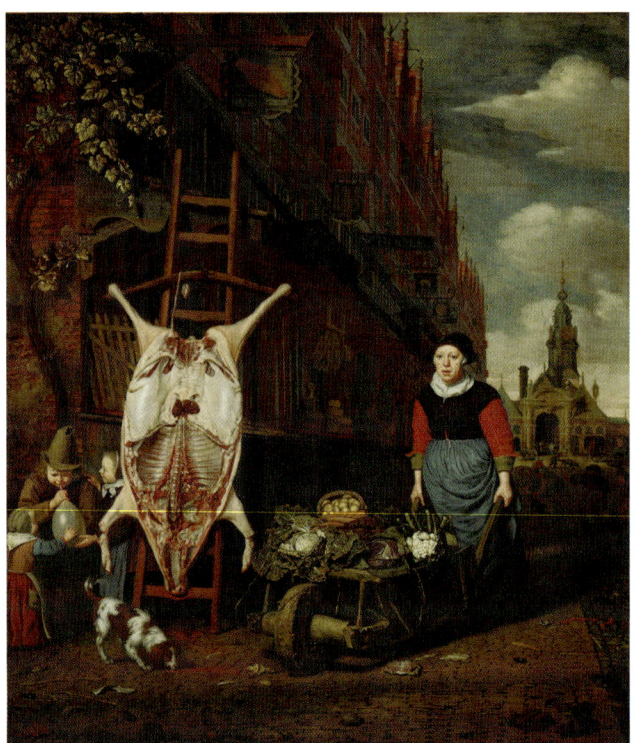

Michiel van Musscher, *A Pig on a Ladder / The Vegetable Market Woman,* 1668. Oil on canvas. Collection Amsterdam Museum (SA 38126).

Trundling her wheelbarrow filled with vegetables, the market woman makes her way through Amsterdam streets near the Haarlemmerpoort. She passes a row of stalls and walks by a disemboweled slaughtered pig suspended from a ladder so its blood might drain away from the carcass. Small children have seized the opportunity to inflate the pig's bladder, which they will use as a toy.

The children ignore the market woman and the dog. The older boy with the tall hat puffs into a straw. He is in charge of this procedure. The younger children touch the slippery organ, marveling as it grows bigger and bigger. The three will probably toss the bladder about like a ball or balloon.

The woman pays no attention to the boy blowing up the pig's bladder and the dog licking up accumulated pig's blood. She was hoping to find customers for her fresh cabbages and cauliflower. A hard-working woman, she has no time for the youngsters' childish frivolity.

Viewers of this painting might have taken delight in the careful rendering of the city gate built on the Haarlemmerdijk between 1615 and 1618. Or they might recall the Dutch saying "What is the world we see? A bag of wind, nothing more . . ." and think about the transitory nature of life and life's pleasures. The pig, after all, is now quite dead, and its bladder, once filled, will also have a short duration as an amusement for the children.

Although inflated pig bladders are associated with scenes of slaughter during November, the traditional month for butchering hogs and preserving their meats for winter use, the artist sets this scene in warmer weather, as indicated by the foliage at the left and the produce in the wheelbarrow. (DRB)

JAN LUYKEN (1649–1712)

De Blaas (The bladder)

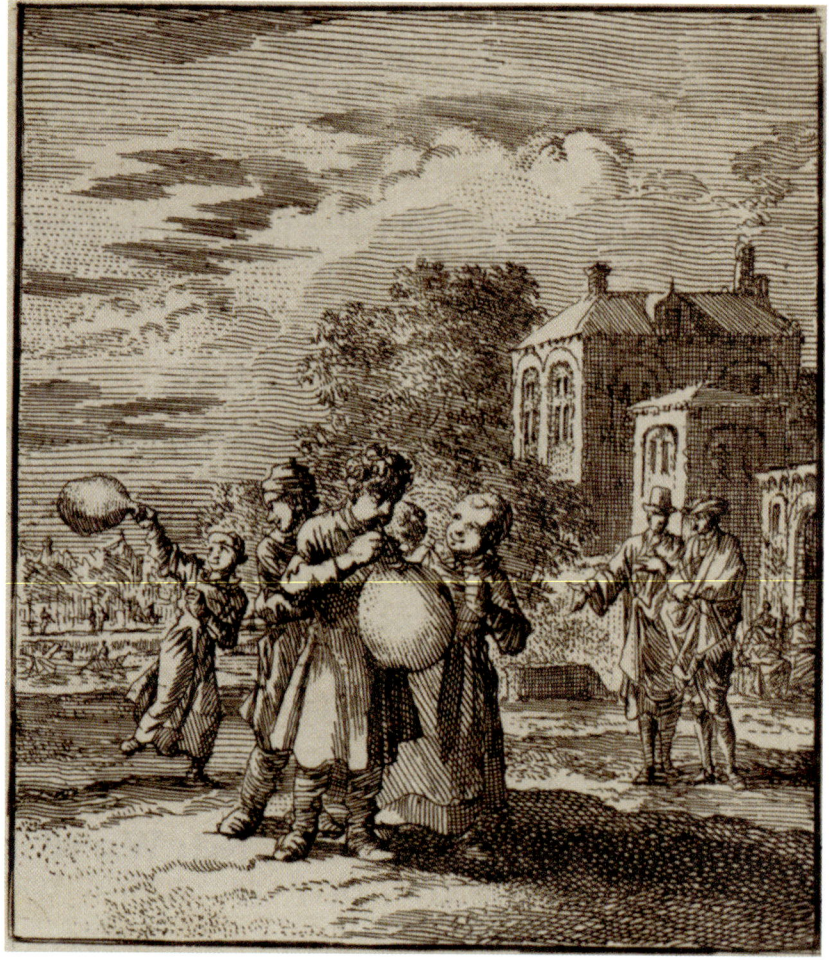

Jan Luyken, *De Blaas* (The bladder). Print, *Des Menschen Begin, Midden en Einde*, 1712. Collection Amsterdam Museum (P4411; A 18956).

One child inflates a slaughtered pig's bladder by inserting a straw into the opening of this organ, blowing through the straw, filling the bladder with air. The second child runs with an inflated bladder, swinging the light, air-filled organ. Once inflated, the bladder opening could be tied off, making a lightweight slippery ball or balloon.

Prior to tying the bladder, dried beans or small pebbles could be inserted to make a rattling noise, or water might be poured into the bladder (especially if it was going to be tossed at someone else), and then the bladder was tied.

Young children sometimes gleefully ran with inflated bladders, swishing them through the air like balloons. The stretched bladder, whether filled with water or not, was slippery. It made an annoyingly sticky "bomb" to lob at friends or rivals, providing a good weapon for mischief.

If the bladder was filled but not tied off, it was possible to squeeze it and produce rude noises as the air escaped. All in all, it was a wonderful "toy" to mark the slaughter of a hog. Many of the pig's other internal organs (such as intestines, heart, stomach, and tongue) were used in the making of sausages and headcheese. The kidneys and liver were quickly pan-fried and eaten as a special treat. All of these porcine delicacies were enjoyed by children and adults.

But bladders, to children's delight, had no useful culinary purposes. That's not exactly accurate: a bladder could be used to seal over a filled earthenware jam jar with a string tied around it, but bladders themselves were not eaten. And a bladder, stretched over a large, tall empty earthenware pot, could be pierced with a stout stick and the entire device made into a rumbling *rommelpot*, which served as a folk musical instrument, producing silly noises that prompted grown-ups and children to laugh.

Dutch artists frequently used the image of an inflated pig's bladder, or a soap bubble, to suggest the transitory nature of human life and human pleasures. Invariably it is a child depicted with the bladder or bubble. (DRB)

JAN LUYKEN (1649–1712)
De Bikkel (Knucklebones)

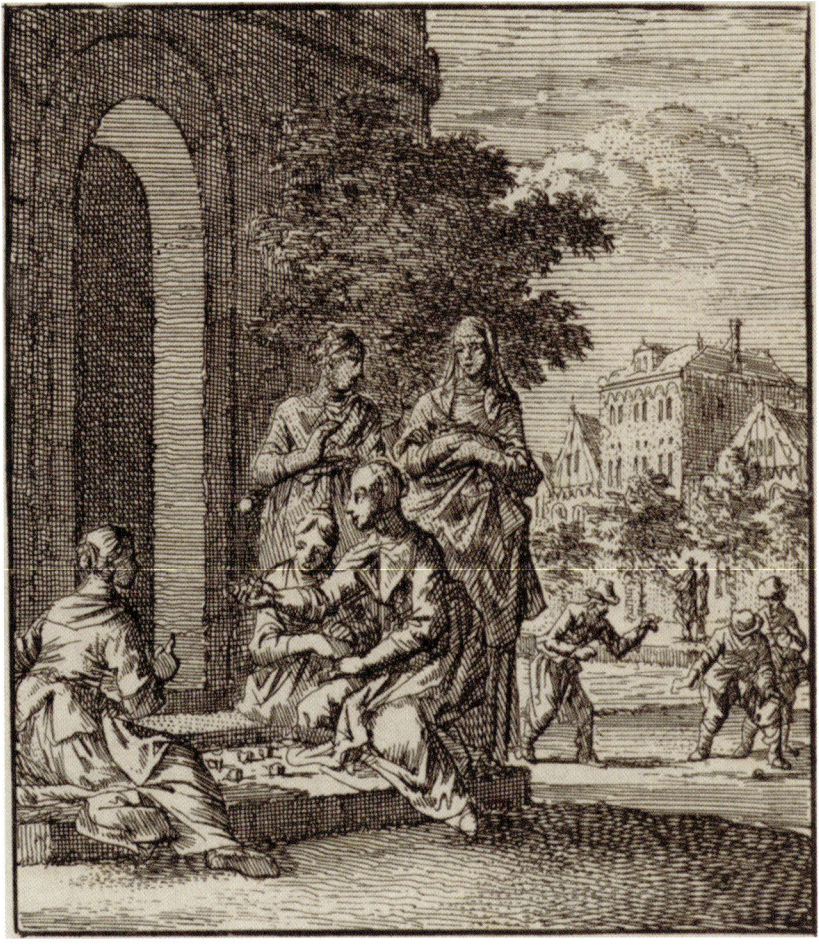

Jan Luyken, *De Bikkel* (Knucklebones). Print, *Des Menschen Begin, Midden en Einde*, 1712. Collection Amsterdam Museum (P 4424; A 18959).

Girls toss knucklebones onto the surface of the front doorstep. They pick them up, one at a time, with one hand, having determined the point value of the upturned surface. Perhaps they used actual animal bones from sheep knuckles or they used cast metal bones made to resemble those of animals. The irregular sides of the bones have different point values.

Improvising games from readily available everyday objects was characteristic of Dutch children, whether they lived in cities, in rural villages, or on farms. Jan Luyken depicted boys playing games on city streets involving animal bones and animal teeth. These items could be cadged from a butcher, especially at slaughter time in November, when many city families purchased slaughtered carcasses of pigs or oxen for preserving in salty brine solutions in a wooden barrel, known as a *vleeskuip*. Rural families raising or fattening their own oxen, mutton, and hogs also slaughtered them in November for preserving. Children not only used animal bones and teeth as playthings, but, as shown earlier, they made use of the pig's bladder which they inflated.

Typically, boys played more vigorous games with these waste animal parts, standing and hurling weighted bones at targets, while the girls would more demurely sit and toss the bone toys into the air. *Bikkel* is a forerunner of jacks.

As shown in Luyken's print, the boys in the background are more actively involved than the seated girls. And it is also significant that the girls' behavior is closely observed by two older women, perhaps a mother and older sister or household servant. Girls' activities were more closely monitored than those of their brothers. Boys were allowed to roam; Dutch girls were expected to stay close to home. (DRB)

JAN STEEN (1626–1679)

A School for Boys and Girls, also known as *The Unruly School* or *The Schoolmaster,* ca. 1670

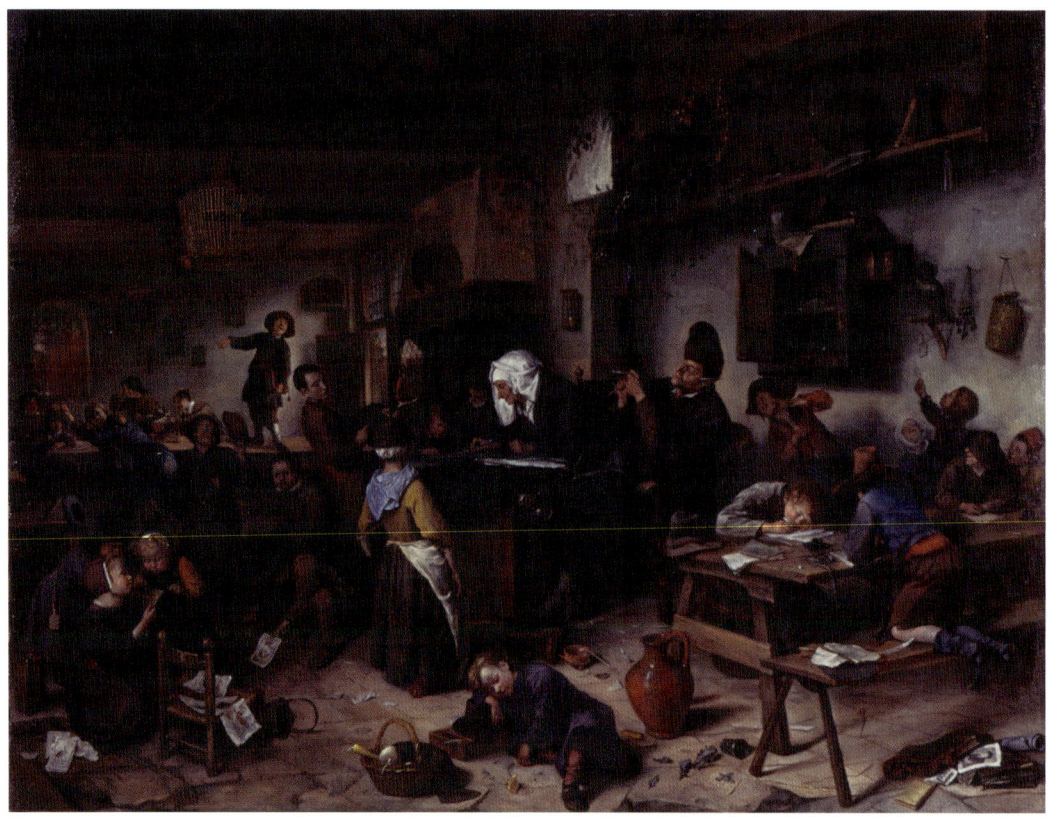

Jan Steen, *A School for Boys and Girls,* also known as *The Unruly School* or *The School-master,* ca. 1670. Oil on canvas, 83.8 x 109.2 cm. National Gallery of Scotland.

The schoolmaster seated at his desk busily sharpens his quill pen, totally oblivious to the chaos all around him. His wife is correcting a few students' lessons. They've come up to the desk; she has a bundle of birch switches to use if the students' work is wrong. Two little kids are on the floor near a small chair. An illustrated reading book is on the chair. Inexpensive catch-penny prints are strewn on the floor. Another small scholar is asleep on the floor— too much pedagogical excitement for him. In the dimly lit background where children are supposed to be working on their lessons, a bold boy has climbed up onto the table. He's not studying anything. Not far away from the school-master, a boy extends a pair of glasses to an owl perched on a wall ledge. His schoolmates, seated or kneeling on a bench near a work table, labor over their schoolbooks. Some kids are fighting or singing or mocking the teachers. The noise must be deafening, and yet the schoolmaster hears none of it.

Jan Steen was not the first to invent such a chaotic image. Indeed a sixteenth-century engraving by Peter van der Heyden after Pieter Bruegel the Elder, *The Ass at School*, depicts similarly chaotic classroom happenings although there the schoolmaster has taken a birch switch to the naked exposed buttocks of a misbehaving ringleader. Perhaps Steen knew the print. He probably also knew that Jan Miense Molenaer, Adriaen van Ostade, and his brother, Isack van Ostade, had explored the theme of classroom cacophony. Steen also created two paintings of a stern schoolmaster who uses a wooden ferule to discipline students who have failed to get their lessons right.

The lantern lit in the schoolroom, like the owl perched near it, are ironic visual comments on the lack of wisdom and learning occurring in this setting. Whether Jan Steen meant primarily to comment on the paintings by his predecessors and rivals or meant also to offer his own commentary on the deplorable possibilities of schooling run amok when schoolmasters don't attend to their pedagogic responsibilities is an open question. That Steen placed atop a pile of books in the lower right foreground a portrait print of Erasmus, the sixteenth-century humanist from Rotterdam, who was taken as a paradigm of wise educational theory, offers a small clue.

The Dutch educational system achieved remarkable results in the seventeenth century, extending literacy to a wider segment of the population than was the case in nearby France, Germany, or England. However, the system was also criticized from time to time by local examiners who visited the schools, sometimes finding teachers who were drunk or indifferent to their responsibilities. Steen's painting might well be considered a humorous, but pointed, reminder to parents to exercise judgment in their selection of schooling for their children.

Jan Steen has been called a "storyteller" because his paintings have such a narrative quality. Frequently the stories told are ones in which children either misbehave or mock the behaviors of adults who are also guilty of misbehavior, whether drunk, quarrelsome, or lecherous. Humor on Steen's canvases often pointed to obvious moral issues, but the viewer also got a chuckle along with the "lesson." How young children viewing Steen's pictures interpreted his images is unknown; perhaps like their elders, they smiled or giggled. (DRB)

JOACHIM WTEWAEL (1566–1638)
Vegetable Seller, ca. 1618

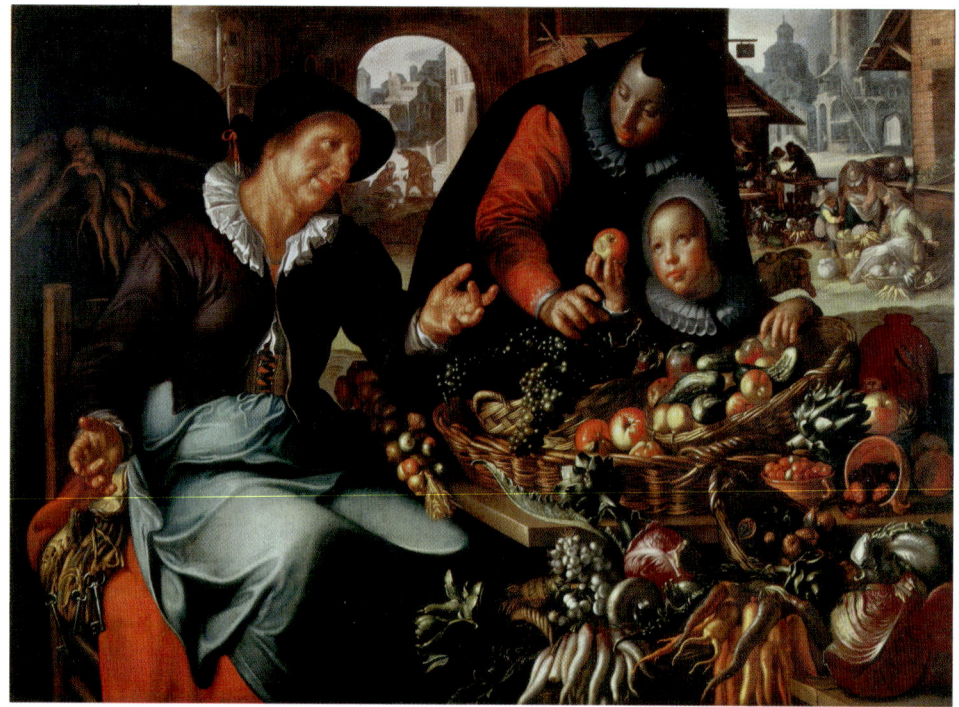

Joachim Wtewael, Utrecht 1566–Utrecht 1638. *Vegetable Seller,* ca. 1618. Oil on canvas. Collection Centraal Museum Utrecht. Image & copyrights Centraal Museum Utrecht/Ernst Moritz.

There is something sanctimonious in the face of the little girl holding up a rotten apple, and the market woman's body language seems to indicate a laissez-faire attitude of "what are you going to do?" although in both Dutch and English there is a proverb that indicates "a rotten apple spoils the barrel" (and should be removed). Apples and other fruit make good snacks and treats, as we also see in Dusart's Saint Nicholas celebration, where the gift baskets contain winter fruit like apples and pears.

In this market scene there are some summery fruits to be found as well, such as the cherries in a typical red earthenware cup for measuring fruit and another such cup filled with what seem to be red and black currants, along with the apples, pears (with gherkins mixed in), and beautiful large bunches of grapes. The carefully arranged vegetables include orange and white carrots, artichokes, and cabbages. It is a beautiful display that celebrates the glories of Dutch horticulture.

De Verstandige Kock (*The Sensible Cook*) has many recipes for these vegetables. Apples, pears, and cherries are used in tarts; red currants are made into juice or syrup. Grapes were eaten as table grapes but also cooked. Unripe grape juice or *verjus* gave sauces and dishes a characteristic acidic flavor. Cabbages were often eaten raw in salads, but also cooked in stews, and so were carrots and onions. The gherkins might be part of a salad but were made into pickles as well. Artichokes were slowly cooked and served with a sauce of butter, vinegar, salt, and pepper. (PGR)

ARTIST UNKNOWN (AFTER ANDRIES DIRKSZ BOTH),
SEVENTEENTH CENTURY

Peasant Man and Child at Market

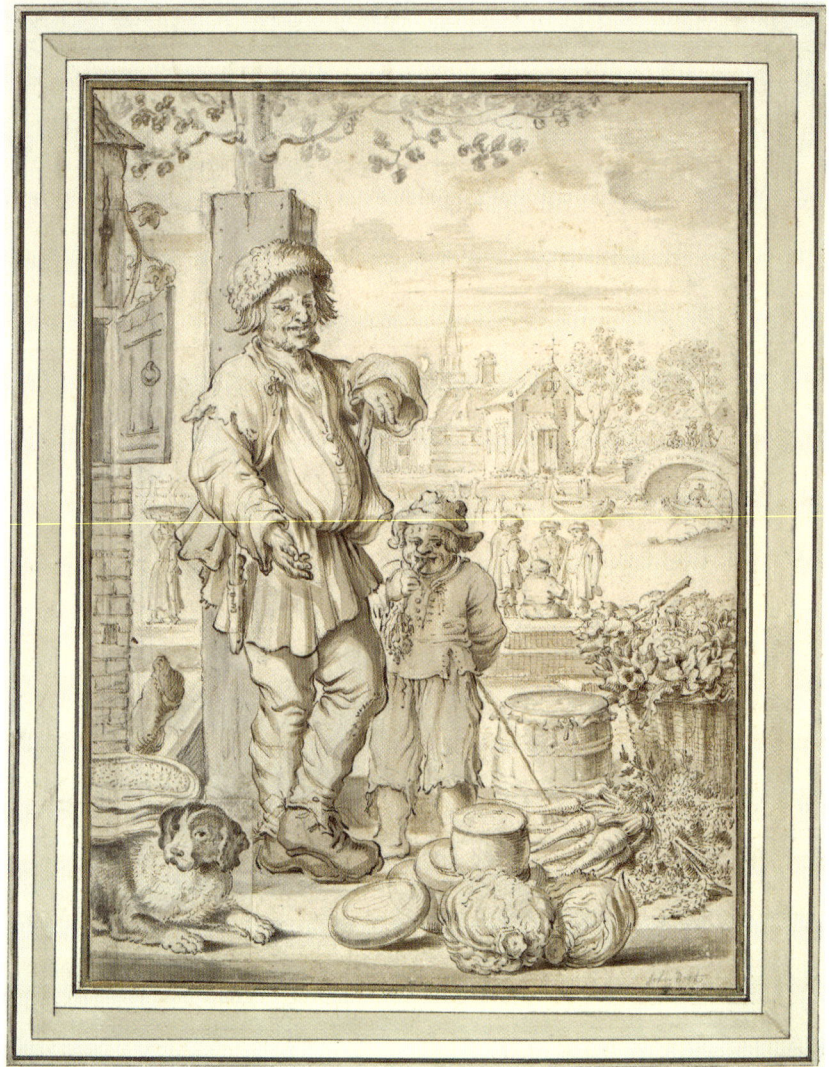

Artist unknown (after Andries Dirksz Both), seventeenth century, *Peasant Man and Child at Market*. Drawing. Yale University Art Gallery, Egmont Collection, Yale Library Transfer.

A vegetable stall offers the shopper only a few choices. The man with a heavy beer belly, leaning against a post, sells cheeses, as well as carrots, artichokes, and large cabbages. (A Dutch saying referring to children with growth spurts says they "grow like cabbage.") Next to the large basket with artichokes on the right stands a barrel that might well contain pickles. Behind the dog, who seems to keep an eye on the merchandise, stands a sack full of hazelnuts, still popular nuts in the Netherlands.

De Verstandige Kock (*The Sensible Cook*) lists cabbage, red or white, in the salad group, while artichokes appear in the section of vegetables to be braised. Carrots would be added to a stew of root vegetables, a mainstay for the poor. Salads were dressed the way we do today with olive oil, vinegar, salt, and pepper. Sometimes a dash of sugar or a handful of (Zante) currants might be added.

In contrast to the beautifully dressed child in the previous painting, the young boy in this depiction is dressed in rags and has bare feet. He is munching on a carrot, which might be a treat in the sense that it is something extra in addition to his usual meager ration, or worse, it might be his meal.

The vegetable stand is situated along a canal, and in the background we see someone rowing a boat. That could very well also have been the way the man and boy transported their wares to this location. (PGR)

LEONARD BRAMER (1596–1674)

Heet garnaalen, heet (Hot shrimp, hot)

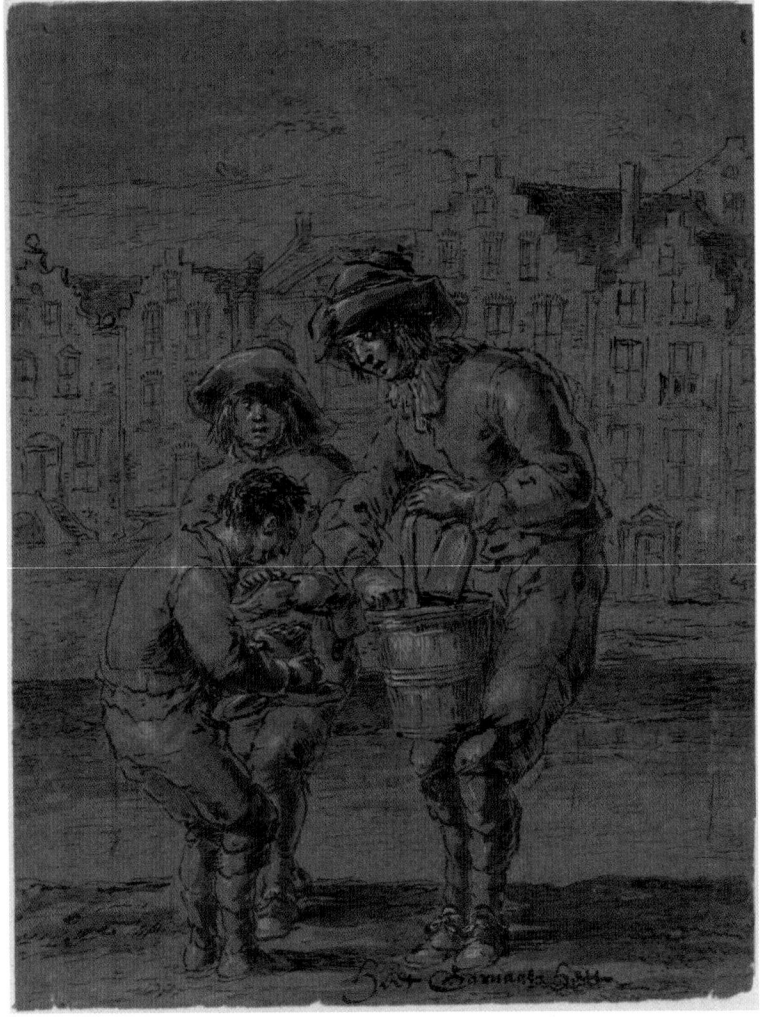

Leonard Bramer, *Heet garnaalen, heet* (Hot shrimp, hot). Drawing
(part of *Straatwerken*). Leiden University Library, PK-T-3605 024.

The title of this drawing (on the bottom in the center) is *"heet garnaalen heet"*
(hot shrimp, hot), which would be the cry of the seller. Standing on a street of
step-gabled houses, he takes some boiled shrimp by the tail from his bucket
and gives them to one of the boys. We may assume he was paid first.

Generally, shrimp were boiled in sea water on board ship or right on the
shore. We also have a lyrical description in Gheeraert Vorselman's book of
1560 on how shrimp should be cooked in salt water: "throw in the shrimp,

make sure they boil as if it were a sea and allow the waves to pass over them three or four times." The recipe suggests eating seafood cold with vinegar, pepper, and chopped parsley.

Parsley was a favorite herb to use with fish in general. One common recipe was for *doopvis* (fish for dunking), which was poached in salted water with parsley. It was served with the poaching water. The fish and the customary accompanying bread were dunked into it. It was a favorite dish served in inns by canal boat stops. (PGR.)

LEONARD BRAMER (1596–1674)

Heet warme waeffelen (Hot warm waffles)

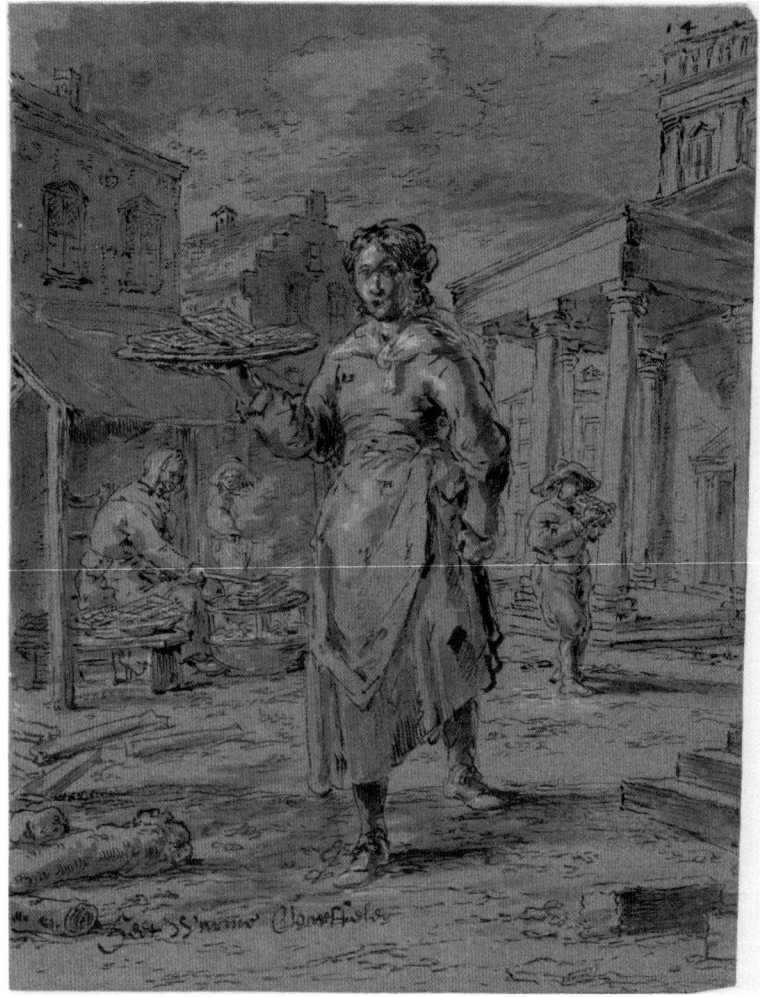

Leonard Bramer, *Heet warme waeffelen* (Hot warm waffles). Drawing
(part of *Straatwerken*). Leiden University Library, PK-T-3605 020.

A woman is seated in the background at a low, portable brazier, stoked with
wood. She shows us how the waffles are cooked over an open fire, like the
pancake woman in Rembrandt's etching, who uses a similar brazier on which
to rest her pan for frying pancakes. Waffle and wafer irons were often given as
wedding gifts. Waffle irons make the waffles we still know; wafer irons make
the now lesser known thin flat wafers or cookies. Both have long handles so

they can easily and safely be used over the fire, or as we see here, over a brazier with hot coals.

The female seller stands in the foreground with her ample platter of stacked waffles. A boy on the right in front of a columned building is taking a bite of his recent purchase. He might have received the money on one of the special occasions when kids go from house to house singing songs and receiving handouts. (A modern equivalent of such activity might be begging for treats at Halloween.)

A waffle recipe in *De Verstandige Kock* (*The Sensible Cook*) calls for flour, milk, melted butter, three or four eggs, and yeast. This recipe makes a sturdy breadlike waffle that could be sold on the street to be eaten out of hand. It was generally topped with a bit of butter. There is no evidence that waffles were drizzled with a molasses-type syrup or a syrup made from apples, nor were they topped with whipped cream and fruit, as is the common American practice today. (PGR)

R E M B R A N D T   H A R M E N S Z O O N   V A N   R I J N   (1 6 0 6 – 1 6 6 9)

The Pancake Woman, **1635**

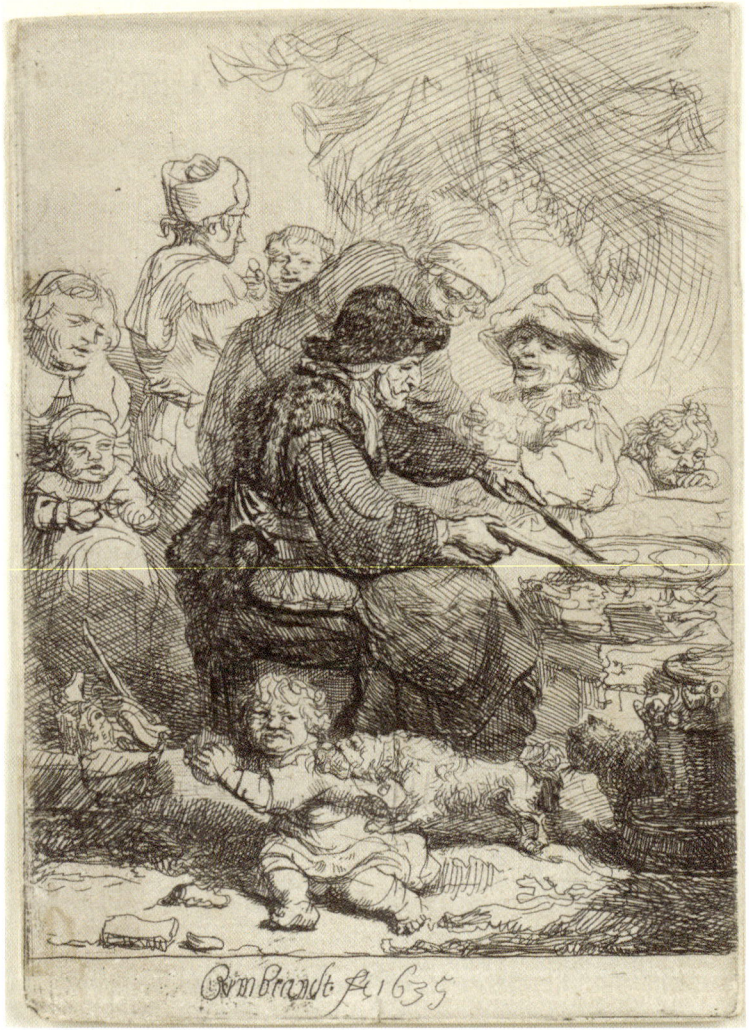

Rembrandt Harmenszoon van Rijn, *The Pancake Woman,* 1635. Etching. Print Collection, Miriam and Ira D. Wallach Division of Art, Prints and Photographs, The New York Public Library, Astor, Lenox and Tilden Foundations.

We include an etching by the Netherlands' most famous painter Rembrandt Harmenszoon van Rijn, who lived well into the second half of the seventeenth century (1609–1669). The image demonstrates once again the popularity of pancakes as a street snack.

The pancake woman uses a long-handled pan like the one in Jan Steen's painting. In both images there are three pancakes in the pan to enable the maker to fill customer demand quickly.

Note how the little dog is trying to get a bite from the pancake the small child in the foreground, sitting on the edge of the sidewalk, is enjoying. Clearly the larger boy on the other side of the brazier finds the lovely smells coming from the frying pan mouthwatering and has taken a large bite from his treats. The smaller child next to him seems to be mesmerized and daydreams while watching the action. A woman holds a toddler her lap, and another child in the background seems to be restrained by an adult, but no doubt eventually everyone will get their share. (PGR.)

JAN STEEN (1626–1679)

The Pancake Woman

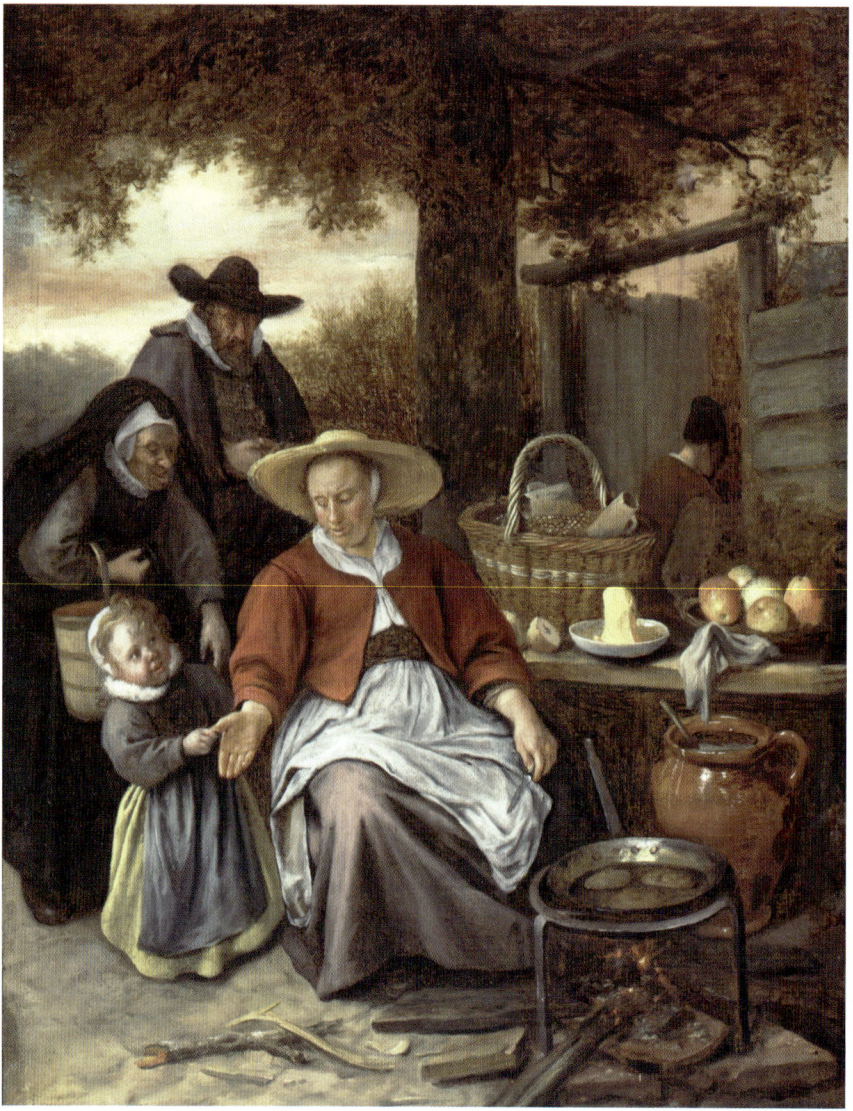

Jan Steen, Dutch 1626–1679. *The Pancake Woman*, ca. 1661–1669. Oil on canvas. 26 1/4 in. x 20 7/16 in. (66.68 cm x 51.91 cm). Memorial Art Gallery of the University of Rochester: Bertha Buswell Bequest, 55.71.

You can almost hear the woman on the far left say to the chubby-faced child "give the money to the lady." In turn, the little one will get one of the small pancakes freshly made from the pan. On the table next to the pancake baker stands a basket with what look like hazelnuts with some mugs for scooping or measuring, a bowl of apples and pears, a large "lump" of butter on a plate (the shape of the butter comes from its traditional mold), and half an apple, probably because the other half was used in the pancakes she is frying.

The butter is used for frying the pancakes but also as a topping, perhaps. As with the waffles, there is no evidence that sugar was used to sprinkle on top, nor any kind of syrup. Nowadays Dutch children write their initials or their whole name on their plate-sized pancakes with thick apple syrup.

The brazier we see here and in Bramer's drawing as well, was made by the blacksmith. It is sturdy, but not too heavy, so that it can be portable and taken from location to location. Pancakes were sold in cold and warm weather and during the day but also in evening markets. From the many depictions, we may conclude that invariably pancakes were made and sold by women. (PGR.)

ABRAHAM BEERSTRATEN (1643–1665)

De Oudezijds of Sint-Olofskapel

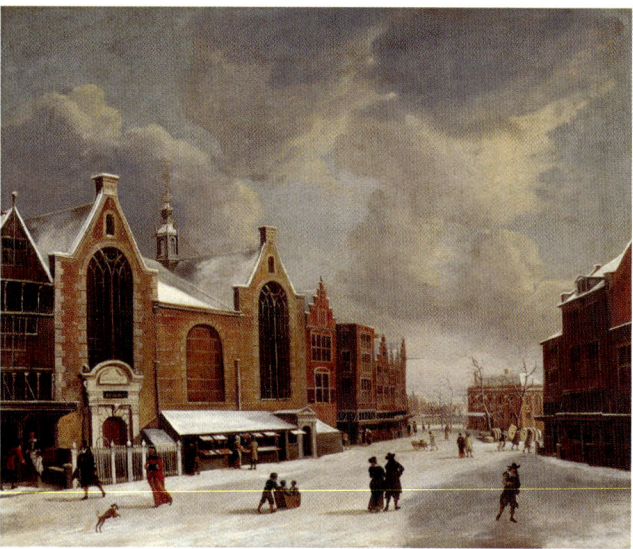

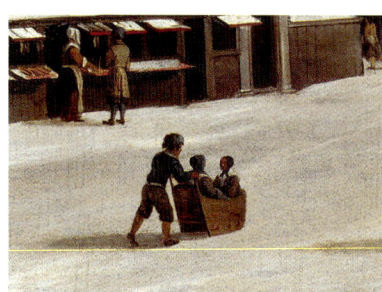

Abraham Beerstraten, *De Oudezijds of Sint-Olofskapel.* Oil on canvas, 89 x 105.3 cm. Collection Amsterdam Museum (SB 6327).

A boy pushes two smaller youngsters in a wooden sled over the snow-covered Zeedijk in Amsterdam. The exertion of the activity will keep the boy warm; his passengers might feel the cold a bit more, but they enjoy the ride. A woman dressed in red protects her hands against the cold by wearing a muff. The cold weather has not deterred people from stopping at the open bookstalls that are alongside this chapel. The light dusting of snow, visible on the roof lines, adds an invigorating nip to the air.

Ice and winter activities were sources of pleasure for both Dutch children and adults during the seventeenth century. Sometimes people went skating on the lakes in the countryside. But when the ice froze in city canals or rivers, which happened only if it was exceptionally cold, city dwellers took to the ice with skates and sleds. Snow-covered streets also provided slippery surfaces for youngsters with sleds.

In 1645 Saint Olof's, initially a medieval Catholic chapel built in Amsterdam by Scandinavian merchants in honor of Saint Olof, was rebuilt along with the chapel next to it, the Chapel of the Holy Sepulchre, to be used as a

Protestant church. It was then commonly called the *Oudezijdskapel.* This is the church shown in Beerstraten's painting.

Cityscapes like this one were purchased by Dutch urban dwellers, who took special pride in their city's historic buildings. That Abraham Beerstraten has taken certain liberties with the perspective here would not have bothered his viewers. They would enjoy seeing the buildings and the view down the Zeedijk in the direction of the Paalhuis on the New Bridge and the harbor. Here the cold gray wintry sky contrasts with the warm glow of the brick buildings. For those viewers, the children with the sled would be simply incidental. For us, they are central. It's all a matter of focus. (DRB)

PHILIPS WOUWERMAN (1619–1668)

Ice Scene

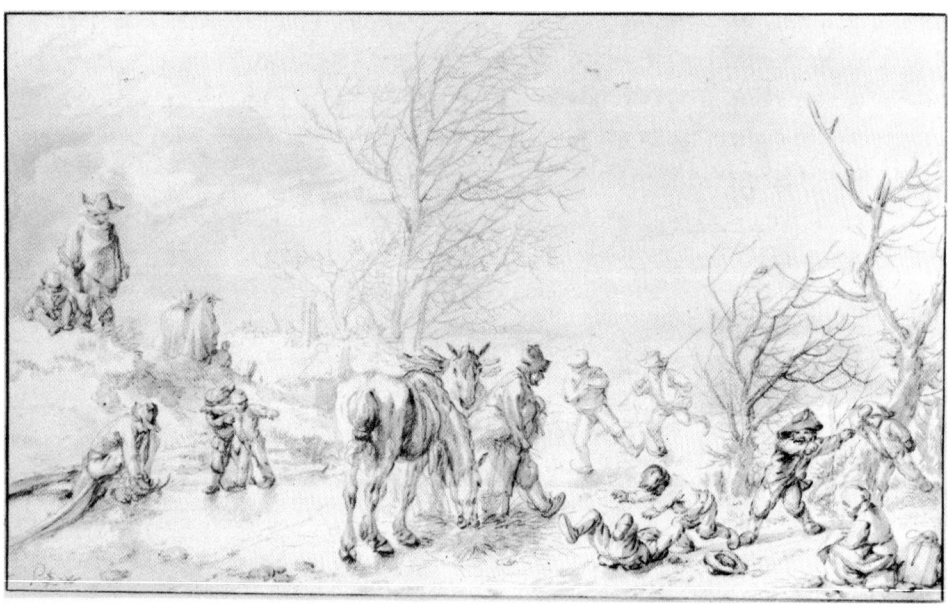

Philips Wouwerman, *Ice Scene*. Drawing. Collection Amsterdam Museum (TA 10389).

Walking along on a cold wintry day, a man is leading his bony horse. He passes boys enjoying themselves skating, or fighting, or watching the antics of one another. Two men skate jauntily in the background. One boy holds onto another boy, whose outstretched arms make it clear he's just learning to skate and find his balance, not easy for a beginner. Another boy sits on a log, strapping on his skates; he is eager to join the fun. Two boys wrestle on the ground and two others cannot wait to join in the melee. They are closely watched by a seated girl. She probably disapproves.

Whether this sketch was meant as a preliminary study for a painting by Philips Wouwerman is not known. The animation of the figures, however, makes for a lively winter scene. Wouwerman's masterful *Winter Landscape with a Footbridge*, now at the Staatliche Museen in Berlin, also depicts two children on the ice, one pushing along in a *prikslee*. Those youngsters are considerably more tranquil than the boys in this lively drawing.

Wouwerman was famous for his paintings of horses. This old nag looks quite tired and not at all amused by the activities of the boys. (DRB)

JAN LUYKEN (1649–1712)
De Kolf

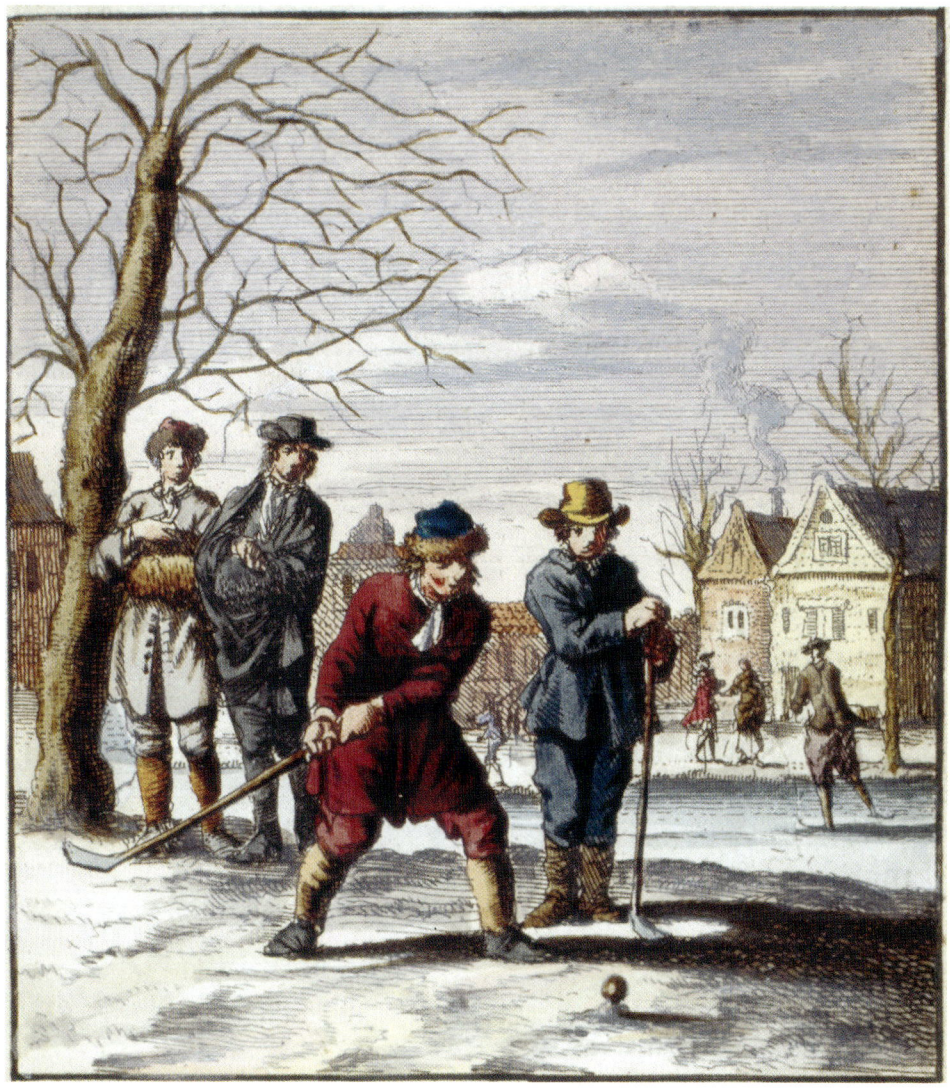

Jan Luyken, *De Kolf* (Kolf). Print (hand colored), *Des Menschen Begin, Midden en Einde* (1712). Collection Amsterdam Museum (P 4427; A 18972).

Taking careful aim, a boy prepares to swing his *kolf* stick, sending the small leather-covered ball flying toward a goal. His opponent, leaning on his own *kolf* stick, watches carefully. His turn is next. He plots his strategy carefully.

   Kolf was a favorite sport for teenage and little boys as well as grown men. During the winter, it could be played on the ice or on frozen ground.

Those playing on the ice frequently did so using skates, but skating was not a requirement.

In warm sunny months, *kolf* could be played on grassy fields. Boys devised temporary rules so improvised versions of the game could be played during the summer on city streets or squares, often to the annoyance of adult house-holders whose windows might be broken with an errant ball. It was definitely not a rainy-day activity. Wherever and whenever *kolf* was played, the fellow taking the fewest strokes to reach the goal was the winner.

Kolf balls were hand-made by specialized producers in some towns who stuffed leather balls with horsehair or tightly rolled wool. *Kolf* sticks or clubs were crafted by workers, often located in other cities, who shaped the wood. Later in the century, iron club heads were affixed to the shaft of the *kolf* stick, thereby adding greater clout to the shot, sending the ball for longer distances.

This sporting equipment was frequently given to boys as a gift from Sin-terklaas on the Feast of Saint Nicholas in early December. Portraits and genre paintings frequently depict boys with *kolf* sticks. Winter landscapes, especially works by Hendrick Avercamp, Isack van Ostade, Jan van Goyen, and Arent Arentsz (called "Cabel") depict men or boys playing the game. While women and girls also skated, they are not shown playing this game. *Kolf* was a dis-tinctly masculine pursuit and pleasure.

Kolf was played in both the Southern and Northern Netherlands, although the Dutch seemed more addicted to the game than their counterparts in Flan-ders. *Kolf* was the forerunner to ice hockey and field hockey as well as to golf. Those games developed later and elsewhere. (DRB)

HENDRICK DUBBELS (1620/22–1707)

The Block Houses in the Amstel during Winter, ca. 1651–54

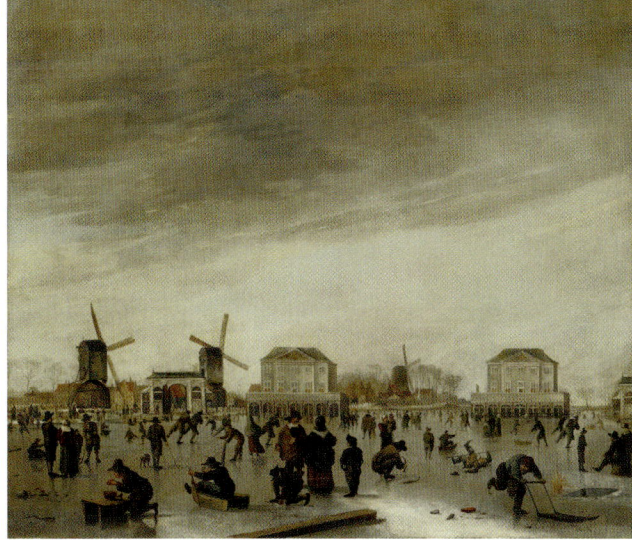
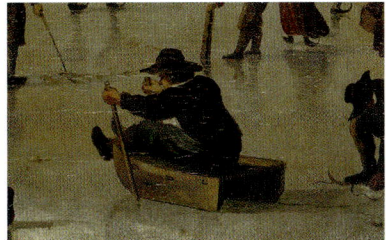

Hendrick Dubbels, *The Block Houses in the Amstel during Winter*, ca. 1651–54. Oil on canvas, 47.5 x 56 cm. Collection Amsterdam Museum (SB 4521)

With the Amstel river frozen, many Amsterdammers have taken to the ice, some to skate, some to fish, some to gossip. A small child pushes along in a wooden sled, goads in hand. At the right, someone has fallen onto the ice, no doubt an embarrassing moment.

Much of the terrain in the Netherlands, especially in the province of Holland, is relatively flat. Downhill sledding was not an option. But by using hand-held sticks or goads to push themselves in small sleds (*priksleeën*) over the ice or having another child or a grown-up push or pull a sled for a passenger, youngsters could enjoy sledding. Adults used similar sleds to transport wooden barrels of beer, sacks of grain, bundles and packages, and an occasional passenger or cow over the ice.

Winter landscapes were a favorite of Dutch paintings collectors in the seventeenth century. Often the winter landscape was set in a rural environment. However, some artists combined a view of prominent buildings in a city with the winter landscape. Here, Dubbels has restricted all his human activity and the windmills and block houses to the lower third of the painting, allowing that wintry, cloud-streaked sky to dominate his canvas. (DRB)

Meet the Artists

Twenty-four artists are represented in this volume; twenty-three are known and one is anonymous. During the seventeenth century and early years of the eighteenth century, in what has been called the Dutch Golden Age, more than a thousand artists produced innumerable works. Some were paintings; others were prints and drawings. It is estimated that anywhere between one and six million works were produced.

We've narrowed our focus to two dozen artists, all carefully chosen because their paintings or prints and drawings help us better understand the pleasures Dutch children experienced during childhood. The artist most heavily used is the author/illustrator Jan Luyken. His emblem book, *Des Menschen Begin, Midden en Einde*, published shortly after his death in 1712, provides many images of children, particularly children playing games or playing with their toys.

In preparing these brief thumbnail sketches, we have relied heavily on information included in *The Dictionary of Art*, edited by Jane Turner, published in thirty-four volumes, in 1996.

We hope that the reader interested in the images will also become interested in the artists who produced them. By consulting museum resources and online data bases, it will be possible to learn more about our artists and the varied works they produced.

Abraham Beerstraten (1643–1665) was the son of Jan Abrahamsz. Beerstraten, a successful painter. Like his father, Abraham specialized in paintings of winter townscapes, sea battles, and southern seaports.

Job Adriaensz. Berckheyde (1630–1693) was born and died in Haarlem. He began his apprenticeship with Jacob Willemsz. de Wet in 1644. He joined the Haarlem Guild of Saint Luke in 1654, following an extensive trip to Germany in the 1650s. While much of his work consists of interior scenes of Saint Bavo's Church in Haarlem or the Amsterdam Stock Exchange, the theme of bakeries captured his attention in the 1680s with *The Baker* (now in

Worcester, MA), the *Baker's Shop* (at Oberlin), and *Baker's Shop with a Woman Making Lace* in the Dutch government's collection.

HENDRICK BERCKMAN (1629–1679) was born in Klundert in North Brabant. He studied in Antwerp with the Flemish painters Jacob Jordaens and Thomas Willeboirts Bosschaert. He was appointed court painter to Hendrick of Nassau, the governor of Hulst. After working in Leiden for two years in the mid-1650s, Berchman moved to Middelburg, where he joined the Guild of Saint Luke in 1655. He was known for his portraits of Dutch dignitaries. He died in Middelburg.

PETER BINOIT (1590/93–1632/39) was born in Cologne, Germany, sometime between 1590 and 1593. He studied in Daniel Soreau's studio in Hanau, Germany. Binoit was clearly something of a man of mystery to those attempting to re-create his biography. He was known for still-life flower bouquets and still-life paintings featuring fruits and vases of flowers with birds, snails, and/ or butterflies. He died in Hanau sometime between 1632 and 1639.

LEONARD BRAMER (1596–1674) was sometimes known as Leonaert, or Leonardo delle notte. As a young artist, he worked in Rome, where he lived from 1619 to 1625. There he was influenced by the painter Adam Elsheimer. He returned to his home town of Delft and became a member of the Guild of Saint Luke in Delft in 1629. After 1635 he produced many drawings; some were cycles illustrating books like the Bible, popular novels, as well works by Ovid and Virgil. He is not known to have had any pupils, but he remained active in the Guild of Saint Luke, functioning sometime as its head man. The images included in our volume are drawn from his sixty-six drawings in the *Straatwerken* series, which, while not bearing a date, has been dated to the 1650s.

HENDRICK JACOBSZ. DUBBELS (1620/22–1707) was born in Amsterdam sometime around 1620–22 and died in Amsterdam in 1707. He was the son of a diamond cutter. He worked in the studios of several artists and was heavily influenced by the painter Jan van de Cappelle. For a short while he worked as a haberdasher, selling stockings, caps, and bonnets until he went bankrupt. Dubbels was known as a painter of cityscapes, winter landscapes in rural settings, and seascapes.

CORNELIS DUSART (1660–1704) was born and died in Haarlem. He was the son of the church organist at Saint Bavo and one of last pupils of Adriaen van Ostade. Dusart was a painter, draughtsman, and printmaker. He became a member of the Guild of Saint Luke in 1679 and served as its dean in 1692. He was influenced by Cornelis Bega and Jan Steen. His graphic oeuvre consists of 119 etchings and mezzotint engravings. He often expresses a satirical side in his art.

GOVAERT FLINCK (1615–1660) was born in Cleve and died in Amsterdam. He was the son of a draper from Cleve (then a Prussian territory). Originally apprenticed in Leeuwarden to painter Lambert Jacobzs., he was a well-known pupil and follower of Rembrandt, whose studio he joined for additional training in 1633. By 1636, he had set up his own studio, painting both history pictures and portraits.

DIRCK HALS (1591–1656) was the son of Franchoys Hals, a cloth worker from Mechelen who had settled in Haarlem by the time Dirck was born. Dirck was the brother of his more artistically accomplished older brother, Frans, who had been born in Antwerp in 1580. Dirck studied with his brother. He was known for small genre paintings that often were based on the "merry company" theme. One of his sons, Anthonie, also became a painter, specializing like his father in genre subjects.

EGBERT JASPERSZ. VAN HEEMSKERK, the Elder (1634/35–1704) was born in Haarlem and died in London. He was perhaps a student of Peter de Grebber in Haarlem. He worked sometimes in London and also worked in Haarlem, The Hague, Weesp, and in Amsterdam from 1665. Heemskerk was known for his scenes of the Temptation of Saint Anthony, images of drinking bouts, and other satirical subjects, somewhat in the manner of David Teniers, Adriaen Brouwer, and Adriaen van Ostade. His son was also a painter and bore the same name.

JAN VAN DER HEYDEN (1637–1712) was born in Gorkum (Gorinchem) and died in Amsterdam. His father, like his maternal grandfather, was an ebony worker and fine cabinetmaker. After the family moved to Amsterdam, and his father's subsequent death, Jan was apprenticed to a glass *schryver*, learning to cut, frame, engrave, and paint on glass. He probably worked in the family's furniture business. He was a painter of Dutch cityscapes and also pleasure-journey paintings of real and imagined locations. A skilled inventor and engineer, he devised both a fire-fighting pumping system to be used in Amsterdam's canals and a system of street lights.

LUDOLF DE JONGH (1616–1679) was born in Overschie and died in Hillegersberg. He was a versatile painter of portraits, genre paintings, and landscapes with hunting scenes. He studied with Cornelis Saftleven in Rotterdam, Anthonie Palamedes in Delft, and Jan van Bijlert in Utrecht. Especially productive while working in Rotterdam in the 1650s, he had an influence on Pieter de Hooch and Jacob Ochtervelt.

JUDITH LEYSTER (1609–1660) was born in Haarlem and died in Heemstede. She was the daughter of Jan Willemsz, a ribbon weaver who had come from Antwerp. Judith was one of nine children. None of her sisters or brothers showed talent for art. It is uncertain from whom she learned the art of painting; it could have been either Frans Pietersz. de Grebber or Frans Hals in Haarlem. In 1629 her painterly talent was recognized in a locally authored historical description of Haarlem, where she was then in De Grebber's studio. She entered the Guild of Saint Luke in 1633 (a most unusual accomplishment for a woman). She married Jan Miense Molenaer, a fellow Haarlem painter, in 1635. So far as is known, she discontinued painting after her marriage but managed Molenaer's studio.

JAN LUYKEN (also Luiken) (1649–1712) was born and died in Amsterdam. His parents were attracted to Mennonite thought and the writings of Jakob Böhme; both were influences on Jan. Luyken learned painting from Martinus Zaagmolen and later developed his skills as an engraver, etcher, and draftsman. He illustrated many books by diverse authors on varied topics, ranging from shipbuilding and accounting manuals to pharmaceutical treatises and versions of the Old and New Testament. He also both wrote and illustrated eleven emblem books, all either religiously or moralistically themed. After the early death of his wife, he raised his son, Casper, training him as an artist. To Jan's grief, his son died a few years after his marriage, leaving a widow and young son. From October 1708, Jan Luyken provided a home for his daughter-in-law and grandson, until his own death in 1712. The last book he was working on at the time of his death was *Des Menschen Begin, Midden en Einde*.

NICOLAES MAES (1634–1693) was baptized in Dordrecht and buried in Amsterdam. The son of a prosperous Dordrecht merchant, he initially learned to draw in his home town before studying painting with Rembrandt in Amsterdam. He is presumed to have entered Rembrandt's studio sometime around 1648–50. By December 1653, he was settled back in Dordrecht as an independent painter. He resided in Dordrecht until 1673. He worked on history and genre paintings and had a productive thirty-five-year career as a portrait painter. When he returned to Amsterdam in 1673, Maes focused on portrait work, producing hundreds of portraits in the 1670s and 1680s.

JAN MIENSE MOLENAER (1610–1668) was born and buried in Haarlem. Molenaer was the son of a tailor. Perhaps he was a pupil of Frans Hals (although that is not known for sure). He married the Haarlem painter Judith Leyster. They moved to Amsterdam in 1636, following some financial difficulties. His fortunes seemed to have improved in Amsterdam, where he continued to paint genre scenes, especially peasant interiors in the style of Adriaen van Ostade, and some commissioned portraits. It is assumed he was also a dealer in paintings.

MICHIEL VAN Musscher (1645–1705) was born in Rotterdam and died in Amsterdam. Van Musscher received his training from different artists, including Martinus Zaagmolen, who was also a teacher for Jan Luyken. He produced both genre works and portraits in 1660s; by 1670s he concentrated almost exclusively on portraits.

MATTHIJS NAIVEU (also Neveu) (1647–1726) was born in Leiden and died in Amsterdam. Naiveu was the son of a wine merchant from Rotterdam. He began his training with Abraham Toorenvliet, a glass painter and drawing master in Leiden. From 1667 to 1669, Naiveu was apprenticed to the Leiden painter Gerrit Dou, who received one hundred guilders per year—a very high sum— for instructing him. In 1671, Naiveu entered the Leiden Guild of Saint Luke and became its head in 1677 and 1678. Later in 1678, he moved to Amsterdam. His depictions of delivery rooms in 1670s was a rare theme in Dutch art.

CASPAR NETSCHER (also Gaspar) (ca. 1639–1684) is assumed to have been born in Heidelberg; he died in The Hague. This Dutch painter of German origin was the son of the German sculptor Johann Netscher, who died when Caspar was very young. At an early age Caspar came to Arnhem, where he was apprenticed to Hendrick Coster, a still-life and portrait painter. In about 1654 Netscher moved to Deventer and completed his training in the workshop of Gerard ter Borch. He moved to The Hague, joining the painters' society, Pictura, in 1662. He initially painted small genre scenes; later, influenced by Gerrit Dou and Frans van Mieris of Leiden, he changed his manner of painting. After 1667, portraits became his main interest, following the aristocratic elegant court style of Anthony van Dyck.

Rembrandt Harmensz. van Rijn (1606–1669) was born in Leiden and died in Amsterdam. The son of a Leiden miller, he was renowned as a painter, draftsman, and etcher. From 1632 he signed his works with his forename, Rembrandt. He studied painting in Leiden with Jacob van Swanenburgh and later studied for six months in Amsterdam with Pieter Lastman (around 1625). He returned to Leiden, where he worked for a few years, often sharing a studio with Jan Lievens. He moved to Amsterdam in 1631 and set up his own studio. Many young artists studied with him. His first etching was made circa 1626; later he experimented with etching techniques and printing on various kinds of papers. His marriage to Saskia van Uylenburgh ended with her premature death from tuberculosis, leaving Rembrandt with a young son, Titus, to raise with the assistance of housekeepers. Eventually he had a long love affair with one of his housekeepers, Hendrickje Stoffels, with whom he sired a daughter, named Cornelia. In his final years, Rembrandt faced bankruptcy and had to sell off many of his possessions.

Jan Steen (1626–1679) was born and died in Leiden, Steen was known for his genre scenes with busy interiors and moralizing themes and also for illustrating Dutch proverbs. He is presumed to have been a Roman Catholic. Steen was the son of a brewer. In all probability Adriaen van Ostade, of Haarlem, was his teacher. In 1648 he joined the newly established painters' guild in Leiden. For a brief period, he ran the Snake brewery in Delft. He worked in many Dutch cities. He frequently included images of his own children and other family members in his paintings. Sometimes he included his own face, frequently smiling broadly, as if winking at—or winking with—the viewer.

Philips Wouwerman (1619–1668) was born and died in Haarlem. He was the eldest son of the painter Paulus (Pauwels) Joostens Wouwerman of Alkmaar. His younger brothers, Pieter Wouwerman (1623–1682) and Johannes (1629–1666), were also painters; Philips was their teacher. Philips Wouwerman was the most accomplished and successful seventeenth-century Dutch painter of horses—in battle scenes, hunting scenes, army camps, smithies, and stables. He also painted some landscapes and genre scenes.

Joachim Anthonisz. Wtewael (also spelled Utenwael, Uytewael, Wttewael) (1566–1638) was born and died in Utrecht and was known as both a painter and draughtsman. More than one hundred paintings and eighty drawings are known to be by him. His subjects tended to be drawn from the Bible and classical mythology, although he also painted some kitchen scenes. He was one of the founding members of the Guild of Saint Luke in Utrecht in 1611. One of his sons, Peter Wtewael, also became a painter, and it is assumed Joachim trained him.

DRB

Recipes

From the beginning we hoped that this book would be enjoyed by adults who would share it with their children or grandchildren. The dozen recipes in this chapter are therefore specifically meant to be adult-child cooking projects.

Cooking with children is a project dear to my heart. I started cooking with my daughter when she was three years old and continued with cooking projects for her and her classmates all through elementary school. In the many cooking classes and workshops I have given over more than three decades, I have always admired and relished the inventiveness and creativity of children. I found that with very few exceptions they will eat what they make and are excited and proud to share their products with parents or siblings.

Use some of the recipes that follow for a family evening meal and make a little menu with the lemon hearts (heart-shaped meatballs), coleslaw, currant-and-beet salad, a starch such as potatoes or brown rice, and the Doornick apple tart or cookies for dessert. For breakfast the sweet bread or pancake recipe will come in handy, the fried green leaves make a nice snack anytime, and a cup of vegetable soup is always a welcome accompaniment for a sandwich at lunch. Most important, please have a good time cooking together!

Recipes appear in alphabetical order as follows:

    Butter/cream making
    Coleslaw
    Currant-and-beet salad
    Currant cookies
    Doornick apple tart
    Fried green leaves
    Lemon hearts
    Letter cookies
    Spiced sweet bread
    Three-in-the-pan pancakes
    Vegetable soup with small meatballs
    Waffles

The main reason to cook with children is that it is an enjoyable activity for everyone. However, there are other excellent reasons: cooking helps hand-eye coordination and finger-thumb dexterity; it reinforces the academic skills learned in school; it teaches nutritional and cultural concepts; it cultivates responsibility and independence and leaves a feeling of pride and accomplishment. In addition, a cooking project is a good opportunity to talk about some simple health and safety rules:

- Washing hands thoroughly before starting to cook;
- Tying hair back and out of the way while cooking;
- Using potholders or mitts when lifting pans;
- Taking particular care that clothing cannot catch fire;
- Turning handles of pots sideways;
- Picking up knives by the handle, not the blade;
- Turning the stove off when cooking is finished.

Above all, have fun together and enjoy this taste of the past!

Butter/Cream Making
(See Jan Steen, *Pancake Woman*)

When cooking with children, particularly in a group, it is wise "to keep the little hands busy." Making butter is an activity that can be ongoing while other things are happening.

> *1 quart glass jar with screw top, jar and lid rinsed with boiling water and dried*
> *   thoroughly with a clean cloth*
> *½ pint heavy cream*

Pour the cream in the jar and screw on the lid. Pass around and have the children take turns shaking it. It will first become whipped cream—give your little helpers a spoonful to taste and then encourage them to keep shaking until it becomes butter.

Coleslaw
(See Michiel van Musscher, *A Pig on a Ladder*)

A description of how the Dutch made coleslaw was found in the 1749 diary of Peter Kalm, assistant to Swedish botanist Linnaeus. As he recalled: it was an "unusual" salad. Children six years and older can work with a knife and help cut the cabbage as thin as possible.

4 tablespoons butter
⅓ cup wine vinegar
Salt and freshly ground pepper
2 cups green cabbage, cut into thin strips
2 cups red cabbage, cut into thin strips

In a saucepan, melt the butter, stir in the vinegar, salt, and pepper, and heat through. Pour the dressing on the cabbage and toss to combine. Make sure the cabbage is at room temperature when dressed and be sure to keep the coleslaw at room temperature, or the dressing will congeal. Allow to stand at least an hour before serving. Stir occasionally.

Currant-and-Beet Salad

All kinds of cooked vegetables can be served at room temperature with a dressing of olive oil, vinegar, salt, and pepper. Here is a salad that uses dried currants as an accent in a mixture of beets and vinegar. Children six years and older can work with a knife and help cut the beets, scallions, and celery.

2 (15 oz.) cans sliced beets, or an equivalent amount of cooked, sliced beets (about
   3 cups), cut into sticks
3 scallions, finely chopped
3 or 4 inner celery stalks with greens, finely chopped
4 tablespoons currants (see note)
Salt and freshly ground pepper
Vinaigrette

In a salad bowl, combine all ingredients and allow to marinate for one hour before serving.

Note: Currants, which are small dried raisins, can be found on the supermarket shelf next to the raisins and are generally known as "Zante currants."

Currant Cookies
(See Job Berckheyde, *The Bakery Shop*)

Amsterdam physician Stefanus Blankaart said in his 1683 book that spiced cookies and currant cookies are better for children than plain ones. My recipe full of currants would certainly get his approval. This is a good recipe for practicing fractions and math skills.

16 tablespoons (2 sticks) butter, softened
½ cup light brown sugar
2¼ cups all-purpose flour
½ cup currants (see note in previous recipe)

In a food processor cream the butter and sugar. Add the flour and process as briefly as possible until the dough forms. Use a wooden spoon to stir in the currants. Remove to a floured board and shape dough into a 1¾-inch high x 12-inch long log. Butter a baking sheet and cut the log in half, then into quarters. Cut each quarter into six slices. Roll each slice into a ball and place on baking sheet; flatten with the flat bottom of a (floured) glass and bake at 350 degrees for 20–25 minutes, until light brown. Remove to racks and cool. Yield: 24 cookies.

Doornick Apple Tart
(See Joachim Wtewael, *Vegetable Seller*)

From the five recipes for *appel-taert* (apple tart) in *De Verstandige Kock* (*The Sensible Cook*) of 1667, I chose the one from the town of Doornick. This recipe already appears in medieval Dutch cookbooks and makes a delicious pastry of apples in a buttery crust.

For the crust:
2 cups all-purpose flour
⅓ cup packed light brown sugar
11 tablespoons lightly salted butter, cut into pats
2 egg yolks, lightly beaten with a fork

Butter a 9-inch springform pan. In the work bowl of a food processor fitted with a metal blade, combine the flour, sugar, butter, and egg yolks. Process just until a cohesive dough forms. Press out the dough on the bottom and 1¼ inches up the sides of the prepared pan. Run your thumb around the rim to even it. (Your helper can do the pressing out of the dough, and together you can finish the crust.)

For the filling:
4 Golden Delicious apples, peeled, quartered, and cored

2 egg yolks, lightly beaten with a fork
4 tablespoons butter, melted and cooled
1 tablespoon ground cinnamon
2–3 tablespoons sugar (depending on the sweetness of the apples)

Preheat the oven to 350 degrees. Cut each apple quarter in half lengthwise and then across into small slivers. Place in a large bowl and add yolks, butter, cinnamon, and sugar and stir (a nice job for your helper) to combine thoroughly. Spoon filling in prepared crust and bake for 50–60 minutes until the crust is golden. Remove to a rack and cool. Serve with large dollops of whipped cream that the child can make by shaking in a jar (see first recipe).

Fried Green Leaves

The following recipe illustrates the sometimes whimsical nature of *De Verstandige Kock* (*The Sensible Cook*). It is a fun project to do with children, who enjoy beating the eggs and fitting the leaves together. Kids love these sugar-strewn leaves as a special snack.

Romaine lettuce leaves (use the smaller inner leaves of a head of Romaine lettuce),
*   washed and patted dry*
2 eggs
4 tablespoons butter
Granulated sugar

With a sharp knife cut out the thick ribs in the middle of the leaves, if necessary. Beat the eggs in a flat dish with 1 tablespoon of water. Dip the inside of two leaves in the egg mixture, then fit the leaves together, the backs facing out. Dip both sides of the package in the egg mixture and shake off excess. Place a frying pan over moderately high heat and melt the butter. Quickly fry the leaves on both sides until lightly browned. Remove from the pan to serving plates and sprinkle lightly with sugar.

Lemon Hearts (heart-shaped meatballs)

Again, here is a recipe from *De Verstandige Kock* (*The Sensible Cook*). I adapted it somewhat to make it suitable for an adult-child cooking project. You can use ground veal, beef, a so-called meatloaf mixture of pork and beef, or ground turkey or chicken to make this dish.

1 pound ground veal, beef (or see above)
2 slices bread, soaked in
⅓ cup milk until soft
1 egg, lightly beaten with a fork
¼ teaspoon each ground nutmeg and pepper
1 teaspoon salt
2 teaspoons grated lemon zest
3 thin scallions with some of the greens, finely minced
3–4 tablespoons olive or other cooking oil

Squeeze the bread until it is somewhat dry, THEN combine it in a large bowl with the meat, egg, spices, salt, lemon zest, and scallions. Knead with a clean hand to combine. Divide into 4 or 6 portions and work with one at a time. Place it on a cutting board and pat it to a 1-inch thickness. Cut it with a heart-shaped cookie cutter and pat extra meat from the outside of the cutter neatly on top, or form meat by hand into a heart shape. Proceed with the other portions in the same way to make 4 or 6 hearts. Heat the oil in a large frying pan, big enough for all hearts. When the oil is hot, carefully transfer to the pan and nicely brown one side, then carefully turn the hearts over and brown the other side. When brown, add about ⅓ cup water; quickly cover the pan and turn the heat down to simmer. Braise for 20 minutes until the hearts are completely done.

Letter Cookies
(See Peter Binoit, *Still Life with Letter Cookies*)

Before you make the next recipe, you might want to practice together, using a piece of string to make the initial of the child's name and discuss how best to form the letters with dough. It is a good project for older children (eight and up).

2 sticks lightly salted butter
1 cup confectioners' sugar
3 cups all-purpose flour
2 egg yolks
(For spiced cookies: add 1 tablespoon ground cinnamon and ½ teaspoon each ground
nutmeg, cloves, and ginger)

Butter a baking sheet. In an electric mixer cream the butter and sugar and add yolks, then the flour in 4 batches. Beat to make a smooth, nonsticky dough that clings to the beater. METHOD 1: Divide the dough into 3 parts and work with 1 part at a time; refrigerate remaining dough. Roll out with a rolling pin about ½-inch thick and cut out with letter cookie cutters. METHOD 2 is more fun to do with an older child: Divide the dough into 3 parts and work with one part at a time; refrigerate remaining dough. Roll each part into an even rope, about ½ inch in diameter, and cut into equal pieces. Use each piece to shape a letter. The dough is very easy to work with. I suggest you look at the painting together and try to decorate the letters in the way they appear there, by using a small knife to cut small grooves in the dough and by giving the ends a small cut in the middle and then curling each side outward.

Preheat the oven to 325 degrees. Place the finished cookies on the buttered baking sheet and bake for 20–30 minutes, depending on size, until lightly browned.

Spiced Sweet Bread (*Zoete koek*)
(See Cornelis Dusart, *The Saint Nicholas Celebration*)

The following sweet bread recipe is my own and very similar to the *zoete koek* of the northeastern town of Deventer. This Hanseatic city has been known for this baked good since the early Middle Ages and is still famous for it to this day. It is seen in Dusart's drawing in the basket on the arm of the girl on the right. Measuring, sifting, and stirring are all good tasks for children when making this recipe.

> *1 cup dark brown sugar, packed*
> *2 cups all-purpose flour*
> *1 teaspoon baking powder*
> *1 teaspoon cinnamon*
> *½ teaspoon freshly grated nutmeg*
> *½ teaspoon ground cloves*
> *1 cup milk*

Preheat the oven to 350 degrees. Sift the dry ingredients together into a large bowl. Slowly add the milk and stir to make a smooth dough. Spoon the dough into a greased 8 x 5 x 2¼-inch loaf pan and bake for about one hour or until a knife inserted comes out clean and the loaf is a deep brown. Cool and store. This is a dense loaf that keeps very well and improves in flavor and texture when stored in an airtight container for a few days.

Three-in-the-Pan Pancakes
(See Rembrandt van Rijn, *The Pancake Woman*)

Here is a modern recipe for a seventeenth-century treat. Three-in-the-pan pancakes are still favorites in the Netherlands. Children enjoy watching the yeast as it starts to bubble and rise. They can stir the batter if they are not old enough to help with the frying. These pancakes make a delicious snack when the children come home from school or make an excellent Sunday breakfast or brunch dish. *Note:* the batter needs to stand for an hour.

> *2 packages dry yeast (not rapid-rise)*
> *¼ cup warm water (100–110° F)*
> *Pinch sugar*
> *2 cups all-purpose flour*
> *Pinch salt*
> *1½ cups milk, lukewarm*
> *1 cup currants or raisins*
> *2 medium Golden Delicious apples, or other firm apples, peeled, cored, and chopped*
> *Butter for frying*
> *Confectioners sugar*

Sprinkle the yeast over the warm water, then sprinkle in the sugar. Let stand 2 minutes, then stir. Leave in a warm place until bubbly, about 5 minutes. Place the flour and salt in a deep bowl. Make a well in the middle and add the yeast mixture. Stirring from the middle, add the lukewarm milk a little at a time until the batter is smooth. Add the currants or raisins and chopped apples and combine. Allow the batter to stand in a warm place for about 1 hour. Heat enough butter in a large frying to amply coat the bottom, about ⅛ inch, and pour out batter to make three small (about 3-inch) pancakes. Fry on both sides until golden brown and serve hot, heavily dusted with confectioners sugar and with just a small pat of butter in the middle. Yield: about 18 little pancakes.

Vegetable Soup with Small Meatballs

This recipe for vegetable soup is ageless. Children love the small meatballs in the soup, and if you remind them about hand washing they'll make short work of rolling tiny meatballs.

For the meatballs:
6–8 ounces low-fat ground beef
Half an egg (beat the egg with a tablespoon of water in a small bowl and use half;
*   the rest can be saved for breakfast,)*
Salt, pepper, and two dashes of ground nutmeg

Combine these ingredients in a bowl and knead. Make small meatballs with this mixture.

For the soup:
2 quarts beef broth (homemade or store-bought)
Vegetables such as: Carrots, leek, celery, Brussels sprouts, tomatoes (not too many),
*   corn, peas, broccoli or cauliflower florets, asparagus, and cabbage, all chopped*
*   into small pieces (use any combination that appeals to you and your helper).*
4 scallions, finely chopped
6 tablespoons minced parsley

In a large pan, heat the broth to boiling and add the meatballs. Cook for 10 minutes. If necessary, skim off any fat, then add the vegetables and the scallions. Gently cook for 10–15 minutes. Add parsley and cook 1 minute more. Taste and adjust seasoning with salt and pepper.

Waffles (*wafels*)
(See Jan Steen, *Twelfth-Night Feast*)

This waffle recipe is from *De Verstandige Kock* (*The Sensible Cook*). Be sure to preheat the waffle iron and to grease it with butter before each use, or the waffles will stick. These waffles are more breadlike than modern ones and not quite as light, but very good. Children enjoy watching the yeast as it starts to bubble and rise and can help with the measuring and stirring.

1 package dry yeast (not rapid-rise)
¼ cup warm water (100 to 110°F)
Pinch sugar
4 cups all-purpose flour
4 tablespoons butter, melted and cooled
2 cups milk
2 eggs, beaten with a fork

Sprinkle the yeast over the warm water, then sprinkle in the sugar. Let stand 2 minutes, then stir. Leave in a warm place until bubbly, about 5 minutes. Place the flour in a large bowl, make a hollow in the middle, and add the yeast mixture and butter. Stir to combine and slowly stir in the milk and then the eggs to make a smooth batter. Allow the batter to stand in a warm place for about an hour. Preheat the iron according to manufacturer's instruction. Brush with butter, ladle in a spoonful of batter, close the iron, and bake the waffle until golden.

Try the first waffle with just a little butter on top to get the authentic taste and then top the waffles as you please.

❧

Have fun and I wish you (in Dutch) *Smakelijk Eten*, or bon appetit.

PGR

Epilogue

The basic premise of this book is that Dutch children in the seventeenth century had many opportunities for pleasurable moments from the early days of infancy through their childhood and youth. Some pleasurable moments were spontaneous or unplanned: a child laughed at the antics of the family dog chasing a thrown stick or smiled when the family cat purred and rubbed its silky fur against the child's bare legs. Other moments were the result of playing with a favorite toy or joining in competitive games indoors or outdoors. Many pleasures were seasonal, tied especially to the activities or treats associated with holidays: the crisp skin of goose roasted for Saint Martin's day in November; the lemony taste of *duivekater*, sturdy waffles, or the spiced *koek* for the Sinterklaas (Saint Nicholas) celebration. Some pleasures belonged to girls; others were enjoyed by boys; and some were gender free.

Sources of evidence for these delights and activities are varied. Pleasurable moments were visually captured in works of art: paintings, prints, and drawings. Others, particularly children's games, were illustrated on hand-painted blue-and-white wall tiles; mentioned in illustrated emblem books; commented upon—often critically—in minister's sermons, which were printed; molded in ceramic figurines or in terra cotta in the activities of cherubic putti used as architectural decorative elements. *De Verstandige Kock* (*The Sensible Cook*) does not mention children specifically in the cookbook but gives ample evidence of the savory foods and sweet desserts, confections, and fruit juices that Dutch people—including children—enjoyed.

Certain beloved sweet treats survive in Holland into the twenty-first century: sugar-coated almonds are sold in candy shops, especially at Easter time; *olliebollen* (the modern word for *olie-koecken*) stands appear at local summer street fairs and in public market squares during the winter season, their deep-fried delights tempting children and grown-ups. Collections of songs sung by children survive. Although winters now are not so cold as once they were, Dutch young people haul out their skates whenever ice gets thick enough to

153

skate on the ponds, rivers, and canals, and some towns have created shallow artificial ice rinks for winter sport.

We hope parents and grandparents will try some of the recipes in the book with their children and grandchildren, re-creating the delicious tastes of the past. The dozen treats in the recipe chapter were adapted by Peter Rose for the modern kitchen.

While much scholarship is summarized in these pages, this is not primarily a scholarly book; rather, it is meant for pleasurable enjoyment. The bibliography indicates scholarly works consulted and certainly can be used by those wishing to learn more about life and art in the Netherlands during the Golden Age. Similarly, the brief artists' biographies, prepared by Donna Barnes, provide names that can be checked further in books, museum collections, museum websites, and Internet databases. Other works by our selected artists give further visual evidence about childhood pleasures and also provide broader views of these artists' visual interests and output.

The images for this book have been selected by both authors not only to give visual evidence of historic Dutch childhood pleasures, but also in the hopes they will generate or stimulate family conversations about activities today's children enjoy and the cherished memories of childhood pleasures of parents and grandparents.

DRB and PGR

Selected Bibliography   ❧   *Index*

Selected Bibliography
Cited and Suggested Works

Seventeenth-Century Dutch Art

Ackley, Clifford S. *Print Making in the Age of Rembrandt.* Boston: Museum of Fine Arts, 1980.

Alpers, Svetlana. *The Art of Describing: Dutch Art in the Seventeenth Century.* Chicago: Univ. of Chicago Press, 1983.

Barnes, Donna R. *The Butcher, the Baker, the Candlestick Maker: Jan Luyken's Mirrors of 17th-Century Dutch Daily Life.* Hempstead: Hofstra Museum, 1995.

———. *Playing, Learning, Working in Amsterdam's Golden Age: Jan Luyken's Mirrors of Dutch Daily Life.* Hempstead: Hofstra Museum, 2004.

———. *Street Scenes: Leonard Bramer's Drawings of 17th-Century Dutch Daily Life.* Hempstead: Hofstra Museum, 1991.

Barnes, Donna R., and Peter G. Rose. *Matters of Taste: Food and Drink in Seventeenth-Century Dutch Art and Life.* Syracuse: Syracuse Univ. Press, in cooperation with the Albany Institute of History and Art, 2002.

Barnes, Donna R., and Ruud Spruit. *Food for Thought: Food and Drink in Seventeenth Century Dutch Art and Life.* Hoorn: Westfries Museum and Peter Sasburg, 2010.

Bedaux, Jean-Baptiste, and Rudi Ekkart. *Pride and Joy: Children's Portraits in the Netherlands, 1500–1700.* Ghent and Amsterdam: Ludion Press, in cooperation with the Frans Halsmuseum, Haarlem, and the Koninklijk Museum voor Schone Kunsten, Antwerp, 2000.

Biesboer, Pieter, and Martina Stitt. *Satire en Vermaak. Schilderkunst in de 17de eeuw: Het genrestuk van Frans Hals en zijn tijdgenoten 1610–1670.* Zwolle: Waanders, in cooperation with the Frans Halsmuseum, Haarlem, 2003.

Brown, Christopher. *Images of a Golden Past: Dutch Genre Painting of the Seventeenth Century.* New York: Abbeville Press, 1984.

Buijsen, Edwin, and Louis Peter Grijp. *The Hoogsteder Exhibition of Music and Painting in the Golden Age.* Zwolle: Waanders; The Hague: Hoogsteder & Hoogsteder, 1994.

Chapman, H. Perry, Wouter Th. Kloek, and Arthur K. Wheelock, Jr. *Jan Steen: Painter and Storyteller.* Edited by Guido M.C. Jansen. Zwolle: Waanders, in cooperation with the National Gallery of Art, Washington, DC, and the Rijks-museum, Amsterdam, 1996.

De Jongh, Eddy, and Ger Luijten. *Mirror of Everyday Life: Genreprints in the Nether-lands, 1550–1700.* Translated by Michael Hoyle. Ghent: Snoeck-Ducaju & Zoon, in cooperation with the Rijksmuseum, Amsterdam, 1997.

Durantini, Mary Frances. *The Child in Seventeenth-Century Dutch Painting.* Ann Arbor, MI: UMI Press, 1983.

Franits, Wayne E. *Paragons of Virtue: Women and Domesticity in Seventeenth-Century Dutch Art.* Cambridge and New York: Cambridge Univ. Press, 1993.

Haak, Bob. *The Golden Age: Dutch Painters of the Seventeenth Century.* New York: Abrams, 1984.

Kettering, Alison McNeil. *The Dutch Arcadia: Pastoral Art and Its Audience in the Golden Age.* Totawa, NJ: Allanheld and Schram, 1983.

Kiers, Judike, and Fieke Tissink. *The Glory of the Golden Age: Painting, Sculpture, and Decorative Art.* Zwolle: Waanders, in cooperation with the Rijksmuseum, Amsterdam, 2000.

Kloek, Wouter. *Jan Steen (1626–1679).* Waanders, in cooperation with the Rijks-museum, Amsterdam, 2005.

Landwehr, John. *Dutch Emblem Books: A Bibliography.* Utrecht: Haentjens Dekker & Gumbert, 1962.

Mandel, Oscar. *The Cheerfulness of Dutch Art: A Rescue Operation.* Doornspijk: Davaco, 1996.

Segal, Sam. *A Prosperous Past: Sumptuous Still Life in the Netherlands, 1600–1700.* Edited by William B. Jordan; translated by P. M. Van Tongeren. The Hague: SDU Publishers, 1988.

Slive, Seymour. *Dutch Painting, 1600–1800.* New Haven and London: Yale Univ. Press, 1995.

Stone-Ferrier, Linda A. *Dutch Prints of Daily Life: Mirrors of Life or Masks of Morals.* Lawrence: Spencer Museum of Art, Univ. of Kansas, 1983.

Sutton, Peter C. *Jan van der Heyden (1637–1712).* New Haven and London: Yale Univ. Press, in cooperation with The Bruce Museum, Greenwich, CT, and the Rijks-museum, Amsterdam, 2006.

———. *Masters of Seventeenth-Century Dutch Genre Painting.* Edited by Jane Iandola Watkins. Philadelphia: Philadelphia Museum of Art and Univ. of Pennsylvania Press, 1984.

Turner, Jane, ed. *The Dictionary of Art.* 34 vols. New York and London: Grove's Dictionaries and Macmillan, 1996.

Van Eeghen, P., and J. P. Van der Kellen. *Het werk van Jan en Casper Luiken.* 2 vols. Amsterdam: Frederik Muller & Co, 1905.

Van Suchtelen, Ariane. *Holland Frozen in Time: The Dutch Winter Landscape in the Golden Age.* Zwolle: Waanders; The Hague: Mauritshuis, The Royal Cabinet of Paintings, 2001.

Weller, Dennis P. *Jan Miense Molenaer: Painter of the Dutch Golden Age.* Raleigh: North Carolina Museum of Art, 2003.

Welu, James A., and Pieter Biesboer. *Judith Leyster: A Dutch Master and Her World.* Zwolle: Waanders, in cooperation with the Worcester Art Museum and the Frans Halsmuseum, Haarlem, 1993.

Westermann, Mariët. *The Amusements of Jan Steen: Comic Painting in the Seventeenth Century.* Zwolle: Waanders, 1997.

———. *Art & Home: Dutch Interiors in the Age of Rembrandt.* Zwolle: Waanders, in cooperation with the Denver Art Museum and the Newark Museum, 2001.

———. *A Worldly Art: The Dutch Republic, 1585–1718.* New York: Harry N. Abrams, 1996.

The Netherlands of the Seventeenth Century

Barbour, Violet. *Capitalism in Amsterdam in the Seventeenth Century.* Ann Arbor: Univ. of Michigan Press, 1950.

Barnes, Donna R. *Street Scenes: Leonard Bramer's Drawings of 17th-Century Dutch Daily Life.* Hempstead: Hofstra Museum, 1991.

Boxer, C. R. *The Dutch Seaborne Empire, 1600–1800.* London and New York: Knopf, 1965.

Carasso-Kok, Marijke. *Amsterdam Historisch.* Bussum: Unieboek, 1975.

Cats, Jacob. *Spiegel van den Ouden en Nieuwen Tyt* [Mirror of the old and new times]. The Hague: Isaac Burghoorn, 1632.

Deursen, A. Th. Van. *Plain Lives in a Golden Age: Popular Culture, Religion, and Society in Seventeenth-Century Holland.* Translated by Maarten Ultee. Cambridge and New York: Cambridge Univ. Press, 1991.

Huizinga, J. H. *Dutch Civilisation in the Seventeenth Century, and Other Essays.* New York: F. Ungar, 1968.

Kistemaker, Renée, and Roelof van Gelder. *Amsterdam: The Golden Age, 1275–1795.* Translated by Paul Foulkes. New York: Abbeville Press, 1983.

Luyken, Jan. *Des Menschen Begin, Midden en Einde* [The beginning, middle, and end of man]. Amsterdam: The Widow of Pieter Arentsz and Cornelis van der Sys, 1712.

———. *Het Leerzaam Huisraad* [The instructive household furnishings]. Amsterdam: The Widow of Pieter Arentsz and Cornelis van der Sys, 1711.

———. *Het Menselyk Bedryf* [The mirror of human trades]. Amsterdam: Jan and Casper Luyken, 1694.

Murray, John J. *Amsterdam in the Age of Rembrandt.* Norman: Univ. of Oklahoma Press, 1967.

North, Michael. *Art and Commerce in the Dutch Golden Age.* Translated by Catherine Hill. New Haven and London: Yale Univ. Press, 1997.

Regin, Deric. *Traders, Artists, Burghers: A Cultural History of Amsterdam in the Seventeenth Century.* Assen: Van Gorcum, 1976.

Schama, Simon. *The Embarrassment of Riches: An Interpretation of Dutch Culture in the Golden Age.* New York: Knopf, 1987.

Visscher, Roemer. *Sinnepoppen.* Amsterdam: Willem Jansz, 1614.

Zumthor, Paul. *Daily Life in Rembrandt's Holland.* Translated by Simon Watson Taylor. Stanford: Stanford Univ. Press, 1994. Original edition 1959; first English translation 1962.

Dutch Food History

Barnes, Donna R., and Peter G. Rose. *Matters of Taste: Food and Drink in Seventeenth-Century Dutch Art and Life.* Syracuse: Syracuse Univ. Press, in cooperation with the Albany Institute of History and Art, 2002.

Blankaart, Stephanus. *De Borgelijke Tafel: om lang gesond sonder ziekten te leven.* 1683; reprint, 1967.

Bredero, G. A. *Moortje en Spaanschen Brabander.* Athenaeum–Polak & Van Gennep, 1617; reprint, 1999.

Burema, Lambertus. *De Voeding in Nederland van de Middeleeuwen tot de Twintigste Eeuw.* Assen: Van Gorcum, 1953.

De Jager, Jef. *Rituelen: Nieuwe en Oude Gebruiken in Nederland.* Utrecht: Het Spectrum, 2001.

Forbes, W. A. *De Oudhollandse Keuken.* Bussum: C. A. J. van Dishoeck, n.d.

Jobse-van Putten, Jozien. *Eenvoudig maar voedzaam: cultuurgeschiedenis van de dagelijkse maaltijd in Nederland.* Nijmegen: SUN, 1995.

Loon, Hendrik Willem van. *The Life and Times of Rembrandt.* New York: Avon, 1957.

McCants, Anne. "Monotonous but Not Meager: The Diet of Burgher Orphans in Early Modern Amsterdam." *Research in Economic History* 14 (1992): 69–116.

Nannings, J. H. *Brood- en Gebakvormen en hunne beteekenis in de folklore.* N.p., 1932; reprint n.d.

Rose, Peter G. *Food, Drink and Celebrations of the Hudson Valley Dutch.* Charleston: The History Press, 2009.

———. *The Sensible Cook: Dutch Foodways in the Old and the New World.* Syracuse: Syracuse Univ. Press, 1989; paperback ed. 1998.

Schama, Simon. *The Embarrassment of Riches: An Interpretation of Dutch Culture in the Golden Age.* New York: Knopf, 1987.

Schilstra, J. J. *Prenten in hout: Speculaas-, taai-, en dragantvormen in Nederland.* Lochem: Uitgeversmaatschappij De Tijdstroom bv, 1985.

Scholte-Hoek, C. H. A. *Het gastmaal en de tafel in de loop der tyden.* Amsterdam: Elseivierpocket U 28, 1967.

Schotel, Dr. G. D. J., and Dr. H. C. Rogge. *Het Oud-Hollandsch Huisgezin der Zeventiende Eeuw.* 2d improved and illustrated ed. Leiden: A. W. Sijthoff, n.d.

Van de Graft, Dr. C. Catherina, and Dr. Tjaard W. R. de Haan. *Nederlandse Volksgebruiken bij hoogtijdagen.* Prisma-reeks. Ultrecht: Het Spectrum, 1978.

Van 't Veer, Annie. *Oud-Hollands Kookboek.* Utrecht: Het Spectrum, 1966.

Van Winter, Johanna Maria. *Spices and Comfits: Collected Papers on Medieval Food.* Devon, UK: Prospect Books, Totnes, 2007.

Vorselman, Gheeraert. *Eenen Nyeuwen Coock Boeck.* Antwerp, 1560. Reprint with commentary by Elly Cockx-Indestege, Wiesbaden: Guido Pressler, 1971.

Vrankrijker, Dr. A. C. J. de. *Mensen, leven en werken in de Gouden Eeuw.* The Hague: Martinus Nijhoff, 1981.

Willebrands, Marleen. *De Verstandige Kok: de rijke keuken van de Gouden Eeuw.* Bussum: Uitgeverij Pereboom, 2006.

Index

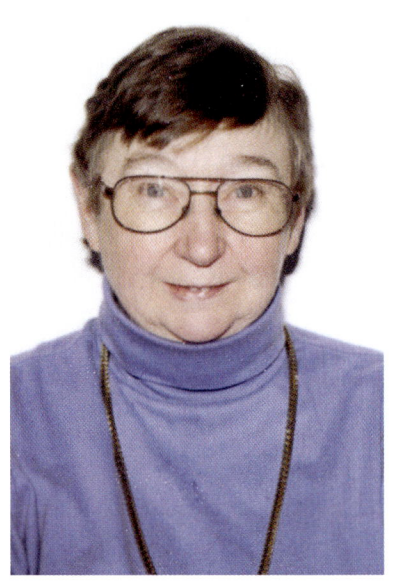

Photograph by Graphicolor Corp.

Donna R. Barnes, professor of education at Hofstra University, has taught a graduate course on childhood and adolescence in historical perspective and a workshop on toys and games, focusing on play and learning in historical and cross-cultural perspectives. She has researched seventeenth-century Dutch art and daily life for twenty-five years. She was the guest curator at four seventeenth-century Dutch art exhibitions at the Hofstra University Museum: "People at Work" (1988); "Street Scenes: Leonard Bramer's Drawings of Dutch Daily Life" (1991); "The Butcher, The Baker, The Candlestick Maker: Jan Luyken's Mirrors of 17th-Century Dutch Daily Life" (1995); and "Playing, Learning, Working in Amsterdam's Golden Age: Jan Luyken's Mirrors of Daily Life" (2004). With Peter Rose, she was exhibition co-curator for "Matters of Taste: Food and Drink in Seventeenth-Century Dutch Art and Life" at the Albany Institute of History and Art (2002), and coauthor of the exhibition catalog, published by Syracuse University Press. In the Netherlands, she was the guest curator for an exhibition of Jan Luyken's prints and drawings at the Amsterdam Museum in 1997. Most recently she was guest curator for "Smakelijk Eten," an exhibition of seventeenth-century Dutch art works at the Westfries Museum in Hoorn (2010–11). She is the principal author of the book accompanying the exhibition. The English-language edition is entitled *Food for Thought;* the Dutch-language version is *Smakelijk Eten.* She has lectured on seventeenth-century Dutch art and daily life at the Amsterdam Museum, the Rembrandthuis Museum, and the Center for the Study of the Golden Age at the University of Amsterdam. In the United States, she has lectured on dimensions of Dutch art and daily life at interdisciplinary conferences at Hofstra University, the New-York Historical Society, the Albany Institute of History and Art, the Rensselaerswijck Seminar of the New Netherland Project, and at other scholarly meetings.

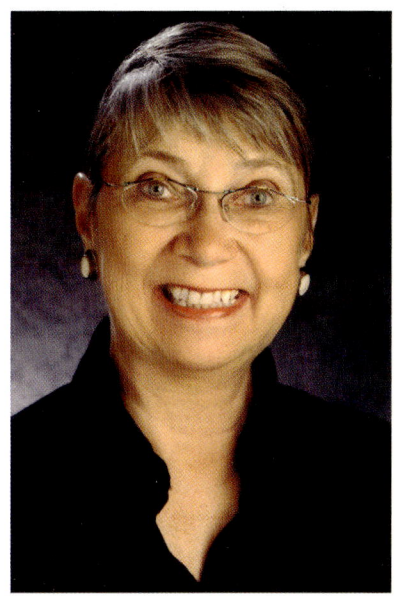

Peter G. Rose has written three books on the subject of the Dutch influence on the American kitchen, *The Sensible Cook: Dutch Foodways in the Old and New World* (Syracuse University Press, 1989); *Matters of Taste: Food and Drink in Seventeenth-Century Dutch Art and Life* (with Donna R. Barnes; Syracuse University Press, 2002) and *Food, Drink, and Celebrations of the Hudson Valley Dutch* (The History Press, 2009). She lectures nationally and internationally on a variety of topics related to Dutch and Dutch-American culinary history at the National Gallery of Art, Houston Museum of Fine Arts, the Smithsonian Institution, the Culinary Institute of America, the Peabody Essex Museum, the Brooklyn Museum, the New York State Library, the New-York Historical Society, as well as at many other historical societies in New York State. In the Netherlands she gave a series of talks at Museum Boijmans-van Beuningen in Rotterdam and lectured at the Mauritshuis in The Hague and the Westfries Museum in Hoorn.

Arthur K. Wheelock, Jr., received his Ph.D. in art history from Harvard University in 1973. He came to the National Gallery of Art in 1973 as a Finley fellow. He subsequently served as a research curator for a year before he was appointed curator of Dutch and Flemish paintings. He is also a professor of art history at the University of Maryland, where he has taught since 1974. Wheelock enjoys an international reputation as an authority on Dutch and Flemish art, particularly of Vermeer and other artists from Delft. Among his many books are *Perspective, Optics, and Delft Artists around 1650* (1977); *Jan Vermeer* (1981); *Vermeer and the Art of Painting* (1995); and the National Gallery of Art catalogues, *Dutch Paintings of the Seventeenth Century* (1995) and *Flemish Paintings of the Seventeenth Century* (2005). He has organized over forty exhibitions that have featured the work of, among others, Hendrick Avercamp, Pieter Claesz., Aelbert Cuyp, Gerrit Dou, Anthony van Dyck, Jan Lievens, Judith Leyster, Gabriel Metsu, Rembrandt van Rijn, Jan Steen, and Johannes Vermeer.